SILENT BUILDER

EMILY WARREN ROEBLING AND THE BROOKLYN BRIDGE

Third Edition

Commemorating the 140th anniversary
of the opening of the Brooklyn Bridge
and the 180th anniversary of
Emily Warren Roebling's birth

Marilyn E. Weigold, Ph.D.

TABLE OF CONTENTS

About the Author   1

Preface to the First Edition   3

Preface to the Second Edition   7

Preface to the Third Edition   11

Introduction   15

Prologue   19

Chapter 1 – Apprentice   23
   Growing Up Along the Hudson   23
   The Washington, D.C., Years   27
   Courtship   28
   Early Married Life   42

Chapter 2 – Journeyman   53
   Genesis of the Bridge Project   53
   Washington Roebling's First Years as Chief Engineer   58
   Emily as Silent Builder   65
   The Attempt to Oust Roebling as Chief Engineer   83
   The Back Story   93
   Opening Day   97
   Emily's Lifelong Involvement With the Bridge   107

Chapter 3 – Master — 138

The Troy Interlude — 139
First Lady of Trenton — 142
World Traveler — 160
Organization (Wo)Man — 170
Law Student — 191

Chapter 4 – Legend — 215

The Family Circle — 215
Emily's Farewell — 221
The Roeblings Without Emily — 228

Chapter 5 – EWR Superstar — 249

All-Around Renown:
The Centennial as Catalyst for Emily's Stardom — 249
Emily Warren Roebling Way:
The Street Sign Dedication — 251
The Roebling Museum — 252
The Emily Warren Roebling School (P.S. 8):
Ribbon Cutting and a Hip-Hop Tribute — 253
Emily Warren Roebling Plaza — 254
Ahead of Her Time — 255

Photo Gallery — 261

The Warren House in Cold Spring — 261
Young Emily Warren — 262
Washington Augustus Roebling — 263
Emily Warren Roebling — 264
John A. Roebling II — 265
Paul Roebling, Son of John A. Roebling II — 265

The Front of the Roebling Mansion in Trenton   266

The Rear of the Mansion   266

The Brooklyn Bridge Window with Emily
    on the Staircase   267

Emily in Her Pink Boudoir   267

Emily in Mid-Life   268

The Proud Graduate of the Woman's Law Class   269

The Graves of Emily and Washington Roebling   270

The Grounds of the Roebling Museum   271

The Entrance to the Museum   271

The Co-Naming of Columbia Heights in Brooklyn   272

Emily at the ASCE convention in 1888   273

George Frederick Kunz   274

Bibliography   275

Index   285

ABOUT THE AUTHOR

Dr. Marilyn E. Weigold is a professor emeritus of history at Pace University. She is the author of books and articles in the fields of regional and local history, environmental history and public works history. Her two most recent books are *Yonkers in the Twentieth Century*, published in hardcover and paperback by State University of New York Press in 2014, and *Peconic Bay: Four Centuries of History on Long Island's North and South Forks*, published by Syracuse University Press in 2015. The latter work resulted in Dr. Weigold's selection as one of 100 authors from throughout the United States to participate in the East Hampton (Long Island) Library Foundation's Authors' Night in 2016.

PREFACE TO THE FIRST EDITION

In the mid-1970s, while preparing to teach a course on the history and culture of New York City, I was struck by Edward Ellis' brief but insightful commentary about Emily Warren Roebling's contributions to the success of the Brooklyn Bridge project. A careful reading of David McCullough's monumental work, *The Great Bridge*, which contains a chapter on Emily, further stimulated my curiosity about this remarkable woman. Seeking answers to the numerous questions that had arisen in my mind, I journeyed to the Alexander Library at Rutgers University in New Brunswick, New Jersey, where, with the assistance of Clark L. Beck Jr., assistant curator, Special Collections Department, I surveyed the sizable collection of letters Emily had written to her son over the years.

In-depth research at Rutgers yielded considerable information about Emily's involvement in the bridge project, as did a thorough study of Mrs. Roebling's scrapbooks at Rensselaer Polytechnic Institute (RPI). Cam Stewart, RPI archivist, was especially helpful as guide and adviser, as were the following individuals, without whose assistance and support this study would not have been possible: Sister Mary Leonard Whipple of Georgetown Visitation Convent, who made Emily's academic record available to the author; Herbert Hands of the American Society of Civil Engineers; Alice Fullam of the Free Public Library, Trenton, New Jersey; Sister Margaret-Mary of the Sisters of St. Joseph of Cluny, who guided the author through Stella Maris, the Newport, Rhode Island, mansion occupied by the Roeblings during the crucial summer of 1882; Douglas Logan of the Cold Spring, New York, Cemetery Association; Gail Myker, reference librarian at Hayes Library, Pace University, White Plains, New York; Ivy Fischer Stone of the Oscard Agency; Lenore Segan, arts consultant to New York State Assembly Majority Leader Daniel Walsh and coordinator of the Emily Roebling exhibition held at the Marymount Gallery in Manhattan in the fall of 1983; and Roebling Exhibition Curator Ann Gabler of the Gallery Association of New York State.

I would like to pay special debts of gratitude to Paul Roebling, a great-grandson of Emily; the late Robert Roebling, who meticulously reviewed the manuscript and offered numerous insightful suggestions; and to the Society of Women Engineers, whose president, Evelyn Murray-Lenthall of the Massachusetts Institute of Technology, has been a strong ally in my quest to publicize the role of Emily Warren Roebling in one of the greatest engineering projects of the 19th century. Lastly, I would like to express my gratitude to the Scholarly Research Committee of Pace University; to Mary Ann Landry, assistant to the vice president for communications, Pace University; to Sister Teresa Brady, professor of English, Pace University; to Sister M. Berchmans Coyle, associate dean, University College, Pace University; to my present departmental assistant, Melea Bolan; and to Marie Cucurullo and Edith Papp, who previously served as my assistants before going on to law school and graduate school, respectively.

Marilyn E. Weigold

PREFACE TO THE SECOND EDITION

It's not often that an author has the opportunity to produce an updated, augmented second edition of a long-out-of-print book but, given the number of inquiries received from individuals interested in acquiring a copy of the first edition, the time seemed right to publish a second edition of *Silent Builder: Emily Warren Roebling and the Brooklyn Bridge.* Moreover, just as the Internet facilitated the discovery of the first edition by would-be readers from as far away as Australia, the Internet also provided access to sources, including the venerable *Brooklyn Daily Eagle*, which has been digitized and indexed. This readily accessible version of the newspaper yielded interesting new information about Emily Warren Roebling's involvement with the Brooklyn Bridge project and her accomplishments in the years following the completion of the bridge.

The Internet also facilitated access to Roebling family documents in the collections of the Rutgers University Libraries and the Folsom Library at Rensselaer Polytechnic Institute. The online finding aids for the collections of both institutions are comprehensive and excellent. I am most grateful to Dr. Fernanda Perrone, archivist, special collections, Alexander Library, Rutgers University, New Brunswick, New

Jersey, for her guidance and detailed answers to my queries. Christine A. Lutz, New Jersey regional studies librarian, and Albert C. King, curator of manuscripts, Special Collections and University Archives, are owed a debt of gratitude as well. At the Folsom Library, Jennifer Monger, assistant institute archivist in the Institute Archives and Special Collections, enlightened me about certain components of the collections and provided a digitized copy of Emily Roebling's brief biography of Washington Roebling. A debt of gratitude is also owed to Kelly Dwyer, a former reference assistant who facilitated the search, in the papers of mineralogist George Frederick Kunz, in Special Collections, Syracuse University Libraries, and directed me to other repositories containing Kunz's papers. Library Reference Services at the New York State Library facilitated the exploration of the papers of Gouverneur Kemble Warren, Emily's brother, and identified correspondence between the two. In Brooklyn, Cecily Dyer, archivist and reference librarian, and Julie May, managing director, library, at the Brooklyn Historical Society were very helpful. In Cold Spring, Putnam County, New York, Rachel Ornstein, executive director of the Putnam History Museum, and the museum's library volunteers provided assistance. And in Washington, Edith Sandler, manuscript reference librarian at the Library of Congress, and Ellen Alers of the archives reference team, Smithsonian Institution, provided assistance regarding the papers of George Frederick Kunz.

In addition to the extremely knowledgeable and accommodating staff members of repositories containing significant collections of material relating to Emily Roebling, a debt of gratitude is owed to Sheila Hu, interlibrary loan/reference librarian, Mortola Library, Pace University, Pleasantville, New York. Sheila obtained dozens of articles and books, including a rare pamphlet containing the full text of Congressman Abram Hewitt's address, in which he praised Emily, at the opening-day ceremonies for the Brooklyn Bridge. As I sat in the campus library turning the pages of this fragile volume I felt as though I was literally holding history in my hands and I am most grateful to Sheila for securing this and so many other works required for my research. Other helpful individuals at the Mortola Library were Steven Feyl, associate university librarian, and Rose Gillen, head of research and information services.

Beyond the research phase of the project and the incorporation of new material on Emily Warren Roebling, plus the writing of a lengthy, extensively documented new final chapter on the history of women in the engineering profession in the United States, the key person in the effort to produce a second edition of *Silent Builder* was Jeff Canning. A fine historian himself, who spent his career as a professional editor, Jeff devoted countless hours to editing the manuscript, catching errors, posing questions and making recommendations that enhanced the final version. For his meticulous work on the manuscript right through the final reading of the proofs, I am exceedingly grateful. I am very appreciative as well of the time my Pace University colleague Dr. Durahn Taylor, associate professor of history, devoted to reading the manuscript and offering helpful suggestions.

I am also appreciative of the enthusiasm and support for this project provided by Varissa McMickens Blair, executive director of the Roebling Museum, an institution that, in the nine years since its founding, has mounted fine exhibits and sponsored educational initiatives designed to acquaint young people with engineering and other STEM fields. The interest displayed by museum trustees in the second edition of *Silent Builder*, with its chapter on women in engineering, is also appreciated. I am especially indebted to trustee Kristian Roebling, great-great-grandson of Emily, who read the manuscript and provided very helpful insights.

Marilyn E. Weigold
August 2018

PREFACE TO THE THIRD EDITION

2023 is an anniversary year for both Emily Warren Roebling and the Brooklyn Bridge. Emily was born in Cold Spring, New York, a picturesque village in the Hudson Valley, 180 years ago and the Brooklyn Bridge, which was such an important part of her life, was completed 140 years ago. Although Emily was very much involved with the bridge long after it was officially opened amidst great fanfare that included a spectacular fireworks display, she remained a rather obscure figure. Beginning with the centennial of the bridge in 1983, however, Emily started to emerge from the shadows of history. The process was gradual prior to the 21st century, when it accelerated. *The New York Times* featured Emily in its Overlooked Women series. The Brooklyn Heights street where the Roeblings lived was co-named Emily Warren Roebling Way thanks to the New York City Council. A public school was named for her as was the final component of Brooklyn Bridge Park, Emily Warren Roebling Plaza, directly below the bridge. By 2023, Emily was at last accorded the recognition warranted by her invaluable contributions to the success of the Brooklyn Bridge project.

In addition to an expanded bibliography, this edition of *Silent Builder* features a new section in Chapter 2 focusing on documentary evidence for the long rumored and often denied story of Emily's presentation to the American Society of Civil Engineers as part of her campaign to prevent her husband from being removed from his position as Chief Engineer less than a year before the opening of the bridge. The author of the document was a prominent and highly respected New Yorker with whom Washington Roebling was associated through the New York Mineralogical Society. The new *Back Story* section of Chapter 2 provides ample information about his fascinating life and career as well as his connection with the Roeblings. The third edition also features a new Chapter 5 providing details of the recognition Emily has received in recent years and analyzing the various titles used to describe her contributions to the bridge project. The new Chapter 5 replaces *Women in Engineering* in the second edition. An expanded version of that chapter was published as a separate volume, *Women Who Engineered Our World*, in 2022.

As with previous editions of *Silent Builder*, this edition reflects the input of individuals who provided assistance to the author. They included Rose Gillen, Director of the Mortola Library at Pace University, who helped me navigate digital databases, Erik Jantzen, Library System Analyst, who created a professor emeritus account that enabled me to utilize all of the university's online resources, and Christina Blinkle, Supervising Librarian for Electronic Services at the Mortola Library. I am also grateful to Dr. Durahn Taylor, Associate Professor of History at Pace, who reviewed the manuscript and offered helpful recommendations for enhancing it, as well as to Dr. Jason Warren, a military historian whose academic career included faculty positions at

West Point and the Naval War College, for providing information about Emily Warren Roebling's ancestors. Jodie Lynn Jacobs, international animal rights advocate and avid reader, reviewed the third edition from the perspective of a general reader. The excellent questions she posed about things that required clarification improved the book and I am most appreciative of her efforts. I am also very grateful to Nancy May, an environmentalist as well as a practitioner of, and enthusiastic spokesperson for, sustainability. An avid reader with wide-ranging interests, Nancy read the manuscript and provided insights that strengthened the final version. Jennifer Lawrence of the American Society of Civil Engineers was most helpful in providing information from the archives of that organization. I also wish to acknowledge graphic artist Phil Rose, well known for the covers he designed for *New York Times* best-selling books, who updated the splendid cover he designed for the second edition of *Silent Builder* to reflect the fact that the new version is an anniversary edition. A debt of gratitude is owed as well to Nancy Rose, rights and permissions expert, who handled issues relating to the use of previously published and new illustrations.

Preparing a book for publication poses many challenges but I have been extremely fortunate to have two superb consultants whose enormous contributions made this project viable. Delaney Anderson, a publishing industry professional specializing in interior book design, is a consummate professional who dealt expertly with all aspects of the volume's design and is a pleasure to deal with. The same holds true for my editor, Jeff Canning, formerly a senior news editor with Gannett and an avid historian, whose expert scrutiny of all components of the manuscript greatly enhanced the final version of the third edition. Jeff has been my editorial consultant for almost two decades. He reviewed proofs for my book on Peconic Bay, published by Syracuse University Press, and a SUNY Press book on Yonkers in the 20th century. For the second edition of *Silent Builder* and the standalone work *Women Who Engineered Our World* he was the editor-in-chief and I am most grateful for his invaluable contributions to the aforementioned volumes as well as to the third edition of *Silent Builder.*

Marilyn E. Weigold, Ph.D.
Professor Emeritus of History
Pace University
May 24, 2023

INTRODUCTION

On May 24, 1983, enthusiastic crowds gathered in New York City to commemorate and celebrate the 100th anniversary of the Brooklyn Bridge. The weather was picture perfect that day as it had been a century earlier when the bridge was dedicated. In 1983 the sun shone brightly on marchers, bands and horse-drawn carriages parading across the bridge and at night conditions were ideal for the huge fireworks display that marked the grand finale of the festivities. Anyone, including myself, who had the good fortune to witness the show that illuminated the sky over the East River was treated to a breathtaking spectacle. For people seated in the VIP section on the Brooklyn side of the bridge or those, like myself, who were on boats, it seemed as though the mighty span was under siege. The cacophony of exploding shells, beautiful though they were, resembled bombardment, conveying the feeling, at least to some onlookers, of being in a war zone. Ironically, 19th century writers had depicted a war torn New York where great structures such as the Brooklyn Bridge lay in ruins. Coinciding with the opening of the bridge, journalist and architectural critic Montgomery Schuyler transported his readers to a future time when only a tower of the bridge served as a silent reminder of what had once been the crowning achievement of the Roeblings, who had designed and built the bridge. In his novel *The Last American*, published in 1889 but set in the mid-20th century, John Ames Mitchell, a co-founder of *Life* magazine, described a New York in which the towers of the Brooklyn Bridge stood as silent sentinels to the destruction of the city.

Amidst the centennial festivities in 1983 the destruction of a great city and its iconic landmarks was unimaginable but within two decades the unthinkable occurred. Even before September 11, 2001, New York was targeted. In February 1993 a bomb hidden in a truck parked in the World Trade Center garage was detonated, killing six people and causing more than a thousand injuries. Horrific though it was, this attack paled in comparison to 9-11 when planes hijacked by terrorists flew into the towers of the World Trade Center, causing the deaths of 2,977 people. In the immediate aftermath of the attacks that toppled the Twin Towers, the Brooklyn Bridge, though itself a potential target, assumed a new role as an escape route for countless people fleeing the chaos of lower Manhattan. Thousands upon thousands of frightened refugees streamed across the bridge to safety in Brooklyn. Among the first wave of people who made it across were some who feared the bridge would be brought down by those responsible for the carnage across the river. Filled with trepidation they, nonetheless, climbed the stairs to the historic structure's walkway. Covered with ash that had coated lower Manhattan, some people held handkerchiefs over their mouths; others wore masks to protect themselves as best they could from the pollutants swirling through the air. On the whole, people were calm, unlike the throng on the bridge on Memorial Day 1883. A boisterous reaction to a minor mishap involving a pedestrian that day reverberated throughout the crowd, causing people to believe the bridge was falling. In the ensuing stampede a dozen people lost their lives.

On 9-11 the scene was very different despite some panic, especially after the second tower fell. There was no turning back, though, and thankfully some of the people on the bridge were take-charge types who practically ordered jittery fellow pedestrians to remain calm and keep on walking. Depending upon their physical or emotional condition, some people strolled across the span while others ran. Through it all, *The New York Times* reported, "The trekkers for the most part remained extraordinarily calm. But once on the streets of Brooklyn, they shook and they walked in circles and they sat down on the curb and wept."[1] Volunteers did what they could to help, providing water and soothing words; for pedestrians needing more than that, ambulances and a triage center awaited them at the foot of the bridge.

One can only imagine what John A. Roebling, who designed the bridge, his son Washington A. Roebling, who became Chief Engineer of the project following his father's untimely death, and Washington's wife, Emily Warren Roebling, who played a vital behind-the-scenes role after her husband was incapacitated by caisson disease, would have thought of the events of 9-11 and the role assumed that day by the 118-year-old bridge to which the Roebling name was still firmly attached thanks to Emily. In the chapters that follow, Emily's story, from her childhood in Cold Spring, New York, through the bridge-building years and beyond to her construction projects in Trenton, New Jersey, and in a Montauk, Long Island, military camp, her world travels, fame as a lecturer, and law student at New York University, is told. In recounting Emily's story, material from *The Brooklyn Daily Eagle*, which was not digitized when the first edition of this book was being researched, and from other sources has been included, along with an updated section on Emily's descendants. This third edition includes a new Chapter 5 that focuses on Emily's growing national and international reputation.

---

[1] *The New York Times*, September 12, 2001, p. 11.

PROLOGUE

On a fine spring day in 1883, less than a month before the Brooklyn Bridge opened, an attractive woman in her late 30s entered the recently completed roadway of the majestic span. She was seated in a grasshopper gig with a retractable hood manufactured by the New York firm of Wood Gibson. Accompanying her was a lively white rooster, the symbol of victory.[1] This unusual spectacle surely must have puzzled workers putting the finishing touches on the bridge.

Yet the woman was no stranger to these men. In the years since her husband had been stricken with caisson disease, the dreaded bends, Emily Warren Roebling had made countless trips to the bridge. She was the liaison between her husband, Colonel Washington Roebling, Chief Engineer of the Brooklyn Bridge, and the laborers, foremen and assistant engineers involved in the day-to-day construction work. It was, therefore, appropriate to accord her the honor of being the first person to drive across the bridge. As with so many tasks she had performed during the preceding 11 years, the assignment was undertaken at the suggestion of her husband, who, according to Emily, "was very anxious to know … the effect of trotting a horse across the Bridge, and it was thought just as well that I should trot … over and that one of the engineer corps should go along to take observations of the effect on the suspenders if any were perceptible."[2] The assistant engineer on the bridge when Mrs. Roebling trotted by could not detect even the slightest vibration of the suspenders.

This was a welcome relief to Colonel Roebling because an earlier Roebling bridge, between Covington, Kentucky, and Cincinnati, Ohio, although perfectly safe, vibrated noticeably whenever a horse trotted across it. The new East River Bridge, as the span linking Brooklyn and Manhattan was first called, represented an important achievement in the evolution of the Roebling bridge-building technique. It is no wonder, then, that Emily felt justified in bringing along a symbol of victory on her fast trot across the bridge.

In a rare interview, Emily told a reporter from the *Brooklyn Union*, "The trotting of a horse on a bridge makes itself felt very easily, but the result of the observations on the day I drove was most satisfactory."[3] When Mrs. Roebling finished speaking, the reporter asked if the new bridge could accommodate locomotives. She replied, "I know that Colonel Roebling is opposed to using locomotives on the Bridge at any time, not because he fears the structure would not sustain the weight, but because they would frighten horses on the roadways and seriously interfere with ordinary traffic across the Bridge."[4]

Rather than elaborate further, she suggested that the reporter accompany her upstairs to her husband's room, where he could speak directly to the Colonel. The elated newspaperman, who discovered Washington Roebling up and about and looking considerably healthier than he had expected, elicited basically the same response from the Chief

Engineer. The only thing husband and wife disagreed on was whether the Colonel would retire from the engineering profession. In response to the reporter's inquiry regarding his retirement, Emily replied, with her eyebrows raised for emphasis: "This is his last as well as his greatest work. He will need a long rest after this is over. He needs it and he has certainly earned it."[5] Yet, when the reporter asked him directly, Washington Roebling said: "I don't know. If I get well there is lots of work in the world to do yet."[6] Emily's reaction to this statement went unrecorded. Most likely, she betrayed no emotion.

When dealing with strangers, it was necessary to convey a positive impression. For Emily Warren Roebling this was a relatively easy task because she had been doing it for more than a decade in a successful attempt to prevent her husband's removal from the position of Chief Engineer of one of the 19th century's greatest construction achievements. Her intelligence, determination and, when required, forcefulness were in no small way responsible for Colonel Washington Roebling's greatest success, and for the honor and respect accorded the Roebling name during the past 135 years. The trials and tribulations of Emily Warren Roebling – a remarkable 19th-century woman and an outstanding model of excellence for women of the next century and beyond – will unfold in these pages.

Endnotes

[1]*True American*, April 15, 1894. Clipping File, Trenton Free Library.

[2]*Brooklyn Union*, May 16, 1883, 1:3.

[3]Ibid.

[4]Ibid.

[5]Ibid.

[6]Ibid.

CHAPTER 1
APPRENTICE

Growing Up Along the Hudson

Although she may not have fully realized it, Emily Warren Roebling's entire life was inextricably bound up with rivers. As an adult she helped her invalid husband bridge the East River separating New York and Brooklyn. During her childhood in upstate New York, the majestic Hudson River played a major role in her life. Near Cold Spring, Putnam County, New York, where Emily was born on September 23, 1843, the Hudson emerges from the Highlands and begins its slow journey to the open sea beyond lower New York Harbor.

Despite the coming of the railroad and various other changes, today's Cold Spring is reminiscent of the little hamlet Emily knew. Indeed, the community, which derived its name from the frigid, crystal clear water bubbling up from a local spring, has aged rather pleasantly. The ruins of the West Point Foundry, where the famous Parrott field gun was produced for the Union Army during the Civil War, are still there, together with the Hudson House River Inn, which was known as the Pacific House when it opened in

1837.[1] Elsewhere in the village, two old Warren family homes are still standing. Along with other charming 19th-century dwellings, they add to the historic character of this quaint community.[2]

A few things have changed since the days of Emily Warren's childhood, however. For one: "[t]hey have blasted away the beautiful Breakneck Mt. at Cold Spring. Such vast quantities of stone are now used for railroad ballast and macadamized roads – nothing is sacred from the stone men."[3] For another, antiques shops and boutiques have replaced the simple shops of yesteryear on Cold Spring's Main Street.

In a letter written to her son a quarter-century after she had first taken the boy there for a visit, Emily said the place had "not changed in a single particular except that the trees are larger and the fences old and tumbled down and most of the family dead and gone."[4] When she wrote these words, Mrs. Roebling was engaged in genealogical research on her paternal ancestors, who included a 13th-century French nobleman and his Huguenot descendant, Claude de Maitre, who settled in New York, where his name was Anglicized as Delamater.[5] Another distinguished ancestor was Richard Warren, Duke of Normandy and great-grandfather of William the Conqueror. A descendant and namesake of this Richard Warren traveled to America on board the Mayflower and was the 12th signer of the Mayflower Compact.[6] Emily Warren Roebling's research on her first American ancestor led her to the Antiquarian Society in Worcester, Massachusetts, as well as Colonial burying grounds in Plymouth, Scituate, Boston, Middleborough and South Duxbury.[7]

Emily's search for maternal ancestors took her to the

historic Old Cemetery at Van Cortlandtville near Peekskill, Westchester County, New York. Of special interest to her were the graves of her maternal grandfather, William Lickley, her great-grandfather, John Lickley, and her great-great-grandfather, John Barret, who, at the start of the Revolutionary War, enlisted in the 7th Regiment, commanded by Henry Ludington.[8]

On her initial visit to the Van Cortlandtville cemetery, Mrs. Roebling had to scrape away the moss to read the inscriptions on the low, old-fashioned tombstones, but it was well worth the effort because, on her great-grandfather's stone, beneath the dates of his birth and death, she discovered the words, "An honest man is the noblest work of God."[9] William J. Blake's *The History of Putnam County, New York*, says something similar about her paternal grandfather, John Warren, who was born in 1765 and died in 1837, just six years prior to Emily's birth. According to the 1849 publication, John aspired to "no higher distinction than that of a plain practical farmer. ... The purity of motives, and the honesty of his heart were never questioned, and in all the relations of life he never gave just cause of offense to his neighbor. He died regretted and beloved by all who knew him."[10] In the course of his lifetime, John Warren became a comparatively wealthy man. A 300-acre farm, a blacksmith shop and a gristmill were his principal holdings. According to his granddaughter Emily, "none of his children, grandchildren, or great-grandchildren ever had so much of this world's goods."[11]

Of the seven children of John Warren and Sarah Nelson Warren, Sylvanus and his brother Cornelius were the most celebrated. Cornelius, who was nearly a decade older than Sylvanus, was a judge in the Court of Common Pleas and a member of the U.S. House of Representatives. Sylvanus was a New York State assemblyman and supervisor of the Town of Philipstown, which included the Village of Cold Spring.[12] In addition to Emily Warren Roebling, the other well-known offspring among the dozen children born to Sylvanus Warren and Phebe Lickley Warren was Gouverneur Kemble Warren. Named for his father's close friend, Gouverneur Kemble, a congressman from New York State, this fourth child of Sylvanus Warren graduated from the U.S. Military Academy second in his class at the age of 20.[13]

Although 13 years older than Emily and absent much of the time while she was growing up because of his school and Army duties, Gouverneur was unusually close to his sister. He especially enjoyed being with her during holidays when relatives and friends gathered for what Emily described in later years as "a family party" attended by "old folks, young folks, and children."[14] It is not difficult to imagine them singing carols and admiring the soft glow of the candles on the Christmas tree. Perhaps afterward some of the younger people piled into sleighs for a moonlight ride. Emily herself was likely to have held the reins since, unlike the stereotypical Victorian who scrupulously avoided activities that could be termed masculine, she was an enthusiastic and expert horse-woman. Throughout her life she enjoyed riding and driving, first horses and horse-drawn carriages, and, later, bikes. Never a thin-stemmed, delicate flower, Emily was robust and amply proportioned as a young woman and remained so for the rest of her life.

The Washington, D.C., Years

Emily's devoted older brother, Gouverneur, junior lieutenant, who would one day become a general of the U.S. Army, offered to send enough money to pay for whatever the younger children in the family needed, including a first-rate education. "If I were to have a choice of ways to spend my money, I would rather, for my own gratification, devote it to advancing my brothers and sisters," he assured his widowed mother.[15]

These were no idle words because, in 1858, Gouverneur Kemble Warren enrolled his favorite sister in the Georgetown Visitation Convent in Washington, D.C. There, at a school in its 60th year of operation, Emily studied Profane History, Ancient and Modern, Geography, Mythology, Prose Composition, Rhetoric and Grammar, French, Algebra, Geometry, Bookkeeping, Astronomy, Botany, Meteorology, Chemistry and Geology, plus subjects calculated to make her eminently marriageable. These included housekeeping and domestic economy, tapestry and crochet work, embroidery, painting in water color, and piano and guitar.[16]

Although Emily studied Christian doctrine for a while, prior to emerging from the school in 1860, after being awarded a Crown and Gold Medal, the highest honors, she dropped the subject since, as a non-Catholic, she was not required to take it.[17] Nevertheless, something of the school's doctrinal orientation rubbed off on her because, later in life, she frequently referred to saints' days in her letters to her son.[18]

Four years after completing her education at Georgetown Visitation, Emily joined the Episcopal Church. Her fiancé,

Washington A. Roebling, eldest son of the famous engineer John A. Roebling, commented on his future wife's sudden interest in religion by observing:

If you are bound to join the Church anyhow, it is just as well that you do it now. In Trenton it would create unheard-of excitement because our family is looked upon as the most monstrous heathens lost to all grace and hopes of future salvation. I think a little religion in a woman is a very good thing. I merely want to stipulate that I won't have to go more than once to church on any one Sunday, and that at least one Sunday in the month I need not go at all. Like yourself I have a religion of my own inclining somewhat toward spiritualism which your little minister no doubt will tell you is rank heresy.[19]

Five months earlier, after Emily had paid a return visit to Georgetown Visitation, he wrote:

How did you find the sisters at the Visitation; did they recognize you anymore or not; my dear, possibly you went there to take the veil and deceive your Wash; but it would do you no good; I would turn Monk at once and we would have the old story of Abelard and Héloïse over again; moreover you are not rich enough to make it an object for them. Do I slander the pious nuns by saying so?[20]

Courtship

It was not unusual for the youthful Washington Roebling, graduate of Rensselaer Polytechnic Institute, class of 1857, to give his sense of humor free rein. But there was one thing about which he was deadly serious – the young woman from Cold Spring, New York, whom he had met while she was visiting her brother, General Warren, on whose staff young Roebling was serving during the Civil War. The initial encounter between Miss Warren and Mr. Roebling occurred at a military ball held on February 22, 1864. Writing to his sister Elvira, Washington described the Second Corps ball where he met Emily as "the most successful ball ever given in any army or by anybody. … In point of attendance nothing better could have been desired," adding that "at least 150 ladies graced the assemblage."[21] But he had eyes for only one of them.

After meeting Miss Emily Warren, Washington Roebling was never the same. If ever there was a case of love at first sight, this was it. He told his sister:

I am very much of the opinion that she has captured your brother Washy's heart at last. It was a real attack in force, it came without any warning or any previous realization on my part of such an occurrence taking place and it was therefore all the more successful and I assure you that it gives me the greatest pleasure to say that I have succumbed; now don't go like a great big goose and show this letter to everyone, will you dear?[22]

Though by no means the most beautiful damsel on either side of the lines during the Civil War, Emily was sufficiently well endowed with looks and personality to capture the young officer almost before he realized what was happening. According to Washington Roebling, the object of his affection was "slightly pug-nosed, [with a] lovely mouth and teeth …

and a most entertaining talker, which is a mighty good thing you know," he told his sister, "I myself being so stupid. She is a little above medium size and has a most lovely complexion."[23]

Besides writing to his sister, Washington sent numerous letters to Emily herself. The correspondence, which began as soon as she returned home to Cold Spring, included an unusually forthright letter in which young Roebling explained how, as a student at Rensselaer Polytechnic Institute, he had been sought out by a homosexual classmate who "committed suicide because he loved me and I didn't sufficiently reciprocate his affection; I advised him to find someone like you for instance," Washington confided to Emily, "but he always said that no woman had sense enough to understand his love."[24] The intensity of his classmate's feeling can be gauged from a letter the young man wrote, in German, stating: "Except for my aged parents, you are the only person in the world whose love and friendship I cherish, and upon whom all my affection is concentrated. Under these circumstances, will you be able to bring yourself to deny my pleas?"[25] He went on to say: "I cannot continue to exist. … The constant uncertainty, in which I find myself, with reference to your attitude toward me, prevents me from working, from thinking – in short from everything."[26] Four days after receiving this letter, Washington Roebling found a suicide note on his table in which his classmate told him, "Keep of my things whatever you like, it is all yours!"[27]

Although his inclinations were decidedly heterosexual, in the aftermath of his classmate's death, Washington Roebling did not fall deeply in love with a member of the opposite sex for almost a decade. In 1864, when he at last met Emily, he confessed, "I had often laughed at other people who said they had been in love and [that] the time would come when I would know what the passion was and would not be able to help myself."[28]

Emily had made a lasting impression on the young officer thanks to a marvelous combination of intelligence, personality and physical presence. The hazel-eyed girl with the fashionable curls encircling her face possessed all the spontaneity and natural looks of a smart, well-brought-up country lassie. Despite her big-city education in the nation's capital prior to the war, she drew the line at affecting urban ways. This suited Washington Roebling, who disliked rouged women, preferring instead honest, down-to-earth women like his German-born mother and the girl from upstate New York who would soon be his wife.

Typical of a young man in love, Washington wrote about his fiancée's attributes and quite humorously at that.[29] In one letter, Wash, the name he preferred in those days, threatened to squeeze her thin. "I have a good deal of the hugging nature in me," he told her, "in as much as a raccoon is called a Wash bear in German – a name derived from the frequency with which he washes his face ..."[30] At one point, after Emily claimed she weighed less than her future husband, Wash insisted, "Your pulling me over proved the contrary very conclusively."[31]

After enduring his teasing about her weight, Emily decided to go on a diet. The results were less than satisfactory. In a letter, in which he referred to her as "Emily the Amazon," Colonel Roebling declared:

If you keep on getting much thinner, you will soon

be nothing but a mess of bones and I really have serious doubts about taking you now; our bargain you remember, was that you should not weigh less than 154 pounds; just weigh yourself quick and let me know if it is less; should it be the case, then I would advise you to contemplate the enclosed picture and grow fat at once –[32]

Despite his lighthearted references to his fiancée, some of Washington Roebling's letters dealt with serious matters such as Emily's habit of going out riding alone, especially when something was bothering her. This greatly troubled Washington Roebling, who warned, "My dear you must be a little more careful in riding; remember you belong to me now and every bone you break hurts me as much as you."[33] The Colonel was convinced that time would solve the problem because five months later he wrote: "What a girl you are for horses; nothing but horses to ride or drive. I have heard tell that when girls get married they get over that and I guess you will."[34] She didn't, but that, like so many other far more traumatic occurrences, was hidden from the eyes of Washington Roebling.

While he was still young, Roebling could brush mishaps and near calamities aside. "That foolish little stallion of mine fell down today causing me to describe a somersault over his head but I was up long before he was and had to kick him to make him get up," he confided in one letter to Emily.[35] But as the Union Army pressed on toward Petersburg, Virginia, something occurred that made riding accidents appear very minor. Despite the presence of General Ulysses Grant, whom Roebling characterized as "Useless" Grant, the troops made little headway and ended up "tired and played out."[36] But that was not the worst of it. Washington came within inches of being killed but he played down his brush with death, saying merely, "I met with no mishap; one bullet intended for me went through my orderly's heart killing him instantly."[37] Although he made light of it in many of his letters, Roebling occasionally betrayed his true feelings about the war. "I feel very much like croaking again about the war," he wrote to Emily in August 1864.[38] "It really looks as if it would never end."[39]

From time to time, Washington described battles, including the engagement at the Spotsylvania Court House. In this and other letters he kept her informed about her brother; "G.K. has a heavy disgust on," he told her, understandable in that "Uncle Robert Lee isn't licked yet by a long shot and if we are not mighty careful he will beat us yet."[40]

Still, even the most serious letters were filled with expressions of his deep love for the girl he would marry. In October 1864, after a brief furlough during which he saw Emily, Washington expressed his undying love for her. Earlier he had insisted, "There is no woman living for whom I would be willing to give you up."[41]

In contrast with the ardent Colonel, Emily appears to have been more restrained. Although her wartime letters to him have not survived, one need only examine his letters to her to realize that she had some misgivings about entering into matrimony. Responding to an issue she had previously raised, he wrote:

You dread our growing cold after marriage; a short
separation from my darling is the cure for that, but

unfortunately the remedy is as severe as the disease; wait until the time comes, you have other feelings which are as yet latent within you. Moreover, I bet you will be tired of me before I will of you.[42]

Despite any misgivings she may have had, by June 1864, counting the months until the wedding, Emily appeared resigned to becoming Mrs. Washington Roebling.

There were still a few hurdles to overcome, however. Breaking the news to General Warren was one. Until this matter was taken care of, Washington begged Emily not to wear the diamond engagement ring he had given her in her brother's presence. She could, however, show it off in front of her future sister-in-law, the general's wife. Indeed, Washington Roebling hoped she would tell her husband that his baby sister was engaged. In this way, Colonel Roebling would not have to approach his commanding officer cold to ask for Emily's hand in marriage. To do so would be unfeeling as well as dangerous given the general's heavy responsibilities. So burdensome were they that Washington confided to Emily that he wondered how long "G.K." could go on without stimulants. Sleeping only a short time, near daybreak, on three chairs pulled up to the fire, the general, in the opinion of the young colonel, was leading a life comparable to that of a Trappist monk.[43] Since he hesitated to interfere with the general's monastic existence, Washington begged Emily to think up a way to let her brother know about their impending marriage. "I know if I had my sister ask me for anything and put her arms around my neck," he told her, "I couldn't have the heart to refuse her anything – no indeed."[44]

Despite his reluctance to approach General Warren,

Washington Roebling was not the least bit hesitant about informing his own parents of his engagement. His father, writing from Cincinnati, where he was building a suspension bridge across the Ohio River, reacted most enthusiastically. Although he had never met Emily, he was quick to endorse the upcoming marriage, provided the union was based on love. To the elder Roebling, "A matrimonial union without love is no better than suicide."[45] His son fully agreed because, a few days later, he wrote to Emily, "Can you conceive of anything more horrible than a woman marrying to please her friends or relations – and still it is done so often – it reminds me of the French system of affiancing children in their cradles – a proceeding so utterly heartless."[46] Such unions were arranged for financial reasons, something young Washington Roebling did not have to think about, since his father was more than willing to lend him a helping hand. Since he needed assistance on the Cincinnati bridge project, John Roebling offered his son, who would be discharged from the Union Army prior to the wedding, a job the minute he learned of the impending marriage. Any money the young man might need in the meantime, he merely had to ask for. Once married, he could look forward to living in his parents' spacious Trenton home and, if that didn't suit the newlyweds, John Roebling offered to build them a house nearby.

Six months before the wedding, Washington informed Emily that they would temporarily live in Trenton following their marriage. A few months later, assuming she would want to return to Cold Spring for a visit with her family, he planned to go to Cincinnati to work on the bridge. He estimated that he would be there eight months. During that time he expected his bride to visit him for a month or two. None of this pleased Emily and she was quick to tell him so. Her letter shocked Washington so much that he declared, "Most of its contents deeply pain and grieve me."[47] He contended that she had misinterpreted his plan to send her off to Cold Spring. "God knows that if I ever had an earnest desire, it is to live together with you always," he told her.[48] But first he had to find a suitable place for them to live in Cincinnati and, as this would take a little time, he thought a visit to her mother and sister was a fine idea.

Emily thought otherwise. She viewed it as a way of getting rid of her for long periods of time, the way John Roebling handled his wife. This accusation prompted Washington to be extremely candid about his parents' relationship. He explained that while his mother, "a yielding and confiding woman," was a perfect partner for "a man of strong passions and impulses" like his father, she lacked his fine education and, since she mastered English imperfectly and many years after they had come to the United States, she was not her husband's equal.[49] Since he always moved in the best social circles wherever his work took him, it was not advisable for John Roebling to have his wife with him. Washington concluded that "a gifted woman" like Emily would have been a more suitable spouse for the middle-aged John Roebling but that, on the whole, his mother was the ideal mate for his father.[50] "I have been thus explicit in regard to my parental relations," he told her, "because I think that some knowledge of the real world will do you good."[51]

In the end, Washington Roebling yielded. He promised to take Emily along despite all the problems it would entail, not the least of which was his father's opposition, which he hoped could be overcome. He estimated that it would take a month or six weeks to find accommodations that would permit him to adhere to the rigid work schedule at the bridge. "I got into more rows with [my] father about that than I ever want to again at Pittsburg," he told her.[52] He was determined to be at the construction site at 6:30 a.m. in the summer and at 7:00 the rest of the year. To do this he would have to live close to the bridge and have an early breakfast, and dinner at precisely 12:30. Since first-class boarding houses did not offer such schedules, he assumed they would have to make some arrangements to live in a private home. It would be well worth the trouble, though, to have Emily at his side because "if I have someone to talk to like yourself, it will take off half the load even if you don't know much about it."[53]

Any objections John Roebling had to his future daughter-in-law accompanying Washington on an extended business trip vanished once he met the woman. A family friend had correctly predicted that Emily would be a "great pet of Father's."[54] The same woman was apparently among the "old fogies of both sexes in Trenton" who were lionizing Washington's fiancée during a 10-day visit to the Roebling home in August.[55] The Colonel did not think much of hometown society; yet before Emily set out for Trenton, he advised her to be especially charming to Charles Swan, his father's right-hand man at the wire factory. She succeeded only too well because, long after she was back in Cold Spring, Swan was sending his regards via her fiancé.[56]

Initially, Washington Roebling feared his Em, as he affectionately addressed her, would feel "like a fish out of water" in Trenton and "would become most dreadfully tired of the place even after a two days' stay."[57] But that wasn't the case. Following a sleepless first night occasioned by the noise of the water in the raceway of the Delaware River, she adjusted beautifully. "I am so glad that you find you can live in Trenton without being homesick," he wrote to her, adding, "if you can do that without my presence you can surely do so when I am there."[58] The woman from Cold Spring adjusted so quickly that she became her old self in short order, even to the point of playing a favorite prank, throwing water, presumably at her fiancé's younger brothers, Charles, Ferdinand and Edmund.

Ferdinand Roebling seems to have developed quite a crush on his future sister-in-law but Emily handled it well when the boys visited her at Cold Spring in the absence of their eldest brother. Their trip was partly a get-acquainted visit and partly an inspection tour, as was the invitation extended to Emily by Washington's sister Laura, who lived on Staten Island with her German-born teacher-husband. Since this visit preceded her trip to Trenton, she derived the erroneous impression that she was marrying into a thoroughly Germanic family. Her husband-to-be hastened to assure her that, with the exception of his mother, the Trenton clan would be different.[59]

This was important because Washington Roebling intended to live there in the old family homestead with his bride, necessitating certain dislocations in the house. Washington initially suggested tossing his sister Josephine out of her room so the newlyweds could have not only a bedroom but a "loafing room. The large front room," he told her, "smells too much of bad tobacco – When Uncle Reidel left us, he left 10,000,000 cigar stumps in the closets, the smell of which has not departed yet."[60] Edward Reidel was actually a cousin and a welcome visitor to the Roebling home because of his ability to function as a medium. Following his wife's death in 1864, John Roebling hosted seances at which Reidel attempted to summon the spirit of Johanna Roebling as well as other deceased family members.[61]

Washington Roebling's interest was in the living, not the dead. Although he sincerely mourned his mother's passing, he had no desire to postpone his marriage to Emily; he was too deeply in love. The attachment was physical as well as spiritual. During periods of their courtship when they were together they were virtually inseparable. "I remember that first tête-à-tête evening at the signal station," he wrote. "When the moon rose I merely ventured to rub my cheek against yours … I know when the ice was broken there was no end to them."[62] Washington was referring to his fiancée's "sweet kisses," which he was utterly incapable of resisting. Early in their courtship, he told her, "My lips have fully recovered from your attacks [and] are in excellent fighting trim to receive you."[63] Months later he wrote, "You ask how it was you came to pet me so much? Why, I always pretended it was such a bore to be kissed by you, so that you made it a point to give me twice as many, which is just what I was fishing for."[64] Interjecting a bit of philosophy, he continued: "A little trouble in getting something always adds to the zest of it. You must not apply that rule though after we are married. I shall claim everything then and bite you if you don't obey willingly."[65]

In preparation for his conjugal duties, Washington Roebling read a book titled *Advice to Married People*. He and some of his comrades in arms stole it from a private home during their sojourn in enemy territory and were reading it "with great gusto."[66] Sometime earlier, upon learning that Emily was reading a rather explicit book, he declared: "I see your taste is perverted past all redemption; a person soon gets tired of reading all piquant and racy books of the kind. I shall, however, constitute myself your purveyor in that line and get you anything you want; I want you to know as much in that line as I do."[67]

Wash's "Sweet Angel of Purity" apparently was well versed in that area. Although there is no reason to suspect that she had been intimately involved with any of her suitors prior to Washington, nor with him, for that matter, before they were married, she was not ignorant about sex. One derives the impression, reading her fiancé's letters, that the reason she asked him to burn her letters was her fear that some of the contents referring to intimacies could be misinterpreted by anyone other than the intended recipient. Whatever the reason, the destruction of her almost daily letters is most regrettable. Yet, happily, his writing yields considerable insight into her thoughts. One learns, for example, that Emily at one point suggested postponing the wedding until after the war ended. Although Washington rejected the idea, Emily's intimations on that subject reflected her ambivalence about committing herself forever to a man she would know less than a year by the time they were married. Yet she somehow overcame her reservations and began to prepare, in earnest, for the wedding.

Seven months before the big day, the jovial future bride-groom told his fiancée, only partly in jest:

I can't help thinking what a time there will be in Cold Spring when you get married to me; there will be such a crowd that I think it would be a good plan to hire out the seats and make enough money that way to pay the expenses of the wedding tour – Where do you want to go to? The summer is a good time to decide where to go in winter and your voice you know is law – let me hear from you on the subject.[68]

As might be expected, the future bride was also permitted to set all the ground rules for the wedding, including the determination of how long her fiancé would have to stay at her home prior to the ceremony. Although he preferred to spend only one night under the Warren roof before running off with the most valuable possession in the house, he was not deterred by the prospect of staying longer in order to claim his prize.

Nor did the chill winds of the Hudson Valley dissuade him. In early September, Emily had written to him about the possibility of frigid weather for their wedding. He reminded her that, as a student at Rensselaer Polytechnic Institute, he had survived four winters in Troy, farther up the Hudson. During the winter of 1856-57, he told her, "The thermometer stood [at] 22 [degrees] in my bedroom, cold enough to freeze both horns and tail off a brass monkey."[69] The frigid weather notwithstanding, Washington was willing, indeed anxious, to head up the Hudson. He even looked forward to seeing "all the notables of Cold Spring and shall no doubt be quite a lion in the character of Em's beau, that is, the real one, not one of the shams you have had heretofore."[70]

As the time for the wedding drew near, Washington, a

newly commissioned lieutenant colonel, left the service. Three-and-a-half years was a long enough commitment to a war that seemed unending. He had more important things to do. Getting married was at the top of the list. Though scarcely able to wait for the big day, he lamented that "the real time that I will have, to get ready for the wedding will after all be quite short, not much over two weeks."[71] Rushed or not, he took time to send Emily these lines by Elizabeth Barrett Browning:

God be thanked, the meanest of His creatures
Boasts two soul-sides, one to face the world with,
One to show a woman when he loves her.[72]

Eleven days later he wrote: "I never realized that I could love you so much and I know after we are married I will love you all the more; it is a feeling that with me increases with the lapse of time. I assure you it is great happiness to know that you fully possess the heart of another human being."[73]

The wedding of Emily and Washington Roebling on January 18, 1865, took place in the red brick Saint Mary's Episcopal Church in the Highlands on Cold Spring's picturesque Main Street, not far from the present church on the corner of Main Street and what is now New York Route 9D. The son of the world-famous engineer, John Roebling, and his new bride quite understandably stole the show but they were not the only couple to emerge from the church as newlyweds. Their wedding was actually a double ceremony in which Emily's brother, Major Edgar Washburn Warren, and Cornelia Barrows were also married.

Early Married Life

For several months after their marriage, Emily and

Washington lived in the Roebling house in Trenton. They eventually moved to Cincinnati, where the bridegroom worked on the bridge his father was building between that city and Covington, Kentucky. Emily was temporarily left behind in Trenton, until her husband could find a suitable place for them to live. Initially, though, his main preoccupation was the bridge. "Our bridge here is an immense thing," he told her.[74] "It far surpasses my expectations and any idea I had formed of it previously. In a short time I shall be accustomed to the enlarged dimensions of everything and then it will be looked upon like anything else."[75]

Regaining his pre-war expertise as an engineer, the Civil War veteran soon settled down to practical matters. Life in the Midwest was far from comfortable between the cramped quarters Washington was forced to occupy when he first arrived and the ever-present soot. "Everything here is black, black; no one wears anything else; it is of no use."[76] He warned Emily: "Your purple silk checked with white would be as black as your black silk in a week. No amount of washing keeps the hands clean."[77] The prospect of being perpetually covered with soot was not enough to deter Emily from heading out to join her husband as soon as he found a livable environment for them to share. For the next two years she remained at his side, apparently with the full blessing of her father-in-law, who spent most of his time at the wire company in Trenton, leaving his capable son in charge of the bridge project.

In 1867, as John Roebling prepared to build an even larger span across the East River linking Brooklyn and New York, he asked his son to travel to Europe to study pneumatic caissons. Always the dutiful offspring, Washington was only too happy to comply with his father's request, especially since the elder Roebling offered to send Emily along and to pay all of their expenses. Although she was expecting a child, the bright, energetic Mrs. Roebling was delighted to undertake the rigors of an Atlantic crossing because "to her the idea of going to Europe is something exceedingly grand."[78] Yet it was no mean feat considering that she suffered from seasickness whenever she set foot on a boat. This trip was no exception; she was "desperately seasick for four or five days."[79] But once they arrived in England, Emily was fine and delighted in touring Parliament and Westminster Abbey. In Paris, the Roeblings visited what *The London Times* called "the Great French Exhibition."[80] From there they went to the German States, where Washington Roebling was given the red-carpet treatment at the Krupp works. Outsiders were never permitted to tour the sprawling Krupp complex at Essen but, for the son of the famous German-born bridge builder, the rules were discarded.

While Washington visited various bridges and factories throughout the German States, the time for the birth of the baby drew near. Three weeks before the child arrived, Emily had a dreadfully traumatic experience, the consequences of which could not be immediately foreseen. While standing at the top of a flight of stairs, she somehow lost her balance and fell down the entire flight, landing on a patch of stone pavement. Since she made a rather rapid recovery from the fall itself, the seriousness of the tumble was not apparent until she went into labor. Fortunately, her husband's cousins, plus several capable German doctors, were able to save both her and the baby boy born in the medieval walled town of

Mühlhausen in Thüringen on November 21, 1867. But the new mother was not out of the woods entirely because, as her husband explained in a letter to Charles Swan, his father's chief assistant and a great admirer of the young Mrs. Roebling:

> While I was away on my travels, Emily had a bad time, all on account of that fall before the child was born; she has been bleeding more or less all the time for the last four weeks which made her excessively weak; it has stopped however and she sat up for the first time yesterday and is getting strength again quite rapidly.[81]

The baby was quite large at birth and robust. His paternal aunt Elvira, on far-off Staten Island, wrote to her father, at her brother's request, informing him of the birth and pointing out that the youngest Roebling weighed 12 pounds and had made his debut with a full head of hair. In view of his concern about Emily, Washington apparently had little time for writing letters. Thus he asked Elvira to be the bearer of the good news to the rest of the family. Her subsequent letter to her father was filled with details about the child born in Europe. Reiterating what her brother had said in his letter to her, she pointed out that the blue-eyed boy had "a thundering voice" and "fingernails that have to be clipped already."[82]

By the time the child was six weeks old, his mother had recovered sufficiently to leave the inn at Mühlhausen in Thüringen where she had been confined since before the birth of her son. On January 5, 1868, she took the baby to the Untermarkts Kirche, an Evangelical Lutheran Gothic structure dating from the 13th century, to be baptized. There, the indomitable Emily strolled into a rather unusual situation. As she approached the baptismal font, with babe in arms, another couple got in front of her and Washington. When the minister asked the name of the child, the parents of the other child who was going to be baptized replied, "Johann August Roebling." Emily quickly realized that the English translation of this was John August Roebling, the name she had selected for her son. She, therefore, shouted, in English, "Stop! You have made a mistake, it is my child who is to have that name."[83] The other couple quickly pointed out that their name, too, was Röbling, which was really not unusual since this was Mühlhausen, the ancestral home of the Roebling family and the birthplace of John Augustus Roebling, the distinguished engineer. At their insistence, the minister baptized their son, Johann August Röbling.

When the time came to hold the son of the American Roeblings over the baptismal font, the perplexed minister called out the same name for the little boy but the name recorded in the church records was James. According to her husband, "It took some time to pacify" Emily.[84] By the following day, however, after a traditional Mühlhausen coffee party to celebrate the baptism, she was in a good frame of mind when she took pen in hand to write to her father-in-law. She informed him that, in accordance with German custom, he had been named the baby's godfather. She delighted in telling her father-in-law that her child bore his name. "The name of John A. Roebling," she declared, "must ever be identified with you and your works but with a mother's pride and fond hopes for her first-born, I trust my boy may not prove unworthy of the name though I cannot hope that he will ever make it famous as you have done."[85] In closing, Emily sent her love to Mrs. Roebling, actually Lucia Cooper Roebling, the daughter of a wealthy civil engineer from Dublin, Ireland, whom John Roebling had married in 1866, following the death of his first wife.[86]

It would be many months before John Roebling and his wife would see Emily's son because the new mother still required considerable rest and ample nourishment. Given her predisposition to seasickness, she would have had a hard time keeping down food even if she had been in the best of health. Under these circumstances, it was deemed safer to postpone the trip to America until she had completely recovered from the energy-sapping ordeal she had undergone following both her accidental fall and John's birth. Being an inherently strong person, physically as well as emotionally, she recovered more quickly than anticipated. In March, the Roeblings were able to sail for the United States aboard the S.S. Weser. Once back in familiar surroundings, her recovery was complete.[87]

At long last, the new mother was able to enjoy the child who, in his father's words, was "a bright little chap."[88] Besides being well-endowed intellectually, the Roeblings' son was physically strong. Robust from birth, the boy was apparently the picture of health. The heart defect that would cause him to lead a rather sedentary life as an adult was not yet evident. At 11 months he was walking considerable distances and fighting with his cousin Sidney, General Warren's son, who was almost two at the time. Emily never hesitated to tell her husband about the child's latest triumphs. When Washington Roebling was away on business, he received numerous letters from his wife. These epistles contained abundant information about John and often ended with a plea for Emily's beloved Wash to return home soon. As might have been predicted before their marriage, Emily usually complained about these forced absences. "I am getting a little homesick for you. It seems so long since I have seen you," she wrote to Washington in the fall of 1868, only six months after their return to America.[89] "I shall be glad when we both get back home and hope you will take no more trips this year."[90] Her wish was soon fulfilled. By 1869, to assist his father with the latest and most challenging of all the Roebling projects, the Colonel and his little family had taken up residence in the city of Brooklyn, directly across the East River from Manhattan.

Endnotes

[1] Additional information about the West Point Foundry can be found in William J. Blake, *The History of Putnam County, New York* (New York: Baker and Scribner, 1849), pp. 240 & ff.

[2] Putnam County Historical Society, *A Cold Spring Walking Tour*, pp. 2-4.

[3] Emily Warren Roebling to John A. Roebling II, October 17, 1894. Special Collections and University Archives, Alexander Library, Rutgers University, New Brunswick, New Jersey.

[4] Ibid., September 28, 1896.

[5] Ibid., March 19, 1899.

[6] Emily Warren Roebling, *Richard Warren of the Mayflower and Some of His Descendants* (Boston: David Clapp & Son, 1901), p. 3.

[7] EWR to JAR II, August 12, 1900.

[8] Daughters of the American Revolution, *Lineage Book*, XXVII (Washington, D.C.: Daughters of the American Revolution, 1896), pp. 342-43 for the Lickleys and p. 129 for Barret. Additional material on Barret can be found in Berthold Fernow, *New York in the Revolution* (New Orleans: Polyanthos, 1976), p. 224.

[9] EWR to JAR II, April 24, 1898.

[10] Blake, *Putnam County*, p. 235.

[11] EWR to JAR II, n.d.

[12] William S. Pelletreau, *History of Putnam County*, New York (Philadelphia: W.W. Preston, 1886), p. 556.

[13] Emerson Gifford Taylor, *Gouverneur Kemble Warren: The Life and Letters of an American Soldier 1830-1882* (Boston: Houghton, 1932), p. 8. Of the dozen offspring born to Phoebe and Sylvanus Warren, there were five surviving younger children for whom Gouverneur Kemble Warren assumed responsibility. Dr. Jason Warren, a military historian whose academic career included faculty positions at West Point and the Naval War

College and whose great-great-great grandfather was a third cousin of Gouverneur Kemble and Emily Warren, noted that the military tradition was very strong in the Warren family and that generations of Warrens had served in the military prior to Gouverneur Kemble Warren. Interview with the author, Aug. 15, 2023.

[14]EWR to JAR II, December 15, 1895.

[15]Taylor, *Gouverneur Kemble Warren*, p. 6.

[16]Georgetown Visitation Convent Archives, Account of Miss Emily Warren.

[17]Georgetown Visitation Catalogue: 1859-1860, p. 13. Additional information about Emily Warren's school career can be found in Eleanore C. Sullivan, *Georgetown Visitation Since 1799* (Baltimore: French Bray Printing Company, 1975), p. 117.

[18]In later years Emily became active in the Georgetown Visitation Alumnae Association. At the organization's second annual meeting, in 1894, she spoke about "The Evolution of a Convent Girl." (Sullivan, p. 118.) At the school's centennial celebration in 1899, Mrs. Roebling, "magnificently gowned in a creation of pale blue silk, covered with point lace … and strikingly set off with superb diamonds," was elected president of the Alumnae Association. (Sullivan, p. 124.)

[19]WAR to EW, September 10, 1864.

[20]Ibid., April 21, 1864.

[21]WAR to Elvira Roebling, February 26, 1864.

[22]Ibid.

[23]WAR to ER, March 5, 1864.

[24]WAR to EW, April 12, 1864.

[25]WAR Letterbook, Rutgers University, p. 195.

[26]WAR Letterbook, pp. 195-196.

[27]WAR Letterbook, p. 178.

[28]WAR to EW, September 6, 1864.

[29]Ibid., November 18, 1864.

[30]Ibid., July 3, 1864.

[31] Ibid., July 18, 1864.

[32] Ibid., July 21, 1864.

[33] Ibid., April 12, 1864.

[34] Ibid., September 6, 1864.

[35] Ibid., July 22, 1864.

[36] Ibid., October 29, 1864.

[37] Ibid.

[38] Ibid., August 27, 1864.

[39] Ibid.

[40] Ibid., May 15, 1864.

[41] Ibid., July 22, 1864.

[42] Ibid., April 12, 1864.

[43] Ibid., April 1, 1864.

[44] Ibid., April 4, 1864.

[45] JAR to WAR, March 30, 1864.

[46] WAR to EW, April 2, 1864.

[47] Ibid., August 2, 1864.

[48] Ibid.

[49] Ibid.

[50] Ibid.

[51] Ibid.

[52] Ibid., August 21, 1864.

[53] Ibid.

[54] Ibid., August 28, 1864.

[55] Ibid.

[56] Ibid., October 11, 1864.

[57] Ibid., August 14, 1864.

[58] Ibid., August 29, 1864.

[59] Ibid., June 19, 1864.

[60] Ibid., August 22, 1864.

[61] Ferdinand Roebling to WAR, January 12, 1867.

[62] WAR to EW, September 19, 1864.

[63] Ibid., March 30, 1864.

[64] Ibid., September 19, 1864.

[65]Ibid.

[66]Ibid., December 16, 1864.

[67]Ibid., October 29, 1864.

[68]Ibid., July 19, 1864.

[69]Ibid., September 6, 1864.

[70]Ibid., October 5, 1864.

[71]Ibid., December 3, 1864.

[72]Ibid.

[73]Ibid., December 14, 1864.

[74]Ibid., March 16, 1865.

[75]Ibid.

[76]Ibid.

[77]Ibid.

[78]WAR to JAR, February 9, 1867.

[79]Ibid., July 19, 1867.

[80]*The London Times*, April 17, 1867, 10:1. Description in *NYT*, April 14, 1867, 6:1; and April 16, 1867, 1:2.

[81]WAR to Charles Swan, December 31, 1867. Description of Mühlhausen in David B. Steinman, *Builders of the Bridge: The Story of John Roebling and His Son* (New York: Harcourt, Brace, Jovanovich, 1945), pp. 3-4.

[82]ER to JAR, December 10, 1867.

[83]WAR to JAR, January 6, 1868.

[84]Ibid.

[85]EWR to JAR, January 6, 1868.

[86]*NYT*, December 30, 1884, 5:1.

[87]G.W. Emlen to E.D. Webster, March 7, 1868.

[88]WAR to C. Swan, n.d.

[89]EWR to WAR, October 14, 1868.

[90]Ibid.

CHAPTER 2
JOURNEYMAN

Genesis of the Bridge Project

The project that occasioned the Roeblings' move to Brooklyn was the fulfillment of a dream, not only for John Roebling but for countless numbers of New Yorkers and Brooklynites who viewed the swiftly flowing East River as an impediment to the ties between their two cities. Before man tunneled beneath the river and threw mighty bridges across it, the only way to travel between Brooklyn, at the western terminus of Long Island, and New York was by boat. In the early Colonial period, private vessels plied the river, eventually replaced by commercial ferries, but, owing to currents, fog and ice, the service was, at best, erratic. The introduction of steam ferries in the mid-19th century improved the situation. The new boats were able to cross the river in approximately five minutes. Fog and frigid winter weather still posed problems but the number of canceled or delayed trips resulting from these temporary conditions was not so great that the public was demanding a bridge. Prior to the advent of steam ferries, there was some talk about building a bridge, mainly among

Brooklynites, but the new boats, for all intents and purposes, put an end to it.

That is how matters stood until John Roebling, manufacturer of wire cable and bridge builder, who had already spanned the Ohio and the Niagara, dashed off a letter to Abram S. Hewitt, a congressman and prominent New York businessman who headed the iron works founded by his father-in-law, Peter Cooper. Hewitt forwarded Roebling's letter suggesting the construction of an East River Bridge to the *Journal of Commerce*, which dutifully printed it just as Horace Greeley gave space in the March 27, 1857, edition of his *New York Tribune* to a Roebling letter calling for a single-span wire suspension bridge linking New York and Brooklyn.[1] These epistles occasioned comment but nothing came of Roebling's proposal because the New York metropolitan area, like the rest of the nation, was being buffeted by the winds of economic change. The onset of a financial panic in 1857, followed by the unsettling effects of the Civil War upon the economy of New York, which had traditionally maintained close trading ties with the South, caused the public to lose interest in an East River Bridge.[2]

Not one to give up, John Roebling decided to approach the problem from the other side of the river. He convinced civic leaders and former Brooklyn Mayor Henry C. Murphy of the benefits of a span linking Long Island with Manhattan. In 1867, Murphy, then a state senator, introduced legislation incorporating the New York Bridge Company for the purpose of building and operating a toll bridge across the East River. Aiding the bill's passage was the unusually severe winter of 1866-67. A veritable glacier impeded navigation and, when the fun of walking over the frozen water wore off, weary travelers endured monumental delays as ferries struggled to get through the ice-choked river. Day after day of not knowing when or whether they would arrive at their destinations convinced even the most skeptical New Yorkers and Brooklynites that a bridge was an absolute necessity.[3] This is precisely the conclusion John Roebling, Senator Murphy, William C. Kingsley, a major contractor, and other proponents of the bridge project hoped the public would come to.[4]

Just about the time old man winter was relinquishing his grip on the metropolitan area, the enabling legislation permitting the construction of an East River span was passed and, a month later, Roebling was appointed Chief Engineer of a project he estimated would take five years and cost slightly under $4 million. (The bridge eventually cost $15 million, or almost $400 million in today's dollars.) Shares of stock in the bridge company were sold to a wide variety of people, including William M. Tweed, the infamous Boss Tweed of Tammany Hall. Eight years after it was established, the company was dissolved following passage of a law authorizing the cities of Brooklyn and New York to create a public corporation to finish and operate the bridge.[5] The Roebling name was still attached to the mighty span but it was not John Roebling who was directing the building of the bridge he had designed. His association with the project was abruptly terminated in July 1869, when he suffered a most unfortunate accident.

The successful German immigrant, who had failed in his attempt to establish a model agrarian community in Pennsylvania, had gone on to utilize the training he had received at the Royal Polytechnic Institute in Berlin to build aqueducts and bridges and pioneer in the manufacture of wire rope.[6] He was doing surveying work on the Brooklyn side of the proposed span as the Fulton ferry approached the pilings on which he was standing. Sensing danger, he stepped back but his right foot became caught on something. Unable to move, he was struck by the ferry as it banged against the slip. Although his foot was crushed, he made light of his injuries. It was his son, Washington Roebling, who spirited him away to a doctor's office. Surgery was advised and the mutilated toes were amputated, at the patient's request, without anesthetic. Then Mr. Roebling was transported to the Hicks Street home of his son and daughter-in-law.

What Emily Warren Roebling thought when she saw the Chief Engineer being carried into her house is unknown but surely she must have been profoundly shocked. To witness a man as physically strong as her father-in-law being reduced to near helplessness was appalling. Yet somehow she coped. Her home became a veritable hospital as specialists came and went, trying to cure the strong-willed patient who believed in the medicinal use of water, thereby rejecting their ministrations.[7] Although the pain was intense, the man who had been one of the philosopher Hegel's favorite pupils in Berlin bore it with an unprecedented degree of stoicism. Day after day of watching him must have instilled patience and resignation in Emily. She would need plentiful quantities of each for many years to come.

Two weeks after the accident, symptoms of tetanus began to appear. At first there were violent headaches and then facial rigidity. After the muscles had tightened, the victim's teeth were all exposed, frozen in a macabre smile, and the brows framing those bright eyes were permanently arched. Despite excruciating pain and convulsive seizures, John Roebling continued making notes as long as he could. The bridge, after all, had to be built, even if he would not be there to supervise its construction.

By the middle of July, there was practically no hope for his recovery. The convulsive seizures were intensifying despite everyone's efforts to keep the house extremely quiet in a vain attempt to prevent the little upsets that they feared triggered the seizures. This was no easy task, particularly since one of the other residents of the house on Hicks Street was a lively two-year-old. Much of Emily's time must have been devoted to keeping the child quiet lest he disturb his grandfather, but it is not hard to imagine her, perhaps in the evening when the boy was asleep, taking her turn in the sickroom of the Chief Engineer, since someone had to be with him all the time. Though she had no inkling of it then, the bright, 25-year-old woman was only beginning her career as a private duty nurse. Until the final stages of the disease, when his mind was affected, John Roebling must have been comforted by the presence of the woman whom he had liked and admired from the moment they met.

In his last hour, though, there was no comfort to be found, as dreadful convulsions sent him catapulting from his bed. His assistant engineer, C.C. Martin, broke the fall and helped put the Chief Engineer back to bed, where he died a few minutes later. Martin was one of a handful of people in the room at the time.[8] Washington Roebling was also there and, although the hour was approximately 3 a.m., Emily may have been in attendance as well. Whether or not she was present, Emily would be profoundly affected by her father-in-law's death.[9]

Washington Roebling's First Years as Chief Engineer

Despite John A. Roebling's statement during his lifetime that he would never have undertaken the East River Bridge project had he not had an engineer-son to aid him, as long as the elder Roebling lived, Washington Roebling did not have to bear the total burden of the bridge. Although his father spent long periods in Trenton, leaving him on his own in Brooklyn, there was no doubt in anyone's mind that John A. Roebling was the Chief Engineer, and his son merely an assistant.[10] With the older man removed from the scene at the age of 63, the younger man was appointed Chief Engineer in his place. For help and advice he had assistant engineers on whom to rely but, for the kind of support he so desperately needed, there was only one assistant to whom he continuously turned – his wife. "Here I was at the age of 32, suddenly put in charge of the most stupendous engineering structure of the age!" declared Washington Roebling. "The prop on which I had hitherto leaned had fallen: henceforth I must rely on myself. … At first I thought I would succumb, but I had a strong tower to lean upon, my wife, a woman of infinite tact and wisest counsel."[11]

In reality, Emily had no choice but to acquiesce in her husband's decision to succeed his father as Chief Engineer.[12] That he would one day assume full control over the project was a foregone conclusion. Years later, Washington Roebling wrote, "At the time of his death he [John A. Roebling] was already arranging to retire and relinquish the work (of the Brooklyn Bridge) to me."[13]

Besides being the son of the recently deceased Chief Engineer, there were three compelling reasons why Washington A. Roebling should be appointed to succeed his father. First, he was "the only living man who had the practical experience to build these great cables, far exceeding in size anything previously attempted."[14] Second, he possessed an enormous knowledge of pneumatic foundations and caissons and third, he had helped his father prepare the designs for the bridge and was "familiar with his ideas and with the whole project – and no one else was."[15]

Although his wife would later claim that Washington Roebling did not merely copy his father's design for the bridge but, rather, adapted the original design as new problems arose during construction, no degree of familiarity with the design, pneumatic foundations, caissons or any other aspect of the project was sufficient to guarantee the successful completion of the bridge.[16] Before the design could be translated into steel and granite, much could and did go wrong. Some of the most serious problems arose in conjunction with the sinking of the caissons, gigantic chambers of wood and iron, boxlike in appearance. After reaching bedrock, the entire interiors of the caissons would be filled with concrete. As the caissons inched their way toward the bottom, they were filled with compressed air to keep the water out. Laborers chipped away at the riverbed from inside the caissons, frequently experiencing breathing difficulties, cramps, muscular pain and other side effects. Nevertheless, there was keen competition for the high-paying jobs beneath the river. Native

New Yorkers and immigrants alike clamored for the privilege of going down into the caissons. Joining them, on a regular basis, was Chief Engineer Washington Roebling.

"While the caissons were being sunk he never left Brooklyn even for an hour and at all hours of the day and night he visited the work going on under the water," his wife explained.[17] From March 1870, when the Brooklyn caisson was launched, until December of that year, Roebling popped in and out of the caissons. Since their European tour in 1867, both he and Emily were aware of the complex illness that sometimes affected men working beneath the water but chose to banish such negative thoughts from their minds. Having already suffered a great loss in the untimely death of John Roebling and a near tragedy in Emily's fall in Mühlhausen, maybe they felt they had already done their share of suffering. Then, too, it is possible that Mr. and Mrs. Roebling may have thought that a healthy man in his prime was unlikely to fall victim to the dreaded bends. In his early 30s, the 5-foot-10-inch Chief Engineer with the "large expressive grey eyes" was in excellent condition.[18] Still, the long hours he was putting in were beginning to take their toll.

Of course, there wasn't much Emily could do about her husband's workaholism, no more than she could slow him down on the European trip or when he was working on the Cincinnati-Covington Bridge. The young officer who had been dreadfully bored by the endless days of inactivity during the Civil War was happiest when he was working hard. This was probably small consolation to his wife, but, if nothing else, in contrast with the war years and part of the time when he was in the Midwest, at least she had him with her. Yet, although they lived under the same roof, days would go by without Emily's really seeing her husband, who refused to be a house- or even office-bound Chief Engineer. His late father had felt perfectly comfortable remaining in Trenton for months at a time at the start of the Brooklyn Bridge project but this simply would not do for his son. He was in charge now and intended to accept his full share of responsibility.

There is the temptation to speculate that Washington Roebling's take-charge attitude may have been a manifestation of a gigantic ego but, at this stage of his life, this does not seem to have been the case. Indeed, the affable Colonel was much easier to deal with than his brilliant, irascible father had been. Having struggled to get through perhaps the most intellectually rigorous undergraduate program in the nation, he knew he was no *genius*, a term frequently used in reference to John Roebling. That he was bright, however, was undeniable. The RPI attrition rate being what it was in the mid-19th century, he had to be merely to stay there. Yet, like the woman he married, though bright, he wasn't smug about his intellectual gifts. The talents both he and Emily had been endowed with were viewed as welcome assets to be utilized for worthy purposes. As the first snowflakes began to whiten the bustling streets of New York and Brooklyn in December 1870, for the Roeblings there was no nobler objective than completing the great bridge. It would not be easy.

On December 1, the Brooklyn caisson caught fire when a workman's candle came into contact with oakum caulking in a seam of the caisson roof. Every other seam had been cemented but this one had somehow been overlooked. Colonel Roebling immediately rushed to the scene and descended into the caisson but, like his assistants, he found it virtually impossible to ascertain the extent of the damage in the choked air beneath the river. Having spent much of the previous day, prior to the discovery of the fire, in the caisson, he had been exhausted to start with and the long night under the river directing firefighting operations proved too much for him. Aides urged him to go home but he was reluctant to do so until the fire was under control. It was not until he was near collapse that he decided to leave. Without the help of his assistants, he would not have made it through the air lock. Once on the surface, he felt better but only momentarily since, without warning, he became immobilized. Unable to walk, he had to be taken home in a carriage.[19]

Witnessing yet another of the Roebling men being carried through the front door of the house on Hicks Street was an ordeal for Emily. Although hardly oblivious to the fact that her husband had been pushing himself to the limit, she had no reason to expect that, like his father, Washington Roebling would become a victim of the still uncompleted bridge. Yet this is exactly what had happened. Fortunately, Emily was a take-charge person. She was not about to sit around and worry. Instead, under her supervision, therapy began immediately. Her husband's entire body was rubbed with a mixture of salt and whiskey for several hours. After this treatment, he was able to get out of bed and return to the caisson. By no means perfectly well, he insisted upon going down again after word was received at Hicks Street that the fire was not out after all. At this point, Emily probably regretted opening the door to the bearer of this unwelcome message but, once received, the communiqué could not be ignored. With the

Colonel on the job again, there was nothing for her to do but wait, worry, pray and tend to the needs of the one Roebling man who was willing to listen to her, three-year-old John.

As for the boy's father, he was reluctantly making the decision to flood the caisson. This could and did extinguish the fire but it resulted in unexpected delays in the construction schedule. Still, by March 1871, the Brooklyn caisson was permanently anchored. In the meantime, there had been other problems to overcome. A scant two weeks after the fire, together with the resumption of work inside the caisson, came a nearly fatal accident occasioned by failure to close a door. The caisson's water shafts began to pour their contents into the chamber where the Chief Engineer and the laborers were working. Believing the river had penetrated the caisson, the men panicked but a coolheaded Washington Roebling saved the day by slamming the door.[20] How much he told his wife about the incident is unclear but there was no hiding the unmistakable symptoms accompanying another attack of the bends.

This seizure came in the New York caisson, which had been launched in the fall of 1871. The following January, after a number of workers had exhibited symptoms of the disease, Roebling engaged Dr. Andrew H. Smith of the Manhattan Eye and Ear Hospital as surgeon for the New York Bridge Company.[21] He remained on the job until the end of May, when the work in the New York caisson was all but completed. During that time he treated over 100 cases of the bends. Toward the end of Dr. Smith's tenure, the Chief Engineer again fell victim to the disease. Writing about the recurrence of the bends, his wife said, "One afternoon in the spring of 1872, Colonel Roebling was brought up out of the New York caisson nearly insensible and all one night his death was hourly expected."[22]

For the third time in three years, Emily Warren Roebling witnessed a doleful procession through the front door of the house on Hicks Street. Her husband had been carried up from the Fulton ferry, which had transported his pain-wracked body across the East River. Now he lay in bed almost unconscious. Surrounded by "anxious friends at the bedside," he was pumped full of morphine for the next 24 hours.[23] No one expected him to survive this attack.[24] For Emily, the prospect of her young husband succumbing was dreadful enough but compounding the horror was the fact that he lay dying in the same house where his father had fought an unsuccessful battle to survive a few years before. The great bridge designed by her father-in-law seemed to be on the verge of claiming another Roebling life. The immediate cause, caisson disease, was different from the tetanus that had killed John A. Roebling, but the remote cause, the bridge itself, was the same.

Identical, too, was the steady stream of visitors to the house. Assistant engineers and others employed on the project filed through the front door only to emerge looking more pessimistic than when they had entered. Years later, when the bridge would at last be finished, Emily paid tribute to these men, saying, "It could never have been accomplished but for the unselfish devotion of his assistant engineers."[25] What she neglected to mention was that, in the period following the second onset of the bends, she became her husband's ablest assistant.

Emily as Silent Builder

It is impossible to pinpoint exactly how and when it happened, but that it occurred is not in doubt. Emily became such a sufficiently visible figure during the remainder of the project that, on the eve of the opening of the bridge, no less prestigious a newspaper than *The New York Times* published an article titled "Mrs. Roebling's Skill." The piece quoted an anonymous Trenton source, a gentleman "well acquainted" with the Roebling family, who declared, "Since her husband's unfortunate illness, Mrs. Roebling has filled his position as chief of the engineering staff."[26]

Whether surrogate Chief Engineer or capable assistant engineer without title, it is truly remarkable that a woman played a role – and especially such a significant one – in the construction of one of the most important landmarks of the 19th century. Equally amazing is the way it all came about. One minute Washington Roebling, the man who would become Emily's mentor, lay dying. Less than a week later the symptoms of the disease subsided, permitting him to pick up where he had left off. In a few weeks, however, the terrifying symptoms reappeared but between attacks he was able to superintend the process of filling in the New York caisson with concrete. Before he became ill, Roebling had made the momentous decision not to push the New York caisson to bedrock. Instead, it would rest on hard sand that had been undisturbed for millions of years and would most likely remain stable in the future. Before making that determination, he thought long and hard about it and most likely discussed the matter with his wife because she noted that this was a time of "intense anxiety" for her husband.[27] Although convinced he was right, he wondered how others would react to his decision. In reality, he had less to fear from adverse public reaction in this instance than to the opposition that would have arisen had the press learned of his true condition following the second attack of caisson disease. Preventing that bad news from leaking out proved to be a full-time job for Mrs. Roebling.

One way of handling the problem was to get the object of speculation out of the public eye. Thus the Roeblings disappeared for several weeks in the summer of 1872. At upstate Saratoga and Richfield Springs, they were far less conspicuous than they had been in Brooklyn. Back on Hicks Street in September, the Colonel appeared ready to resume full-time work. Then, suddenly, the symptoms reappeared and, before the end of the month, he was putting in only three or four days a week on the job instead of the usual six. Before the year was over, he had to give up going to the construction site. He was plagued by fatigue, depression, irritability, stomach trouble, pain and loss of feeling in his limbs. These were the protracted symptoms of caisson disease. At the onset of the bends, severe vomiting, vertigo and cramps are common. If the patient lives, these symptoms disappear, but a host of other ills takes their place. Under these circumstances, the patient cannot function normally, no matter how determined he is.[28]

Such was the case with Washington A. Roebling. Although he steadfastly refused to step down as Chief Engineer, he simply could not function as he had previously, nor could he even put in an occasional appearance at the bridge offices on Water Street.[29] While construction was suspended for the winter, he could perhaps get away with this but, once work resumed in the spring, he would be pushed out unless he had powerful backing. For this reason, Emily was dispatched to confer with Henry C. Murphy, president of the New York Bridge Company. She came away with an assurance that her husband could stay on as Chief Engineer provided no untoward developments occurred during construction.[30] It is not difficult to imagine Emily charming old Senator Murphy as she had once mesmerized a young Union officer during the Civil War.[31] An attractive woman of 29, she undoubtedly donned a lovely frock and her best jewels and set off to dazzle the senator.

At this point in Washington Roebling's illness, his wife's persuasiveness was extremely important because, had Emily failed in her mission, her husband might have given up everything. Her success gave him the impetus to take pen in hand, despite pain and depression, to write a comprehensive and detailed set of instructions for the completion of the bridge. Until his eyes began to weaken, this worked. The written notes, together with oral instructions given to the assistant engineers who paid regular visits to the Hicks Street house, kept things moving along. Eventually Emily stepped in as pupil, secretary, messenger and finally surrogate engineer. By the spring of 1873, she was the only person whose presence he could tolerate since he was now suffering more from nervous exhaustion than from the physical effects of the bends.[32] Lengthy conversations with anyone else exhausted him. Noise bothered him as did conversation. Thus the visits of the assistant engineers were terminated.

At the urging of his doctors, he applied for a leave of

absence from his position as Chief Engineer in April 1873.[33] Emily, too, was feeling the strain by now because many years later, when she accidentally came across her son's baby curls, which she had "cut off before we started for Europe in 1873," she admitted, "I was very ill then and feared I should never return home again."[34] The Roeblings' specific destination in Europe was Wiesbaden, Germany, whose magical waters they hoped would have a beneficial effect upon the Colonel. The trip was a terrible ordeal for Washington Roebling and the six months spent at the old spa resulted in no noticeable improvement in his condition. Given the cost of remaining in Europe and the meager benefits of the treatment at Wiesbaden, the Roeblings embarked for America in the autumn of 1873.

Once back in Brooklyn, they bought a home at 110 Columbia Heights, approximately half a mile from the bridge and situated so that the rooms facing the back of the house on the upper floors afforded a magnificent view of the East River.[35] After taking title to the house, however, the Colonel did not stay around long enough to enjoy the view nor superintend the construction of the bridge through a large telescope from his bedroom window; the latter was the popularly held view. Restless from his seemingly insurmountable health problems, he heeded his doctors' advice to once again get away from Brooklyn. This time he headed to his former home in Trenton, New Jersey. There, in the community where the Roebling Mill was located, he spent the next three years. During that time both the Brooklyn and New York towers of the bridge were completed. Although Washington Roebling was not present to supervise the enormous blocks of granite being put in place, the job was done in accordance with his instructions.

Determined to remain in charge of the project and see it through to completion, he painstakingly dictated correspondence to his wife. Day after day Emily faithfully took down notes because, according to her husband's own admission, "For 15 years I had eye trouble, could neither read nor write nor sign my own name."[36] In a rare interview granted a few years before his death, Washington Roebling elaborated further upon his visual problems, saying: "There were ten years from the time I was forty till I was about fifty, that I never stirred out of one room. There was a time when I thought I'd be blind."[37] To prevent his sight from deteriorating further, the Colonel even refrained from reading what his wife had written. Instead, he had her read everything back to him. Then, after he suggested revisions, she incorporated them before rereading the material to the Colonel and once again, if he felt changes were in order, his wife made them and then wrote out the final version.[38] Given her bright mind and all the repetition involved in this process, Emily amassed an enormous quantity of information about bridge building.

An anonymous Trenton man, quoted by the *Times* shortly before the bridge opened, elaborated upon Emily's mastery of the conceptual aspects of bridge building, saying, "As soon as Mr. Roebling was stricken with that peculiar fever which has since prostrated him, Mrs. Roebling applied herself to the study of engineering and she succeeded so well that in a short time she was able to assume the duties of chief engineer."[39] The Trenton source went on to give an example of her expertise. "When bids for the steel and iron work for the structure were advertised for three or four years ago, it was found that entirely new shapes would be required, such as no mill was then making," he explained.

This necessitated new patterns and representatives of the mills desiring to bid went to New York to consult with Mr. Roebling. Their surprise was great when Mrs. Roebling sat down with them and by her knowledge of engineering helped them cut out with their patterns and cleared away difficulties that had for weeks been puzzling their brains.[40]

Thus, at an age when most women of her station would have been devoting themselves to social life, philanthropic and other pursuits outside the home, and a growing family, this mother of an only child and wife of an incapacitated man, who was defying the odds to build one of the greatest monuments of the epoch, had been launched upon a new, albeit clandestine, career as a silent bridge builder. Although news of Emily's conferences with key people leaked out periodically, the work she did was largely behind the scenes. As the epitome of Victorian womanhood, her objective was to obtain neither glory nor immortality for herself, but to give her husband an opportunity to realize the dream for which his father had given his life and for which he himself had sacrificed his health. This explains why she shielded him from the press and from the public and, to a great extent, even from the trustees of the bridge.

Yet, while keeping him out of the limelight, she steadfastly maintained that her husband was not "a helpless paralytic. ... He has never been paralyzed for even one moment and there never has been a time when he has not had the full use of every member of his body. ... He has never needed to 'peer through a telescope' at the bridge from his bedroom window and one glance of his practiced eye would tell him if anything was going wrong on the work. ... Since 1873 his house has been the office where all the engineering plans for the bridge have been discussed and perfected."[41] Still, Washington Roebling was far from well.[42] In fact, the return trip from Trenton in the fall of 1876 was made by boat rather than by train because it was feared that he could not stand the rapid movement of even the finest padded Pullman car.[43] Another factor may have entered into the decision to travel by boat, however. It would give the Chief Engineer an opportunity to scrutinize the bridge he had been building in absentia. As he sailed down the East River on a tug and gazed up at the mighty towers, it is not difficult to imagine a great feeling of satisfaction coming over him. Without the help of his patient wife, none of this would have come to pass. In the years since Washington Roebling had been brought up from the New York caisson, she was the single most effective weapon he had in the fight to prevent his removal from the post of Chief Engineer.

Following their return from Trenton, the Roeblings lived with the Colonel's old commanding officer, General Warren, Emily's brother, until June 1877.[44] The general's residence on the West Side of Manhattan did not afford its occupants a view of the East River but, although the Chief Engineer's big project was out of sight, it was hardly out of mind. Two years earlier, though, he may have been on the verge of resigning; the scratch copy of a letter contains the Colonel's offer to step down.[45] She could have been attempting to persuade him to resign and may have prepared the letter for him, or maybe he dictated it himself. No matter who was responsible, the Colonel was determined to stay on the job to the point of fighting back when bridge trustee Lloyd Aspinwall proposed the appointment of a consulting engineer to work with Roebling.[46] Writing to Henry C. Murphy from his brother-in-law's home at 33 West 50th Street, the Colonel admitted:

I consider the motion of Mr. Aspinwall quite natural. Neither he or some other of the New York Trustees know me save by reputation nor have ever seen me. It is known that I have been sick for the two years these gentlemen have been members of the Board and even for some time previous. It is therefore quite excusable that he should feel a little alarmed both as to the future management of the work and the troubles that might possibly arise in case I die before the Bridge is completed.

Despite these conciliatory remarks, the Colonel went on to say, "The idea of an associate, or even of a consulting engineer, is quite opposed to the spirit of American engineering."[48] If the board of trustees insisted upon appointing an associate engineer, Roebling felt he would have to resign. Referring to this possibility, he said:

It is a step that could only inure to my great benefit because no sick man can lead even a passable existence or have the slightest hope of ever recovering his health, who does as much work and under as great disadvantages as I am constantly forced to do. Continuing to work has been with me a matter of pride and honor![49]

It was also a matter of his wife's tender devotion, brilliance and capacity for the kind of work opponents of higher education for women claimed would cause the collapse of the weaker sex. Without Emily's assistance, Washington Roebling would not have come through the Aspinwall episode unscathed. Although he stated in his letter to Henry Murphy that he would give the trustees "ample warning" if he could not "do full justice to my duties as Chief Engineer," he earnestly wished to retain the number one position, especially now that the "Bridge is almost half built and every month's work lessens the amount of responsibility that would have to be assumed by my possible successor."[50]

But there would be no successor. Instead there would be a faithful surrogate working behind the scenes to assist the Chief Engineer with the work that lay ahead. Together they would ride out controversies about a possible conflict of interest between the Colonel's stock holdings in the family Mill and the submission of bids for the bridge's steel wire by the John A. Roebling's Sons Company. Washington Roebling sold his stock in the family firm and the company ended up providing much of the wire that went into the bridge after it was discovered that another mill had been supplying an inferior product.[51] When this came to light, the usual fears about the strength of the bridge were expressed but no ill effects were felt. Yet quite aside from the wire matter, it was necessary to reassure the public about the safety of the span. A cable break in June 1878 had resulted in several casualties and people were frankly apprehensive about the bridge.[52]

A giant step in the direction of quieting their fears was taken when Master Mechanic Edwin Farrington gave a series of lectures on the bridge. Utilizing lantern slides to illustrate his talks at Cooper Union in Manhattan, and at the Brooklyn

Music Hall on the other side of the river, he enlightened the public about the majestic span at its doorstep. Although the first two lectures in Brooklyn, delivered late in 1879 and illustrated by diagrams on cloth and by 35 stereopticon views, were not well attended, the second series, at Cooper Union in March 1880, attracted upward of 2,000 people.[53] The public relations effort surrounding the talks, plus the lectures themselves, may have been the work of Emily Roebling, who was rumored to have written the presentations.[54] This is not in the least implausible in view of the fact that Farrington, who had been a carpenter and machinist before becoming a celebrated bridge mechanic, was more a doer than a thinker or writer. In any event, his lectures in New York were a great sensation. Providing the audience with an impressive overview of the entire project, he began with a brief history of suspension bridges going back to one built in Thibet, India, in A.D. 65.[55] Then he went on to discuss the East River Bridge.

The lectures also included considerable information about caisson disease without elaborating on the Chief Engineer's collapse and his wife's subsequent involvement in the project.[56] Had the audience been told that a woman was playing a major role in the construction of the bridge, the lecturer might have been greeted by uproarious laughter; had the listeners believed him, public confidence in the great project might have been lost. In this epoch, although it was taken for granted that lower-class women worked, even after marriage and motherhood, it was unthinkable for respectable middle-class and wealthy women to engage in any serious work. Home and hearth were viewed as their only legitimate areas of concern. Even childless women or those with small families were told their place was in the home. With only one son to care for and servants to run the household, a woman as bright and determined as Emily Roebling would have found some outside interest had she not single-mindedly devoted herself to her husband and his great project. Her son, after all, required less maternal care as time went on. Indeed, during the period that the bridge was being built, John A. Roebling II grew from babyhood to the verge of manhood. Only two when his parents moved to Brooklyn, he was almost ready for college when the bridge was at last finished. During that time, he had attended the Collegiate School in New York and the Brooklyn Boys' Preparatory School.

Watching out for the two men she loved was a major occupation for Emily Warren Roebling and one that was directly related to the bridge. Her son, after all, bore the name of the designer of the span and her husband was struggling to get it built. Is it any wonder, then, that she wanted to get the true story of the bridge before the public? The amiable Farrington may have been her vehicle for doing just that. Perhaps she first selected him as a spokesman and then wrote the lectures. This is not inconceivable because Emily possessed a good grasp of the importance of favorable public opinion and Farrington was already a popular figure.

The spotlight was initially focused on him in the Roeblings' absence during the summer of 1876. The country was then celebrating its Centennial and crowds rushed to the Philadelphia Exposition but throngs no less enthusiastic turned out to watch the master mechanic travel in a boatswain's chair between the Brooklyn and New York towers of the bridge. Less than two weeks before, the first wire rope linking the two anchorages had gone across the river. This greatly cheered Washington and Emily Roebling but, in terms of popular enthusiasm, Farrington's trip was more significant. Seated precariously in the makeshift conveyance, which would be used to transport him across the river, he waved and threw kisses to the crowd. When he reached New York safely, people on both sides of the river erupted into a noisy chorus of hurrays. One newspaper reported that "on the top of the New York and Brooklyn towers, crowds were also collected, many ladies being on the former."[57] Although the wife of the Chief Engineer was not among them, she may indeed have penned the description of the crossing Farrington used in his lecture. "The ride gave me a magnificent view, and such pleasing sensations as probably I shall never experience again."[58] "It also gained for me what was in my position a troublesome and annoying notoriety, and I was well pleased when public attention was attracted to other events of more importance."[59] The master mechanic was being unduly modest because he seems to have enjoyed himself immensely back in August 1876 and maybe almost as much three years later when he delivered his lectures.

Emily, too, was adapting well to her role as silent builder. The same year that Farrington gave his initial lectures, the Edge Moor Iron Company, which played a key role in the bridge project, was accused of dishonesty. In an attempt to dispel the cloud of suspicion, the company communicated directly with Mrs. Roebling, bypassing her husband. Addressing her as "Dear Madam," W.H. Francis of Edge Moor assured her that "the report regarding this company asking a higher price … is utterly and unqualifiedly false."[60]

That Edge Moor's previous dealings had been with the wife of the Chief Engineer rather than with the great man himself is evident, and this was probably not the only firm she negotiated with because, as the *Times* pointed out when the bridge was finished, "Among those who have had occasion in the course of business at various times to test Mrs. Roebling's engineering skill is Frederick J. Slade, Treasurer of the New Jersey Steel and Iron Company."[61]

Aside from handling negotiations, Emily aided her husband by boosting his spirits during a number of real crises. One of them resulted from a suit to remove the bridge because it interfered with navigation.[62] This eventually came to naught, as did an attempt to prove that the assistant engineers were taking bribes and that the John A. Roebling's Sons Company was involved in the whole messy business, but the Chief Engineer and his wife had to suffer through it all.[63] From the standpoint of the public, perhaps the most serious crisis the Roeblings had to endure was an indirect one occasioned by the collapse of the Tay Bridge in Scotland. Several weeks after the disaster occurred, *The New York Herald* asked if such a collapse could happen here. A letter to the editor urged that the greatest possible margin of safety be built into the East River Bridge, something the Roeblings had already done.[64]

The Tay Bridge disaster gradually faded from the pages of the New York and Brooklyn newspapers to be replaced by something considerably more cheerful, the visit of Ferdinand de Lesseps to the United States. When the famed builder of the Suez Canal came to this country to obtain support for the Panama Canal, he toured the East River Bridge construction site. Looking very dapper in an exquisitely tailored topcoat and high hat, the 76-year-old diplomat-turned-builder climbed to the top of the New York tower in February 1880.[65] His enthusiastic praise of the bridge went far toward dispelling doubts about the stability of the span and Emily and Washington Roebling were appreciative of the international seal of approval his visit gave the bridge. Mrs. Roebling attended a dinner honoring de Lesseps and was part of a group of women who walked beside him as he entered the dining room.[66]

Emily was not present at an important dinner that was held in New York a year after de Lesseps' visit to the city. It was a gathering of the Rensselaer Polytechnic Institute Alumni and the principal address of the evening was given by Francis Collingwood Jr., one of Washington Roebling's assistant engineers, who positively lauded his chief. Emily's turn came the following year when Rossiter W. Raymond, an engineer, though not an alumnus of RPI, and a celebrated orator, paid Mrs. Roebling the highest compliment, telling the RPI alumni something many of them already knew:

> I think it may be said of us in this, our time, whatever may have been the subjection and insignificance of women of other days, or whatever it may be today in other lands, that no good man here and now does any good thing but does it under the inspiration and with the help of a woman.[67]

To illustrate his point, Raymond singled out one woman. Referring to the assistance she was rendering the Chief Engineer, Raymond said:

> In the pictures of the master workman, directing from

his bed of pain the master work, I see another figure – a queen of beauty and fashion – become a servant for love's sake; a true helpmate, furnishing swift feelings and skillful hands and quick brain and strong heart to reinforce the weakness and the weariness that could not, unassisted, fully execute the plans they form, but that stand with this assistance, almost as in the vigor of health.

Gentlemen, I know that the name of a woman should not be lightly spoken in a public place. I am aware that such a speech is especially audacious from the mouth of a stranger, but I believe you will acquit me of any lack of decency or irreverence when I utter what this moment half articulates upon all your lips, the name of Mrs. Washington Roebling.[68]

Things were looking up. Indeed, they had been for about a year. Criticism of the project had subsided and, in addition to the Chief Engineer and his faithful surrogate, the bridge itself was being praised. *The Brooklyn Daily Eagle* called the span "Pons Maximus – the greatest engineering project of ancient or modern times."[69] On the other side of the river, some of the papers were less enthusiastic. The *Herald* asked, "Will they ever be finished?" and half answered the question by declaring, "The Brooklyn Bridge drags its slow length along between the two cities in a way that is exceedingly suspicious."[70] Such articles disturbed Emily but this and hundreds of others were carefully clipped from the New York and Brooklyn papers, and occasionally from the out-of-town press. By the time the bridge opened, Mrs. Roebling had two gigantic scrapbooks filled with clippings pertaining to the entire project from its inception. She also had bitter memories of some of the incidents described in those articles. Yet, through it all, she could take pride in the fact that it was she and she alone who kept her husband going during the 11 long years between the second attack of the bends and the completion of the bridge. Most of the time that was a difficult task because, just when one crisis seemed to pass, another one took its place.

In April 1881, for example, there was talk among the trustees of reducing the Chief Engineer's $10,000 annual salary.[71] Washington and Emily Roebling naturally viewed this as a ploy to force the Colonel out. The Chief Engineer, therefore, wrote to Henry Murphy telling him, "For me to consent to a reduction of salary now that the bridge is so nearly completed would look as if the trustees could get along very well without me now, but I, feeling anxious to stay, make them a bid to keep me by offering to work for anything they see fit to pay me."[72] In effect, Roebling offered to work for nothing, informing Murphy, "If I live long enough to direct the important work still to be done I know it will be finished cheaper and better than it will be if left to some engineer who has not had my experience."[73]

Toward the end of 1881, the still-salaried Chief Engineer vicariously enjoyed a bit of glory and satisfaction. His wife told him all about it when she returned home. There was no one better acquainted with what went on at the bridge on the afternoon of December 12, because she was the principal actor in the little drama played out on the span's new plank walkway, which had been placed over the steel superstructure. The other actors were the members of the board of trustees.

At the conclusion of their meeting, they were invited to take a stroll high above the East River between the two towers of the still-uncompleted bridge. Most, but not all, of the members accepted the invitation. Those who did formed a compact party that made its way "up the winding stairway beside the Brooklyn tower, and when they arrived at the level of the roadway, it was met by Mrs. W.A. Roebling, the wife of the Chief Engineer," according to *The New York Star*. The paper went on to point out that "this lady's husband is still confined to his house in Brooklyn Heights from the disease he contracted in the caissons of the bridge in the early stages of its erection."[74]

Insistent though it was upon informing readers that Washington Roebling was still an invalid, the *Star* carefully noted Mrs. Roebling's exuberance and energy as she led the trustees across the span. Unnerved by the height and the narrowness of the walkway, some members of the party held back, preferring to stroll leisurely across while trying not to look down. The brave souls who did glance at the river saw swirling currents and whitecaps caused by brisk winds buffeting the New York metropolitan area. Although the temperature was almost springlike, the stiff breeze and the threat of rain made the day unpleasant. Happily, though, the heavens did not open up while the silent builder and her male admirers hiked across the span.

When they reached the New York tower, in the company of Mayor William R. Grace of that city and his counterpart, Mayor James Howell of Brooklyn, both of whom were members of the board of trustees, champagne awaited them. Despite the threatening weather, everyone sipped a bit of the bubbly, pausing between glasses to toast not only the great bridge, but Emily Warren Roebling. The champagne was supposed to have been served not at the tower, but on the bridge itself where the gap in the roadway had been closed. The messenger delivering the ice-cold bottles, however, was delayed and the members of the party merely continued to the other side of the river where they, at last, found refreshments awaiting them.[75] This no doubt pleased Mayor Grace but may have upset some of the Brooklyn trustees as well as the chief executive of that city because some members of the Brooklyn contingent chose not to tarry in the alien city of New York. After draining their glasses, they headed straight across the bridge. The less adventurous Brooklynites in the group waited for the ferry.[76]

Several of the metropolitan dailies played up the walk across the bridge. The *Eagle*, however, treated it as a kind of footnote to the other bridge news of the day, saying, "But on the other side we have the better news, that the trustees and the wife of the chief engineer crossed the bridge from tower to tower yesterday on the permanent roadway."[77] Less satisfactory but more important in the paper's estimation was the revelation that the trustees' meeting preceding the stroll over the bridge had concentrated on the twin problems of weight and safety of the span. The trustees demanded to know who had modified the plans to permit the addition of 1,200 tons of steel.[78] There was considerable discussion at the meeting but no real answer was forthcoming. Yet disgruntled board members clearly pointed an accusing finger at Washington Roebling. Had he been deceiving them? Were his calculations incorrect, or was the man too ill to continue functioning as Chief Engineer?

The Attempt to Oust Roebling as Chief Engineer

If Seth Low had his way, the answer to all those questions would have been yes. The brilliant, abrasive, 32-year-old son of a well-to-do silk merchant had been elected mayor of Brooklyn in the fall of 1881. His new position brought with it an automatic seat on the bridge's board of trustees. After attending board meetings from January until June 1882, he became increasingly impatient with the slow progress of the bridge. With this thought in mind, Low proposed that the board of trustees require the Chief Engineer to submit monthly reports on the progress of the bridge and that he be asked to attend a special meeting of the board at the end of June.[79] The board planned to put Roebling on the hot seat about delays in the delivery of steel by the Edge Moor Iron Company. Some board members felt this was the crux of the problem but at least one of them, Robert Roosevelt, resigned from the board, contending that the most serious difficulty was the lack of a functioning Chief Engineer. The board president, Henry C. Murphy, stoutly denied the charge.[80] He insisted that Roebling was in complete control of every phase of the project.

Although controversy was once again swirling about her husband, Mrs. Roebling was more relaxed than she had been in ages. With the completion of the bridge only a matter of time and the really demanding work already done, she was looking forward to a pleasant summer in Newport, Rhode Island.

No doubt she longed for this summer to be like the ones she had known as a child in the waterfront community of Cold Spring. Emily chose a three-story house at 91 Washington

Avenue, across the street from Narragansett Bay. Sitting on the large veranda or wandering across the street to what is now a public park, but what was then part of the property the Roeblings had rented for the summer, Emily may have reminisced about childhood walks down to the Hudson to see the towering form of Storm King Mountain looming above the opposite bank.[81]

There was even someone around to help Mrs. Roebling conjure up mental images of her childhood. Her Army officer brother, General Warren, was living in Newport while overseeing the construction of the Block Island breakwater. His presence was undoubtedly a factor in Emily's decision to vacation in Newport. An equally compelling reason was the ease of transporting the Colonel from Brooklyn to the Rhode Island resort. Train travel was simply too hard on the man, but a pleasant journey by sea was just what the doctor ordered. Once Washington Roebling arrived in Newport, he would have to journey overland in a carriage to his final destination. Since this would be the hardest part of the trip, the clear-thinking Emily, who by now truly possessed the logical mind of an engineer, plotted the whole thing out. In choosing a place, she calculated the time and distance from the steamboat wharf to the house. The large fashionable mansions out on Bellevue Avenue were too far away. Thus the Roeblings ended up on Washington Street, an older residential neighborhood, "a section where merchant princes built their homes, shops, and wharves."[82]

In a sense, this was the other side of the tracks because, although the homes were handsome and spacious, they were not in the same class as the palazzi built by the Vanderbilts,

Astors and Belmonts elsewhere in town. Some of the houses on Washington Street dated from the Colonial period, and one had even been used as naval headquarters for the French who arrived in Newport in 1780 to lend a helping hand to the Americans during their struggle for independence from England. Washington Street's interesting past must have delighted Mrs. Roebling. Another interest was the social life of Newport though she had no opportunity to become part of it.

The Roeblings' Newport idyll was broken by a summons to appear before the trustees on June 26. With Emily's assistance, the Colonel fired off a "brief and mysterious telegraphic dispatch" to the board president saying that he simply could not be there.[83] Later, in a letter, he explained that he still was not well enough to attend meetings.[84] None of this set well with trustee General Henry Slocum. When the Colonel's original telegram arrived and was passed around at the June 26 board meeting, Slocum insisted that the Chief Engineer was an employee and, as such, had to answer to the trustees.[85] Slocum was not alone in his views. He had the support of Seth Low and others on the board, many of whom had never met Washington Roebling since they had become members after the second onset of the Colonel's caisson disease. The feeling among these men was that, if Roebling was well enough to journey to Newport, Rhode Island, he could surely make it to a trustees' meeting.

At the July 10 meeting of the board, an angry Seth Low asked for a report on the progress of the construction work during the past month, but a red-faced Henry Murphy was unable to produce it since the Chief Engineer had not submitted one.[86] Had he deemed it necessary to submit reports, the Colonel could have relied upon Emily and the assistant engineers to prepare them but, suspicious of Seth Low's and Henry Slocum's gubernatorial ambitions, he was unwilling to kowtow. This almost proved to be the Chief Engineer's undoing because, not only did the newspapers revile him for his seeming indifference to the board, but Seth Low, after prevailing upon the trustees to pass a resolution requiring the submission of monthly reports by the Chief Engineer, went to Newport to confront Roebling face-to-face.

Low's mission was a secret one. He slipped out of Brooklyn quietly around the first of August and was back within 24 hours. According to Washington Roebling's account of the meeting with Low in Newport, the young mayor threatened to have the trustees fire him if he did not agree to step down as Chief Engineer. [87]

In a fit of rage, the mayor declared that Roebling would be removed if for no other reason than to please himself. After the mayor stormed out of the house, Emily attempted to pick up the pieces as her husband took to his bed, where he stayed over the next few weeks due to the bad press he was receiving in New York and Brooklyn.[88]

Years later the Colonel would tell his son, "You are not old enough yet nor as yet have mingled enough among men to fathom the true causes and motives of their actions, but be assured that it is invariably self-interest disguised in a thousand different forms."[89]

Low's interests were political, something Mrs. Roebling could not abide. To her dying day Emily would abhor the man. She viewed him as the great enemy who initiated the offensive to rob her husband and, indirectly, herself of the glory of having built the Brooklyn Bridge and within less than a year of the span's completion.

Years later, when Low was running for mayor of New York City, Emily told her son: "Seth Low's treatment of your father is one of the campaign songs of New York! I almost have to shed tears, when I read in the papers of the very cruel way I was treated while struggling to finish the bridge and save my husband's life and reason from the fierce onslaught of the Low family."[90] This revealing statement indicates the scope of Mrs. Roebling's involvement in the bridge project. By choice and necessity she remained behind the scenes but, as the silent builder of the Brooklyn Bridge, she was an incredibly strong force. Without her, the Colonel would have been pushed aside by Seth Low.

To add to Emily's problems, while the papers and the public were calling for Roebling's removal as Chief Engineer, Emily's brother, General Warren, died unexpectedly on August 8, 1882.[91] In his early 50s, he left a wife and three small children. Before Warren's death, a military court was investigating the validity of General Philip Sheridan's action in relieving him of his command following the Battle of Five Forks in the Civil War. For years Emily's older brother had been trying to have the matter reopened. Sad to say, the court's full exoneration wasn't published until November 1882.[92] The delay was a cruel blow from which Emily Roebling never fully recovered. For the rest of her life she would labor to restore her late brother's reputation, particularly where his alma mater, the U.S. Military Academy, was concerned.[93] In the immediate aftermath of his death, however, she had little time to mourn since her husband desperately needed her as a strong, clear-thinking ally in the battle to keep his position as Chief Engineer.

Once back in Brooklyn, Low began in earnest to try to oust Roebling. On August 21, the day before a meeting of the bridge board of trustees, the *Eagle* published an article whose title posed a question: "Is Chief Engineer Roebling to be Removed?"[94] According to the paper a rumor was making the rounds at City Hall that "Mayor Grace of New York, would to-morrow support a resolution of Mayor Low to discharge Engineer Roebling. The probabilities are that the meeting will be a very interesting one."[95] When the trustees met on August 22, Low called for the appointment of Assistant Engineer C.C. Martin to be Chief Engineer to replace Roebling, who, in turn, would be named consulting engineer. Former Brooklyn Mayor William J. Hunter attempted to dissuade Low by reminding the trustees that John Roebling had given his life for the bridge and that his son had sacrificed his health. To replace the person possessing the most comprehensive knowledge of the project at this juncture was the height of folly in Hunter's opinion. "I think that Mr. Roebling is being made a scapegoat for the trustees, who were directly responsible for changes made in the work while it was in progress."[96] Brooklyn Comptroller Ludwig Semler also defended the Chief Engineer, contending that the delays in the construction schedule were not the fault of Roebling but the failure of supplies to arrive on time. Overriding the objections of New York Mayor William Grace, who felt it was high time to vote on the subject of Roebling's removal in order to permit the "appointment of a man who will be constantly on the ground," the trustees voted to table the matter until September 11.[97]

The delay may have given the trustees time to reflect upon the *Eagle*'s coverage of the August 22 meeting. After noting that the completion of the bridge had not been delayed by the engineering staff but, rather, the "weak and stupid" business management, the paper declared:

> A radical change in the business management of bridge affairs is demanded, and the taxpayers of this city will sustain Mayor Low in bringing it about. But no generous man will willingly degrade Roebling, on the eve of the completion of an enterprise, which, to him and his, will be as the victorious flag of his country to the soldier whose frame has been shattered in its defense.[98]

Before Washington Roebling could claim the flag of victory, he and Emily had to endure a very tense time. The weeks leading up to the trustees' September meeting would be one of the most difficult periods in their married life. Not since Washington Roebling had been carried out of the New York caisson near death had Emily faced such a crisis. Although she and her husband were geographically removed from the place where the drama affecting their lives was being played out, she kept abreast of developments. The goings-on in New York and Brooklyn were more important to her than the fact that President Chester Arthur, accompanied by his son and two private secretaries, was visiting Newport and was the guest of honor at a reception given by Cornelius Vanderbilt Jr. Her husband's problems, however, proved to be of sufficient interest to the editor of *The Newport Daily News* that he included a small article about the dissatisfaction expressed by the mayors of New York and Brooklyn over the interminable delays in completing the bridge.[99]

Far more significant was the interpretation metropolitan area newspapers placed on the recent trustees' meeting. Still distraught over the death of her brother, Emily must have felt completely depressed reading about "Roebling's Probable Removal" in the *Herald*, "Engineer Roebling to Go" in the *Star*, and "Engineer Roebling – Mayor Low Proposing to Supersede Him Because He Cannot Perform His Duties" in *The New York World*.[100] Fortunately for both herself and her husband, she was not the kind of person to sit and wait while trouble brewed. She immediately sat down and dashed off a letter to Ludwig Semler thanking him for his defense of the Colonel and telling him that she would like to speak with him directly. "I will go over to Brooklyn any day you can give me a little of your time," she told him.[101] Before this could happen, Semler took it upon himself to go to Newport, where he met not only Mrs. Roebling but the celebrated Mr. Roebling. A comparatively new member of the bridge board of trustees, Semler had never met the Colonel before. Although it was evident to him that Washington Roebling was suffering from some sort of nervous condition, he came away convinced that the man was brilliant, lucid and in full possession of his faculties. To the Roeblings' delight, Semler said as much to the press.[102]

Undoubtedly because they believed favorable publicity was what they needed at this point, Emily and the Colonel were willing to admit a reporter from the *World* to their rented home in Newport. For a decade the Chief Engineer had avoided the press, denying all requests for interviews, but he was willing to make an exception provided the reporter did not directly quote his views on the politicking he believed was going on among the board of trustees. A bit more circumspect than her husband, Emily was skeptical about this arrangement. After the interview was concluded, she spoke with the reporter alone, getting him to reiterate his pledge not to use direct quotes. But when the article appeared, the Colonel's vigorous denunciation of the gubernatorial aspirations of certain members of the board was quoted verbatim.[103]

This nearly finished Washington Roebling. Any hopes he entertained of staying on as Chief Engineer were abandoned. Emily said as much in a letter to Trustee William Marshall, a very nonpolitical member of the board. Although she vigorously defended her husband to Marshall, noting that "he has no idea of doing anything for the sake of policy," she admitted, "I was very much alarmed lest something Mr. Roebling said should be turned to his disadvantage."[104] Emily, contrite, concluded that the outcome of the effort to remove the Colonel was up to the Almighty. Although her statements about all of the problems resulting from her husband's illness were unquestionably true, it is entirely possible that the apologetic letter to William Marshall was "General" Emily's last shot in the war to save the Colonel by playing on Marshall's sympathy.

Perhaps Emily's last shot struck its target, since, at the crucial meeting of the board on September 11, Marshall vigorously defended the Chief Engineer, asserting that he had not been responsible for any of the delays in the construction schedule. The other trustee over whom Emily had exerted her personal influence, Ludwig Semler, also came forward on behalf of the Colonel. Fearing Roebling would be fired at that meeting, he proposed referring the question to a special committee of the board.[105]

Shortly before the crucial meeting of the trustees on the 11th, Washington Roebling's spirits were abysmal, judging from a letter he wrote to the board before a vote was taken on Seth Low's resolutions. In it he said:

> I cannot see why Mayor Low in his resolution took the trouble to offer me the position of consulting engineer after I had positively refused it in the interview at Newport, when he announced to me that I must be put out at once. I am an invalid, and certainly it would be to my advantage to be well, but I should like some facts to sustain his judgment that my absence from the post of active supervision is necessarily a source of delay. I have made every possible arrangement to prevent a work of such magnitude being exposed to any of the vicissitudes of my health.[106]

Roebling concluded with a plea to the board to vote not on the question of making him a Consulting Engineer, but on the simple question of whether he was to stay on as Chief Engineer.

In the end, the board voted on all of Low's resolutions. They were defeated, 10-7.[107] The *Eagle* reported that the outcome of the vote "has been received by the public with ... genuine satisfaction."[108] Praising the Chief Engineer, the paper went on to say, "Since his illness does not in any way militate against the public interests, the public is more than willing that he should retain such honors as his genius and fidelity have earned."[109] The paper said nothing about his wife's genius and fidelity, but that was how Emily wanted it. She was content to remain the silent tower of strength as sturdy as either of the bridge anchorages; but behind the scene she had not been completely silent in the period leading up to the vote on the resolution to remove her husband as Chief Engineer.

The Back Story

In addition to lobbying board members to ensure that her husband retained his position as Chief Engineer, Emily made a presentation to the American Society of Civil Engineers. Her appearance at an ASCE meeting in Manhattan was long rumored and often dismissed as a mere legend. That it actually occurred was corroborated by Emily's great-great-grandson, Kristian Roebling. In 2018, in a conversation following the dedication of the new Brooklyn Heights street sign honoring Emily, Kristian Roebling explained the importance of transmitting family history orally from generation to generation, noting the family's certainty that his great-great-grandmother had addressed the ASCE.

Besides the Roebling family's oral history, documentary testimony to Emily's presentation to the ASCE exists in the form of a letter to the editor of *The New York Times* upon the death of Washington Roebling in 1926. Emily had predeceased her husband 23 years earlier and Washington's friend, George Frederick Kunz, convinced of the need to respect the Roeblings' privacy, waited to recount the back story of Emily and the ASCE. Kunz's letter revealed that he was present

when Emily and Washington went through various itera-
tions of the statement she presented at the ASCE meeting.
According to Kunz:

> The writer clearly remembers hearing him dictate to
> his wife a final statement, after many dictations, telling
> what he was doing on the bridge and why he should not
> be displaced. Mrs. Roebling read this paper before the
> American Society of Civil Engineers in the American
> Institute Fair Building at Sixty-third Street and Third
> Avenue. It produced an immense sensation because it
> was a splendid statement and well delivered by Mrs.
> Roebling, who was young and handsome. It was not
> always the case at that time when a woman spoke in
> public.[110]

As a witness to a long-concealed episode of Brooklyn
Bridge history, Kunz was credible. An internationally
renowned mineralogist and gemologist, his expertise was
recognized quite early by Tiffany and Co., where he was
appointed vice president at age 23 and served in this position
until his death, in 1932, at age 76. A self-taught mineralogist, Kunz was awarded honorary degrees from universities
in Germany and the United States, including Columbia
University. His awards also included the Legion of Honor
of France and an appointment as honorary curator of the
precious gemstones collection at the American Museum of
Natural History. In addition, he was a prolific author and
a civic-minded individual who served as president of the
American Scenic and Historic Preservation Society and was
instrumental in preserving New York City's High Bridge.[111]

George Frederick Kunz and the Roeblings had a lot in

common. They had dealt with challenges, loss and sadness. Kunz's 24-year-old daughter Elizabeth was killed, along with his secretary, when the carriage Elizabeth was driving on a country road outside Peekskill, New York, overturned after the horse pulling it became frightened. Before fleeing, the horse stepped on the accident victims.[112] Just as George Frederick Kunz's life was impacted by a tragic accident, for the Roeblings, the accident that led to the slow, agonizing death of John A. Roebling was overwhelming, as was Washington Roebling's caisson disease. The experience of tragedy was not the only thing the Roeblings and Kunz had in common. Emily Roebling, like Kunz, was active in historical associations. The common thread linking her husband with Kunz was mineralogy. In her brief biography of her husband, Emily wrote, "as a mineralogist he is nearly as widely known as he is as an engineer."[113]

Washington Roebling sought Kunz's advice about purchasing minerals and with Kunz's urging loaned some of his rare minerals "for investigation" to the American Museum of Natural History.[114] In 1917, when the New York Mineralogical Club, of which Kunz was president, elected Roebling to honorary membership, a "surprised and highly pleased" Roebling said in a letter to Kunz that he thought he recognized "your master hand in the flattering announcement."[115] In 1926, when Roebling donated $45,000 in bonds to the Mineralogical Society of America, Kunz, writing on the stationery of the New York Mineralogical Club, praised Roebling for his "most munificent gift, a great aid to mineralogy and mineralogists."[116] Kunz ended his letter to Roebling by saying, "May you live long to enjoy the fruits of your gifts."[117] Washington Roebling died five months later. His impressive collection of minerals was donated to the Smithsonian Institution.[118]

That there was a connection between the Roeblings and George Frederick Kunz is undeniable, as is Kunz's credibility. Given the details included in his letter to the editor of *The New York Times*, it's not difficult to picture Emily addressing the American Society of Civil Engineers. The ASCE would not, however, have wanted this in its official records. Allowing a woman to appear before an all-male professional organization was something that could not be admitted. By omitting any mention of Emily in its records, the ASCE could claim she never appeared before the association. If ASCE members in attendance at her presentation spoke about it in public, the ASCE had plausible deniability. Since rumors that a woman was building the Brooklyn Bridge continued to circulate, loose-lipped ASCE members would have fanned the flames, intensifying concern about the stability of the bridge, and yet, without that woman, the bridge would not have been completed in accordance with her husband's uncompromising instructions regarding its safety. Interestingly, Emily is included in the ASCE's list of Notable Civil Engineers.[119] She is also in a photograph of attendees at the ASCE 20th annual convention, which was held in Milwaukee in 1888. The article in which the photograph appeared stated: "Once lost to history, we now know many of the ASCE members who took part in a photograph commemorating its 20th annual convention in 1888 – including two identifications that likely push back the record of women and minorities as members of the Society."[120] Emily, who was seated in the front row, was one of those identifications. Also, the Roebling award, established by the ASCE's Construction Institute in 1987, was created "in memory of 3 outstanding constructors," John and Washington Roebling and Emily, "who, in effect became the field superintendent in support of her crippled husband's effort."[121]

Opening Day

Emily's lobbying efforts on behalf of her husband produced the desired result. With Washington Roebling's position assured, following the failure of the vote on the resolution to remove him as Chief Engineer, Emily was able to prepare for the opening of the bridge. In the months leading up to the big day, things returned to normal at the Roebling house on Columbia Heights. Emily resumed the duties she had been performing for more than a decade. Besides acting as her husband's secretary, she was a tireless messenger when necessary, making several trips a day to the bridge offices to see the assistant engineers or to see the span itself. By this time she knew so much about engineering and construction that her husband felt perfectly comfortable sending her across the newly completed roadway a few weeks before the bridge opened to ascertain the effect, if any, of trotting a horse over the roadway.[122] This was one of a host of last-minute details that had to be taken care of prior to opening day. Most had to do with the dedication ceremonies planned for May 24, but some were directly related to the bridge itself. In this category was the installation of electric lamps. Thomas Alva Edison had begun supplying power to subscribers in the area surrounding his Pearl Street generating station in lower

Manhattan but the U.S. Illuminating Company was given the job of lighting the bridge, not only because its bid was lower, but because the Chief Engineer viewed its proposal to install electric arc lamps more favorably than Edison's suggestion for incandescent lamps.[123]

On the night of opening day a different kind of illumination was planned, a gigantic fireworks display. Washington Roebling was so alarmed when he learned of it that he had Emily dash off a strongly worded note declaring that the fireworks extravaganza over the East River should be held the night before the official dedication. In this way the public could be kept off the span until everything was over. Especially dangerous, as far as the Chief Engineer was concerned, was the possibility of large numbers of people remaining on the bridge if it were opened immediately after the dedication ceremony. Emphasizing the seriousness of the matter, Roebling stated:

> I fear it will be impossible to clear the crowd off again before night. I will not be responsible for the consequences if people are allowed to crowd on just as they like. It would be possible for one hundred thousand people to get on the main span of the bridge and cover every available foot of space, cables, and tops of trusses. This would make a load three times greater than the live load calculated for.[124]

As these words were written, Emily Warren Roebling surely must have wondered how she and her husband had come so close to reaching their goal of seeing the bridge completed and opened only to be confronted by still another problem. Yet, in comparison with the difficulties they had to contend with over the years, this one, while serious in terms of the potential threat it posed for the bridge and for public safety, was easily solved when the trustees decided to take the Colonel's advice and tweak the opening-day schedule. Thus, the massive fireworks display took place that evening as planned and ended at 9 o'clock. The bridge was formally opened to the public at midnight.

With this problem solved, Emily could concentrate on more pleasant things, including plans for what she called a bridge party. This was to be a formal procession of carriages on opening day. With the son and wife of the Chief Engineer in the lead, sharing the same victoria she had used on her first trip over the roadway, two dozen carriages, filled with relatives and friends of the Roeblings, proceeded from 110 Columbia Heights to the Brooklyn entrance to the bridge. Among the guests was Mrs. Rossiter Raymond, wife of the man who had praised Emily at the RPI alumni dinner. Another was Mrs. William G. Wilson, who received a most cordial hand-written note from Mrs. Roebling inviting her to participate in the bridge party. Signed "Yours affectionately," the brief letter, dated exactly one week before the scheduled opening of the bridge, also invited Mrs. Wilson to assist Emily in receiving guests at a gigantic reception at the Roebling home following the dedication ceremonies.[125] Although she personally preferred hand-written to printed invitations, the size of the guest list necessitated a Tiffany-engraved invitation. Printed in script, it was adorned by both pictures of a serious-looking Washington Roebling and the bridge. Sharing top billing in terms of the size of the print were "The East River Bridge" and "Col. & Mrs. Washington A. Roebling."[126]

The invitation, also done by Tiffany, sent by the "trustees of the New York and Brooklyn Bridge," was adorned by pictures of the span and the seals of the two municipalities linked by the bridge, but nowhere on it was the Chief Engineer's countenance found.[127] His name appeared at the very bottom of the invitation, below those of the trustees and mayors. In the official program for the opening ceremonies, his name was also toward the bottom of the list, preceding only those of the assistant engineers.

Washington Roebling did not attend the actual dedication ceremonies. As usual, his wife took his place while, according to the press, he watched the dignitaries assembling at the Brooklyn terminus of the span, where the ceremonies were held. President Chester A. Arthur, Governor Grover Cleveland and Mayor Franklin Edson of New York walked across from the New York side, accompanied by the Seventh Regiment. Mayor Seth Low of Brooklyn greeted them on the other side. Thousands of ticket-holders who had been admitted to the roadways flanking the promenade cheered. Following a musical rendition by the Twenty-third Regiment Band and an invocation by A.N. Littlejohn, Episcopal bishop of Long Island, the speeches commenced. The masses for whom the bridge had been built were being honored today, but, nevertheless, John and Washington Roebling were singled out by the speakers for their remarkable contributions to the project. One orator, Congressman Abram S. Hewitt, heaped praise upon another Roebling, Emily. Of her he said:

> One name, however, which may find no place in the
> official records, cannot be passed over here, in silence.
> In ancient times when great works were constructed,

a goddess was chosen, to whose tender care they were dedicated. Thus the ruins of the Acropolis today recall the name of Pallas Athene to an admiring world. In the Middle Ages, the blessing of some saint was invoked to protect from the rude attacks of the barbarians, and the destructive hand of time, the building erected by man's devotion to the worship of God. So, with this bridge will ever be coupled the thought of one, through the subtle *alembic* of whose brain, and by whose facile fingers, communication was maintained between the directing power of its construction, and the obedient agencies of its execution. It is thus an everlasting monument to the self-sacrificing devotion of woman, and of her capacity for that higher education from which she has been too long debarred. The name of Mrs. Emily Warren Roebling will thus be inseparably associated with all that is admirable in human nature, and with all that is wonderful in the constructive world of art.[128]

At long last the world knew of Emily's contributions to the success of the great project and she was positively delighted, except for one thing. Abram Hewitt's use of the word *alembic* puzzled her. An alembic is a device with a beaked cap that was once commonly used in distilling. What Abram Hewitt meant was that Emily's sharp mind had distilled an infinite variety and quantity of complex theories, figures and details during the construction of the bridge. A dozen years after the span opened, Mrs. Roebling had occasion to send her son a copy of Hewitt's remarks. In her covering letter, she pointed out, "Your father crushed me, by telling me, an alembic was 'a thing with a long nose and a big belly.' Nevertheless, when I have a crest, it shall bear a 'bridge rampant' somewhere on it, and an alembic on an azure field!"[129]

Taking a cue from Abram Hewitt, the *Eagle*, in its coverage of the opening day ceremonies, devoted considerable space to Mrs. Roebling. After quoting Hewitt's remarks, the paper observed:

> Among the many hundreds of thousands of people who have read or will read this tribute of esteem and regard, there are very few, perhaps, who will quite understand and appreciate its significance without a word of explanation. The *Eagle*, we are sure, will be acquitted of any desire to invade the privacy of Mr. Roebling's home in making the explanation. It is rather with a purpose to make known the facts that more than entitle the admirable lady to this worldwide praise that we refer to the subject.[130]

The paper went on to term Mrs. Roebling's devotion "a public benefaction." Praising her intellect, it said:

> Great emergencies are the opportunities of great minds. Mrs. Emily Warren Roebling met this difficulty as nobody else could. She addressed her remarkable intelligence to the acquisition of the higher mathematics; her luminous mind was well-adapted to its profound and often desperate labyrinths. She mastered this most bewildering of sciences, applied it to the bridge, was in rapport with her husband, and dazzled and astounded the engineers by her complete and intelligent conception of their chief's theories and plans.[131]

Referring to her other contributions, the paper declared:
Day after day, when she could be spared from the sick-room, in cold and wet, the devoted wife exchanged the duties of chief nurse for those of chief engineer of the bridge, explaining knotty points, examining results for herself, and thus she established the most perfect means of communication between the structure and its author. How well she discharged this self-imposed duty the grand and beautiful causeway best tells.

The *Eagle* proceeded to ask "why this charming bit of romance ... never before found its way into print" and promptly answered the question by stating:
The true woman possesses, above all attributes, that loveliest and most womanly characteristic – modesty. Out of deference to Mrs. Roebling's aversion to posing in public and standing apart from her sex, those who have long been aware of her noble devotion and the incalculable services she rendered to the people of the two cities, to the world indeed, have discreetly kept their knowledge to themselves.[133]

Many admirers familiar with Emily's contributions to one of the century's most impressive engineering projects flocked to the Roebling home in Brooklyn Heights immediately after the official opening day ceremonies. Ostensibly they came to pay honor to the Chief Engineer but Emily received congratulations as well. Yet, consistent with the modesty that the *Eagle* had praised, there was no bust of the silent builder adorning the gracious home. It was Emily's idea to place marble likenesses of her husband and father-in-law on the mantel in the drawing room. The new oil painting of the

Colonel was also her idea, as was the profusion of flowers that greeted the thousand-plus guests. President Chester Arthur, who arrived shortly after 5 p.m. to pay his respects to the Chief Engineer, was most enthusiastic about the spring blossoms whose fragrance wafted through the air along with music. Several of the major newspapers scarcely mentioned the entertainment but all of them noted the decorations. The *Tribune*, for example, observed:

> The house was handsomely decorated outside with flags and lanterns, as were all the neighboring houses, making the scene one of much beauty. Inside the long drawing room, the floral decorations were numerous. Both mantels were banked with red and white roses, wisteria and white lilacs, and there was a large cluster of white callas in the center. On either side of the folding doors was a large shield of ... roses. In front of the large mirror was an immense basket of gilt-straw filled with ... roses and lilacs, and vases of cut flowers were disposed about the rooms.[134]

Outside, dozens of police were required to hold back the immense crowd of onlookers who had come by to catch a glimpse of the president of the United States, New York's governor, members of the city councils of New York and Brooklyn, the mayors of those cities, and hundreds of other invited guests. A canopy running from the front door down to the end of the sidewalk shielded the guests from the crowd.[135] In the confusion, guests alighting from carriages most likely failed to notice that "the coats of arms of New York and Brooklyn were surmounted by flags, while over the street hung the Stars and Stripes," or that "streamers were flying from windowsills, and hung down in loops."[136]

Once they were safely inside the house and out of the public glare, guests were welcomed by Mrs. Roebling. She was attired in "a dress of heavy black silk, trimmed with crepe, and worn with a large bunch of purple violets."[137] The *World* reported, "Mrs. Roebling attended the ceremonies at the bridge for a short time, but did not stay until the conclusion of the ceremonies, as her husband required her attendance."[138] He was doubtless eager for her to get home to lend him moral support before the guests started arriving.

If Washington Roebling had a bad case of the jitters, it is perfectly understandable. He had not faced a crowd in more than a decade. During the preceding 11 years, his wife had been his emissary and chief supporter. He more or less acknowledged that, in body language, by leaning on her as he descended the stairs from his bedroom to the ground floor of the house, where he and Emily seated themselves on a sofa in the drawing room.[139] The Chief Engineer's 15-year-old son was physically big enough to lean on but he was passed over in favor of his mother, which is maybe only fitting considering the role she had played since 1872. In any event, the silent builder did not seem to mind. She chatted amiably with the guests while her husband attempted to conserve his strength. According to some press accounts, the Colonel looked "very feeble," and appeared "pale."[140] But at least one paper, while speaking of the "invalid engineer and his accomplished wife," said "he looked well and seemed in high spirits."[141] At any rate, he survived the reception though he did not get outside to the back lawn overlooking the river to see the magnificent new bridge, which veritably glowed in the late afternoon sunlight. A large refreshment tent had been set up on the grass. Underneath the marquee was a buffet table dominated by a three-foot-long model of the bridge constructed of sugar.[142] The rotund president of the United States must have been duly impressed but how much nibbling he and the other high-ranking officials did is questionable because they were expected for dinner at the home of Seth Low.

After a sumptuous repast, they viewed the brilliant fireworks display, held in honor of the bridge opening, from the upper stories of the mayor's residence. The Roeblings watched from 110 Columbia Heights as tens of thousands of pounds of rockets and flares illuminated the sky over the East River. On this day, the swiftly moving water separating the two great metropolises on opposite sides of the river ceased to be a barrier. Thanks to the prematurely aged man with the full gray beard and the strong, gifted woman who, even now at the completion of the century's most fabled engineering project, stood by faithfully, New York and Brooklyn had been linked. Not one of the brilliant bursts of rockets spelled out a tribute to the silent builder but it is an unquestionable verity that, had Washington Roebling selected a less accomplished and devoted woman for his wife, he would not have been showered with praise that very afternoon. His removal from the position of Chief Engineer would have occurred long before.[143] As the silent builder of the Brooklyn Bridge, Emily Warren Roebling viewed this as her crowning achievement. Five years before her death she asserted:

> I am still feeling well enough to stoutly maintain against all critics (including my only son) that I have more brains, common sense, and know-how generally

than any two engineers civil or uncivil that I have ever met, and but for me the Brooklyn Bridge would never have had the name of 'Roebling' in any way connected with it! It would have been 'Kingsley's Bridge' if it had ever been built! Your father was for years *dead* to all interest in that work.[144]

Emily's Lifelong Involvement With the Bridge

In the period immediately following the opening of the bridge, and, indeed, for more than a century afterward, the association of the name Roebling with the majestic span would prove to be a double-edged sword. Although the Roeblings would be lauded for the beauty and stability of the bridge they had designed and built, they would receive a disproportionate share of the blame when anything untoward occurred on the span. Tragedy first touched the bridge on Decoration Day, 1883, exactly one week after it was opened to the public. Late in the afternoon, as tens of thousands of curious people, many of them using the holiday to get their first look at the bridge, crowded onto the span, the sound of a high-pitched voice penetrated the warm spring air. A split second later, panic ensued as the crowds of men, women and children, both on the span itself and on the staircases leading to the promenade, attempted to flee the bridge, which they evidently feared was about to give way under the heavy weight of pedestrians, wagons and the U.S. Army's Twelfth Regiment.

In the aftermath of the tragedy, which left a dozen people trampled to death, various theories were advanced to explain what had happened. According to one version, the military was to blame because by marching across the bridge they caused it to sway, thereby alarming members of the public and causing them to lose faith in the stability of the great span. While it is true that soldiers were on the bridge, it is highly unlikely that they were marching despite the contention of the *Times* that they "were marching over the south drive of the bridge ... and were within a short distance of the spot where the panic occurred."[145] The letter Emily had written almost a month before, when the trustees were finalizing plans for the opening celebration, contained a very emphatic warning about marching. If the military took part in the ceremonies, "it must be with the distinct understanding that they are not to <u>march</u> across the bridge either before, after, or during the ceremonies." To emphasize the point, not only was the word <u>march</u> underlined, but the trustees were reminded that "on no existing suspension bridge are troops allowed to march to music in crossing and it should not be permitted here."[146]

If the soldiers were not to blame, then who was? This is a question that would baffle the trustees, Washington and Emily Roebling and a coroner's jury for quite some time. Trustees, bridge employees and eyewitnesses were summoned to report on various aspects of the events of May 31. Many told the story of a woman stumbling and then falling down the wooden steps on the New York side of the bridge. To get her out of the way so that she wouldn't be trampled, a policeman rushed to her assistance. Unable to carry her through the dense crowd, he was compelled to pull her along. Another woman, seeing the officer dragging a middle-aged female down the stairs, let out an awful shriek. Before long people were shouting, "The bridge is falling! The bridge is falling!"[147]

Plausible though this explanation was, the incident opened up a whole Pandora's box. Eclipsing the question of the immediate cause of the panic was the long-range concern over the stability of the bridge. General Egbert Viele, a noted civil engineer, addressed this issue. Although he found no fault with the strength of the bridge, he regarded "the placing of the steps where they are, an engineering blunder."[148] Furthermore: "the footpath is too narrow for the travel that is to pass over it. Here is a structure built to last fifty or one hundred years, and it is found to be too small for the necessities of today. Think what the travel will be fifty years hence."[149] At the coroner's inquest there was considerable discussion about the width of the promenade. Although trains wouldn't actually start running until September 1883, a decision had been made several years before the completion of the bridge to accommodate this mode of transportation across the span, thereby confining pedestrians to what many deemed an inadequate walkway.[150] In the end, the coroner's jury placed the blame on the narrow staircase where the incident originated, and on the comparatively small number of police employed by the bridge trustees to patrol the span. The implication was that the men, who had been working 12-hour shifts for $2 per day, were both overworked and underpaid.[151]

At the very moment that the coroner's jury was deliberating, the Brooklyn Common Council, which had evidently discounted the possibility that the Chief Engineer was in any way to blame for the Decoration Day tragedy, was proposing to commission a life-size portrait of Washington Roebling for the Brooklyn City Hall. In passing the resolution authorizing the expenditure of up to $1,000 for the painting, Alderman

McCarty declared that "Mr. Roebling was eminently entitled to this honor, and that it should be granted so as to remove a stigma which was cast upon him some time ago by asking his withdrawal from the position of chief engineer."[152] This surely must have been gratifying, not only for the Colonel, but for his wife, who had recently agonized with him over the senseless loss of life in the bridge panic. Understandably, the Roeblings were reticent about the events of May 31, which they regarded as a tragic accident and one that could have been avoided. Watching the Decoration Day activities on the bridge from his home, the Chief Engineer became alarmed about the crush of people and advised Assistant Engineer Martin to allow pedestrians onto the roadway to alleviate overcrowding.[153]

Thirteen years later, when she was a guest at the coronation of Tsar Nicholas II of Russia, Emily witnessed a stampede of peasants in Moscow. Commenting on the dreadful incident to her husband, she said: "Today we are all sad over the terrible accident that occurred yesterday at the people's fete when two thousand peasants were trampled to death. It was just such an accident as the crush on the Brooklyn Bridge."[154]

Although the Roeblings viewed the Decoration Day stampede as an accident, they could not help but wish that the Colonel's role in the bridge project had ended on that happier day a week before the tragedy when the span was officially dedicated. Once it was thrown open to the public, the bridge was the responsibility of the trustees, unless, of course, some structural problem threatening the stability of the bridge was discovered; but this was not the case. Even with approximately 20,000 people scrambling to get off it on the afternoon of May 31, the bridge had proven as sound as a dollar. Yet, there was lingering public apprehension which was allayed by a procession of P.T. Barnum's circus animals across the bridge a year after the stampede. In all, twenty-one elephants, including the famous Jumbo, seven camels and ten dromedaries made a night time trek from Manhattan to Brooklyn. By this time the Roeblings had no official connection with the bridge.

A little more than a month after the opening of the span, Emily Warren Roebling performed what she was convinced would be her last act as her husband's chief assistant. She sat down and wrote his letter of resignation. Now that the bridge was completed and open, there was nothing more for the Chief Engineer to do. For him to step down at this point was right, proper and prudent. The Roeblings were severing their ties with the bridge board of trustees at precisely the time they planned to do so. Had the vote on Mayor Low's resolution the previous autumn gone against the Colonel, his resignation would have taken place according to the board's timetable. Now it was entirely different. Instead of forcing him out, the trustees graciously accepted his resignation and appointed him to the unsalaried position of Consulting Engineer. His deputy, C.C. Martin, the board's candidate for Chief Engineer the previous fall, was appointed to that position now.[155]

Gone but not forgotten would perhaps be the best way to describe Washington Roebling's relationship with the bridge for the remainder of his life. From time to time, Martin and others contacted him for advice about problems that arose. Often, it was Emily who dealt with these matters, just as it was she who continued to fight for the kind of recognition she felt her husband deserved. Since Washington Roebling preferred to stay out of the limelight, she took it upon herself to guarantee that he would not be forgotten. For that reason Emily wished to see "two bronze bas reliefs on the sides of one of the tower[s], one being the bust of her husband, the other of the other Roebling."[156] According to the *Eagle*, "Mrs. Roebling offered to defray all the cost of this beautiful and appropriate memorial of the two Roeblings – but some political influence at work defeated this design. Who was it? Is Brooklyn unwilling to honor the man who honored her?"[157] The newspaper hinted that Seth Low, who had been reelected mayor of Brooklyn in 1883, was the obstacle, which is not surprising.

There would eventually be memorials to the Roebling men and Emily on the bridge but following its completion and Washington Roebling's resignation as Chief Engineer, while he was not forgotten, all sorts of nonsense was written about him. The press frequently confused him with his father and many an article claimed that both men were long dead. The minute she learned of any erroneous information in print, Emily sat down and wrote a letter to the publication in question to set the record straight.

Sometimes the fault lay not with the newspaper but with the actions of members of the Roebling family. "Your uncle Ferd is masquerading on the Pacific coast as the Engineer of the Brooklyn Bridge," Emily told her son a dozen years after the bridge was completed:[158]

In the *Los Angeles Herald* of Monday, February 25, 1895, this was the heading in large letters: "He built the Big Bridge." Among other things, it said: "Mr. Roebling is a quiet unassuming man. ... He would be passed in a crowd without remark, yet his name is familiar to scientists the world over." This I consider a real tribute to his fine insignificance. ... No one would pass W.A. in a crowd, without remark, even if that remark was not complimentary![159]

Having mastered the fine art of diplomacy during the bridge years when she had to contend with trustees, assistant engineers, foremen and so forth, Mrs. Roebling handled this incident carefully. Instead of revealing the identity of the bogus Chief Engineer to the editor of the *Herald*, she merely told him, in her inimitable way, that he had been had and that the real Chief Engineer had not been out of Trenton all winter long.[160]

To while away the time that winter, the Colonel was busily replying to letters from people interested in building suspension bridges over the Hudson River.[161] Emily helped with the correspondence but attempted to remain as uninvolved as possible with bridges other than the one across the East River. Yet she continued to be vitally interested in the Brooklyn Bridge, sending her son a handsome picture of it and encouraging one of her grandsons to build a model of the span. In order not to stifle the child's creativity, however, she suggested that he "build his bridge after his own fashion quite to his satisfaction even if it differs widely from the laid-down plans."[162]

Mrs. Roebling remained interested in any event that was connected to the bridge. In February 1896, she informed her son, "The wire rope cable has been taken off the Brooklyn

Bridge and they are running the cars with a trolley electric system."[163] When highly technical engineering questions arose, Washington Roebling did not hesitate to dispatch his engineer-son and Emily to look into the matter. In the summer of 1898, Mrs. Roebling wrote to John:

> I have been to the Bridge twice but neither time was there half the load on it you and I saw. That suspender has slipped by the slip joint plate in some way so it no longer chafes it. The fresh-cut plank has cut fully a quarter inch more than when you saw it and dozens of suspenders have the paint scraped off more than half round so you see the twines in the strands bright and glittering.[164]

Truly this was a case of one engineer talking to another and both of them, as well as the Colonel, were concerned about the stress imposed upon the bridge by heavy usage. Fully loaded trains closely following each other were a special worry. At the end of August 1898, Emily went to the bridge to have another look at the situation. Then the Colonel and one of his old assistants from the bridge-building days, draftsman Wilhelm Hildenbrand, who had emerged as quite a famous engineer in his own right in the meantime, calculated the effect of the loads.[165] The New York City Bridge Department made its own calculations and, in December, Brooklyn Bridge Chief Engineer C.C. Martin issued a report claiming that "the bridge is entirely safe and no one need have any apprehension that it will ever break from the strain to which it is now subjected."[166]

The newspapers dutifully reported the results of the investigation but, before the findings were publicly announced, they had a field day alarming the public about the safety of the span. To judge from Emily's letters, there was reason for concern. She dubbed Martin's report "Christian Science engineering. Just keep on saying a thing cannot fall and it will hold all you can put on it!"[167] After reviewing an advance copy of the report, she confided to her son that the Colonel "never figured out a larger margin of safety than 3 for the weakest part and after fifteen years of use and an added weight of 430 tons it is now 3.57."[168] After discussing the entire matter very thoroughly with her husband, she told their son, "[The] Colonel says Martin assumes in his calculations that the strain on the middle cables and the outside ones are the same which is all wrong and Hildy says he makes no allowance for the effect of a sudden jar which is worse than a strain."[169] Washington Roebling put all of this in writing to Martin but otherwise held his tongue because, to use his wife's words, he did not want "to create a panic nor make the bridge out worse than it is."[170] Emily noted, "I hear that there is to be a great exodus from Brooklyn to New York next spring. People are growing distrustful of the bridge and the ferry facilities have become so poor they are next to nothing."[171]

The solution to the problem was to remove some of the burden from the Brooklyn Bridge and shift it to the two new bridges planned for the East River: the Williamsburg, which would be finished in 1903, and the Manhattan, to be completed in 1909. Although these spans were the work of L.L. Buck, the John A. Roebling's Sons Company received the contract to provide the wires. When the contract for the Williamsburg Bridge was awarded, neither Emily nor the

Colonel was ecstatic. Washington Roebling admitted that the new undertaking was

> an overwhelming responsibility, which I did everything in my power to ward off, but it was inevitable. When I think back to the tortures I endured in Brooklyn, my heart sinks within me. ... Fortunately, it is only the cables. They however are the most important part of a Suspension Bridge. Mr. Buck frankly confessed that he knew nothing of cable making, and as I was the only one who did, I had to do it![172]

Telling his son of this development, the Colonel ended a lengthy letter by admitting: "I ask myself the question, why do you do this for Buck, but there is no answer. If it is ever done it will be as much a Roebling as a Buck bridge! because the cables are the most important part."[173] As an afterthought, the Colonel observed: "Your mother is furious because she knows it will kill me."[174]

His assessment of his wife's feelings was quite accurate. She, herself, told John, "I am brokenhearted the John A. Roebling's Sons Co. got the contract for the cables of Buck's bridge."[175] Although her husband's health was considerably better, she declared:

> I totally disapprove of his whole connection with the contract, and the work but I have requested him not to talk to me on the subject, and I will keep my opinions to myself. ... I shall now feel free to do many things I have long wanted to do, as your father's plans will take him quite out of my world.[176]

Emily's opposition to the new project was twofold. An extremely straightforward person, she abhorred the political wheeling and dealing she was convinced had preceded the awarding of the contract. On top of that, she feared that her husband's health, which was fragile at best, would break down under the strain of hard work and deadlines and that she would once again be forced to step in. "No more public work for me with a broken reed like the Colonel," she declared.[177] A short time later, she reported to her son that his father "is more than half sick with his preliminary work on the cables. I think he will last about ten days when he gets finally in the field and take to his bed as he did in Brooklyn!"[178] Although her husband's health roller coasted up and down, he managed to provide the cables for the new bridge. In the spring of 1901, he personally supervised the installation of the first set of cables, and he and Hildenbrand were on the barge that transported reels of cable across the river.[179] Emily was not well enough to go along for the ride but told her son that the whole business was "a great success."[180]

Illness also prevented Mrs. Roebling from accompanying her husband to the Brooklyn Bridge in July 1901. At the time there was considerable public concern about the safety of the span because of overcrowding at the Manhattan entrance to the bridge.[181] Soon a new problem arose. A cable snapped and became detached. Despite Chief Engineer Martin's assertion that the bridge "is not going to fall down," the newspapers played up the safety angle to the point that bridge officials felt they had to do something to counteract the adverse publicity.[182] The logical thing was to get the old Chief Engineer back on the job as a consultant. "He wanted me to go with him," Emily told John, dismayed that she was not quite up to it.[183] On a subsequent trip to the bridge, which she was also unable to make, the Colonel "found things not half as bad as the newspapers had made them out but he was asked to make any changes and repairs he thought best."[184] Hildenbrand, who was now in charge of supplying the cables for the Williamsburg Bridge for the John A. Roebling's Sons Company, was given the additional job of "making plans for roller connections for the suspenders" of the Brooklyn Bridge and the Colonel was asked to prepare a written report "so as to restore public confidence in the stability of the work."[185] This was indeed a new role for the bridge office, for as Emily noted, "they never seemed to care what your father feared or the public thought."[186]

Like her husband, Mrs. Roebling cared about the well-being of the people who used the bridge, just as she cared what they thought about the span and those responsible for it. Is it any wonder then that she was delighted with the suggestion to rename the bridge in honor of its builders? In telling John about this development, she sent him, along with other press clippings, "best of all, an article from the *Troy Daily Times* begging that the Brooklyn Bridge should be immediately named the 'Roebling Bridge' in honor of John A., W.A., and Emily Warren Roebling."[187]

The editorial noted that

The big city is bound to have several big bridges in (the) course of time, and the proper way is to give each a distinct name. And nothing could be more appropriate than to call the original structure the Roebling bridge. The Roebling family is inseparably connected with its history. It was conceived and partly executed by John A. Roebling, one of the greatest of engineers, who fell a victim to his fidelity to duty and close watchfulness of the work. Then his son, Col. Washington A. Roebling, a worthy successor, and one of the famous graduates of Rensselaer Polytechnic Institute of Troy, took up the task. His health was wrecked by disease contracted during his labors in building the mighty structure, and for years he was an invalid confined to his room, where through others he directed operations. His most efficient assistant was his gifted wife, who, in order to aid him, acquired the technical knowledge of an expert, and so carried out the plans which her disabled husband perfected.

Devotion like this to a vast undertaking should never be forgotten, and it would be altogether fitting to call it the Roebling bridge, although that would be but a small recognition of the service the Roebling family has done to millions of people.[188]

First, last and always, it was the people who really counted. The bridge for which Emily Warren Roebling had sacrificed a dozen years of her young life, the majestic span whose public image and stability interested her for the rest of her days, had been constructed for the masses of New York and Brooklyn by a remarkable family whose most surprising member was the silent builder. In 1915, the Board of Aldermen of New York voted to officially designate the East River Bridge the Brooklyn Bridge, a name then in common use. A more fitting appellation, the Roebling Bridge, or perhaps the John, Washington and Emily Roebling Bridge, would have to await a future day when the silent builder's light would be hidden no longer.

Endnotes

[1] *New York Tribune* letter in EWR Scrapbook, RPI.

[2] The most comprehensive account of the story of the Brooklyn Bridge is David McCullough's *The Great Bridge* (New York: Simon & Schuster, 1972). Other good sources include: David B. Steinman, *Builders of the Bridge: The Story of John Roebling and His Son* (New York: Harcourt, Brace, Jovanovich, 1945); Alan Trachtenberg, *Brooklyn Bridge: Fact and Symbol* (Chicago: University of Chicago Press, 1965); and *Stanley Edgar Hyman, "Profiles: This Alluring Roadway,"* The New Yorker, May 17, 1952, pp. 39-84.

[3] Another bad winter, that of 1876-77, caused *The Brooklyn Daily Eagle* to declare, "Let the structure be carried to completion with all proper rapidity." EWR Scrapbook, January 3, 1877.

[4] David McCullough recounts the story of Kingsley's supposed visit to Murphy on a wintry December night in 1866 to convince him of the need for a bridge. At that point, Murphy had reservations about a project from which Kingsley, as Brooklyn's largest contractor, stood to reap enormous financial benefits. (McCullough, pp. 112-13.) Washington Roebling said of the inception of the project: "The financial part of the Bridge project was started by Mr. W.C. Kingsley of Brooklyn, who expected to make money and gain fame but got little of either. He associated with ... some of the prominent men of Brooklyn." (WAR to General James F. Reisling, January 23, 1916, WAR Letterbook, p. 512.)

[5] *Eagle*, January 19, 1877, EWR Scrapbook.

[6] *National Cyclopaedia*, IV, p. 404.

[7] WAR to James F. Reisling, January 23, 1916, WAR Letterbook, p. 510.

[8] Hamilton Schuyler, *The Roeblings: A Century of Engineers, Bridge-Builders, and Industrialists* (Princeton, New Jersey: Princeton University Press, 1931), pp. 139-40.

[9]Obituary of JAR, *The New York Times*, July 23, 1869, 4:6.

[10]In a letter to R.T. Crane., Esq., of Chicago, Washington Roebling said his father made the original designs for the bridge "with perhaps a little assistance from myself and [draftsman] Mr. Hildenbrand." (WAR to R.T. Crane, November 12, 1904.)

[11]Reflection on death of JAR, WAR Letterbook, p. 614.

[12]She also had to accept his decision to become the legal guardian of John Roebling's youngest son, Edmund, an often troublesome young man, who, after his father's remarriage, ran away from boarding school and disappeared for a year. When he was considerably older than Edmund, Washington Roebling had been driven out of the house by his father and forced to enlist in the Union Army. The Colonel explained this in a letter to General James. F. Reisling, February 18, 1916, WAR Letterbook, p. 408. In a memorandum of July 20, 1898 (Ibid., p. 592), he refers to his guardianship of Edmund. For part of the time the Colonel and Emily were residing in Brooklyn, "Eddie," as he was called, lived with them.

[13]WAR to William Couper, July 26, 1907.

[14]WAR to General James F. Reisling, January 23, 1916, WAR Letterbook, p. 511.

[15]Ibid., and WAR to R.T. Crane, November 12, 1904.

[16]EWR Biography of WAR, Roebling Collection, Institute Archives and Special Collections, Rensselaer Polytechnic Institute, Troy, New York. According to Emily:

When Mr. John A. Roebling met his sudden and tragic death in July 1869, Col. Roebling was left with three burdens on his shoulders. The settlement of his father's Estate, the care of the manufacturing business in Trenton and … the longest bridge in the world, on which not a stroke of work had been done, the plans of which were most general in character and not a detail of which had been considered. … It has often pleased the average penny a liner [newspaper reporter] to remark that there is nothing new in the East River Bridge and that Col. Roebling only copied his father's plans. The fact is there is scarcely a feature in the whole work that did not present new and untried problems.

[17]Ibid.

[18]Ibid.

[19]David McCullough masterfully recounts the full story of the fire in Chapter 10 of *The Great Bridge*, pp. 231-47.

[20]Report of the Chief Engineer, June 5, 1871, p. 28.

[21]Smith obituary, *NYT*, April 9, 1910, 11:4.

[22]EWR biographical sketch of WAR.

[23]Ibid.

[24]WAR: *Pneumatic Tower Foundations of the East River Bridge*, p. 88; and *Sun*, September 22, 1882, EWR Scrapbook.

[25]EWR biographical sketch of WAR.

[26]*NYT*, May 23, 1883, 1:2. Same article in *Trenton Times*, May 22, 1883, 4:2. Commenting on the publicity accorded Emily, Erica Wagner states: "At a time when it was unusual for a woman to speak in public, it was unheard of for a woman to assume the duties of a chief engineer." (*Chief Engineer Washington Roebling: The Man Who Built the Brooklyn Bridge*, New York: Bloomsbury, 2017, p. 205.) Wagner goes on to say that Emily "was invaluable to her husband; whether it is fair to call her an engineer is another question." (Ibid.)

[27]EWR biographical sketch of WAR.

[28]Analysis of caisson disease, *Sun*, August 1, 1877.

[29]WAR memo, July 20, 1898, p. 592.

[30]EWR biographical sketch of WAR.

[31]Referring to "the engineering conversations I used to have with Mr. Murphy," Emily told her son years later, "He had one of the finest legal minds I have ever known, but could never learn whether wire was 'wrought iron' or 'cast iron.'" EWR to JAR II, August 4, 1901.

[32]EWR Scrapbook.

[33]New York and Brooklyn Bridge Proceedings, Meeting of the

Board of Directors, April 21, 1873, p. 339.

[34]EWR to JAR II, July 12, 1894.

[35]Description of Columbia Heights in Clay Lancaster, *Old Brooklyn Heights: New York's First Suburb* (New York: Dover Publications Inc., 1979), pp. 67-72. Canceled mortgage and deed in Box 3, Folder 6, RPI.

[36]WAR to James F. Reisling, February 18, 1916, WAR Letterbook, p. 415.

[37]*Trenton Times*, June 13, 1921, 3:3.

[38]*True American*, March 2, 1903.

[39]*NYT*, May 23, 1883.

[40]Ibid. Emily's grasp of matters relating to the bridge was noted in a letter to her brother, Gouverneur Kemble Warren, in which she wrote: "Everything is going on splendidly at the Bridge except a little hitch about money for the stone and iron contract which may delay work a little." (EWR to GKW, May 6, 1875, Gouverneur Kemble Warren Papers, New York State Library, Albany, New York.)
At times Emily wrote to her brother about the volume of correspondence she was handling for her husband. In the spring of 1878, she told him: "I have to write so much for Wash I fairly hate the sight of a pen." (EWR to GKW, May 21, 1878.) Three years later she wrote: "I have had a great deal of writing to do for Wash lately and I have had to neglect my own correspondence." (EWR to GKW, September 8, 1881.)

[41]EWR biographical sketch of WAR. Maybe so, but it is likely that he was in a wheelchair because, years later, when her husband was housebound because of malaria, Emily told their son: "It seems odd to have your father again an invalid. His life now is very similar to the way he lived in Columbia Heights ... I fear the wheeled chair is going to be established in the dining room again." EWR to JAR II, November 12, 1893.

[42]Ibid.

[43]Unidentified *Tribune*, EWR Scrapbook. From this time

onward, rumors about the Chief Engineer's condition abounded. The *Union*, on January 18, 1877, calling for Roebling's removal, declared: "[h]e may have been dead or buried for six months. He is surrounded by clouds impenetrable." (EWR Scrapbook.) Refuting the *Union's* contention, a letter to the editor of the *Eagle* pointed out, "The fact is, there is no better talent in the country than is now engaged in the construction of the New York and Brooklyn Bridge." (January 23, 1877, EWR Scrapbook.) Few readers understood that part of the talent was female.

[44]*Eagle*, May 20, 1877, EWR Scrapbook.

[45]WAR to Henry C. Murphy, December 1875, RPI.

[46]New York and Brooklyn Bridge Proceedings, 1867-1884, pp. 384-86.

[47]WAR to HCM, November 21, 1876.

[48]Ibid.

[49]Ibid.

[50]Ibid.

[51]*The Union and Argus* viewed Roebling's move as "an effort to keep the great structure in one family." May 22, 1878, EWR Scrapbook.

[52]*NYT*, June 15, 1878, 8:3; and June 16, 1878, 2:7; *Union and Argus*, June 14-15, 1878, EWR Scrapbook.

[53]Edwin F. Farrington, *Concise Description of the East River Bridge: Two Lectures at Cooper Union: 1880* (New York: C.D. Wynkoop, Printer, 1881), p. 1.

[54]*Star*, December 17, 1879; and *Eagle*, December 16, 19, 1879, EWR Scrapbook.

[55]Farrington, *East River Bridge*, p. 2.

[56]Ibid., pp. 26-28.

[57]*NYT*, August 26, 1876, 8:1; *Sun*, August 27, 1876; *Tribune*, August 22, 1876; *Eagle*, August 25, 1876, EWR Scrapbook.

[58]Farrington, *East River Bridge*, p. 36.

[59]Ibid.

[60]W.H. Francis to EWR, October 28, 1879, EWR Scrapbook.

[61]*NYT*, May 23, 1883, 1:2.

[62]Ibid., April 1, 1880, 3:3. Other articles dealing with the bridge's potential for disrupting navigation appeared in the following articles included in EWR's Scrapbook: *Eagle*, April 24, 1876; *Eagle*, May 22, 1876; *Herald*, June 10, 1876; and *Sun*, May 4, 1878.

[63]*Sun*, May 4, 1879, EWR Scrapbook; *Star*, May 6, 1877.

[64]*Herald*, January 11, 1880.

[65]*New York Daily Graphic*, February 28, 1880, EWR Scrapbook.

[66]The *Star* observed, "Count de Lesseps pronounces the Brooklyn Bridge one of the grandest and most audacious engineering conceptions of the age." (February 26, 1880.) Although the paper disagreed with him, some of the engineers accompanying de Lesseps paid a return visit to the bridge and "pronounced the enterprise much greater and a more difficult engineering feat than the proposed Panama Canal." *Sun*, March 1, 1880, EWR Scrapbook.

[67]*Sun*, February 18, 1881, EWR Scrapbook; Engineering News, February 26, 1881, EWR Scrapbook.

[68]*True American*, March 2, 1903. The Annual Alumnae Bulletin of the Georgetown Visitation Convent for 1903 observed, "Mr. Raymond's parents made an engineer of him, but heaven made him a poet, and he told the story of a woman's devotion in a way that secured it immortality," p. 24. The *Engineering and Mining Journal* quoted Raymond's praise of Emily, adding, "To which the *Engineering and Mining Journal*, in common with all who heard the words, and all who will see them, heartily says, Amen." *Engineering and Mining Journal*, Jan. 21, 1882, p. 34.

[69]*Eagle*, April 17, 1881, EWR Scrapbook.

[70]*Herald*, June 19, 1881, EWR Scrapbook.

[71]Washington Roebling contended that his actual expenses exceeded his salary by 100 percent. Memorandum, July 20, 1898, WAR Letterbook, p. 592.

[72]WAR to HCM, April 15, 1881, RPI.

[73]Ibid.

[74]*Star*, December 13, 1881.

[75]*Sun*, December 13, 1881, EWR Scrapbook.

[76]When a temporary footpath was opened several years earlier, the trustees were deluged with requests for passes to cross it. Some people who attempted to make the crossing became so nervous that they had to turn back or be rescued. Emily preserved in her Scrapbook an article from *The New York Illustrated Times* of August 18, 1877, featuring a large picture of a woman fainting on the footpath. The article quoted a bridge workman who observed, in contrast with the illustration, that "the women are the soonest at ease and you'll see them swinging their parasols carelessly where brave men hold on wih [*sic*] both hands. Surely it must be that the women havent' the sinse [*sic*] to know what danger they're in." Commenting on the bridge itself, *The Commercial Advertiser*, in an attempt to be humorous, observed, "God helps those that help themselves, but God help the man that steals the Brooklyn Bridge." (September 17, 1881, EWR Scrapbook.)

[77]*Eagle*, December 13, 1881.

[78]Earlier consideration of this: *World*, December 6, 1881, EWR Scrapbook. This important topic had been tabled from a previous meeting, held the week before. On that occasion the report of the Chief Engineer was read and, according to *The New York Times*, it "provoked animated discussion such as is not often heard in the board's rooms." In providing its readers with a comprehensive analysis of the Chief Engineer's report, the *Times* incorrectly gave his name as John A. Roebling. (*NYT*, December 6, 1881, 8:1.) Although the first Chief Engineer had been dead for a dozen years, the confusion between him and his son would continue indefinitely. It greatly troubled Emily and, in later years, whenever newspapers made such errors, she endeavored to remind them that her husband, the builder of

the Brooklyn Bridge, was very much alive.

[79]New York and Brooklyn Bridge Proceedings, June 12, 1882, p. 468.

[80]*Herald*, June 14, 1882; *Tribune*, June 14, 1882; *Sun*, June 16, 1882, EWR Scrapbook.

[81]*Atlas of Newport and Environs*, 1921; *The Green Night*, 1976.

[82]Antoinette Downing and Vincent J. Scully, *The Architectural Heritage of Newport, Rhode Island: 1640-1915* (Cambridge, Massachusetts: Harvard University Press, 1952), p. 191. In reporting the Roeblings' trip to Newport, *The Star* headlined an article "Roebling Hopelessly Sick – At Times He Loses All Control Over His Mind and Is Really as One Dead," July 3, 1882, EWR Scrapbook. *The Knickerbocker* said nothing about his health but noted, "Colonel W.A. Roebling, chief engineer of the Brooklyn Bridge, has taken the Meyer Cottage for the season, and proposes to remain there, far from the maddening crowd." July 13, 1882, EWR Scrapbook.

[83]*NYT*, June 27, 1882; *Sun*, June 27, 1882, EWR Scrapbook.

[84]New York and Brooklyn Bridge Proceedings, pp. 473-74.

[85]*NYT*, June 27, 1882, 8:1.

[86]Ibid., July 11, 1882, 8:3.

[87]WAR notes on meeting with Low, August 8, 1882, RPI.

[88]*World*, August 23, 1882; and *Evening Post*, August 23, 1882, EWR Scrapbook.

[89]WAR to JAR II, January 12, 1898, p. 584.

[90]EWR to JAR II, n.d., probably fall 1900.

[91]Obituary, *NYT*, August 9, 1882, 5:2.

[92]Taylor, *Gouverneur Kemble Warren*, p. 248; and WAR to James F. Reisling, February 18, 1916, WAR Letterbook, p. 413.

[93]Many years later, Washington Roebling explained that the victory at Five Forks was "won by Warren and not by Sheridan and the only victory won by Grant's army in this campaign up to that time. I have already felt that if I had been there the outrage perpetrated by Sheridan could have been forestalled as I was

well aware of the jealous motives that governed." WAR to James F. Reisling, February 18, 1916, WAR Letterbook, p. 413.

[94]*Eagle*, August 21, 1882, p. 4.

[95]Ibid.

[96]*Star*, August 23, 1882, 1:1.

[97]*World*, August 23, 1882, 5:3.

[98]*Eagle*, August 23, 1882, p. 2.

[99]*Newport Daily News*, August 24, 1882, 2:1.

[100]*Herald*, August 23, 1882, 9:1; *Star*, August 23, 1882, 1:1; and *World*, August 23, 1882, 5:3.

[101]EWR to Ludwig Semler, n.d., RPI.

[102]Semler told the *Eagle*: "I found him a man of wonderful clearness of thought," despite the fact that on the day Semler visited, Washington Roebling "had just had a very trying interview with one of the engineers of the German Empire who is attached to the embassy at Washington, that he did not feel as well as he otherwise would have felt. The interview was held in the German language and, lasting several hours, somewhat exhausted him." (*Eagle*, September 12, 1882, p. 4.) Additional articles dealing with this critical period appeared in the *Eagle*, September 4, 1882; the *Evening Post*, September 7, 1882; and the *Sun*, September 8, 1882, EWR Scrapbook. Other articles dealing with the attempt to remove Washington Roebling appeared in the *Tribune*, August 23, 1882, 1:6; the *Sun*, August 23, 1882, 1:4; and the *Eagle*, August 23, 1882, 2:5.

[103]This article was part of a series on alleged bridge frauds published shortly before the New York State Democratic Convention at which General Henry Slocum, a bridge trustee, made an unsuccessful bid for the gubernatorial nomination. Although Grover Cleveland, mayor of Buffalo, was eventually nominated, a serious contender was Congressman Roswell P. Flower, a friend of financier Jay Gould, who at this time owned the *World*. After the election, the *World* dropped the whole business about the bridge frauds, and a subsequent investigation

failed to uncover any instances of fraud. Emily preserved the articles on the bridge frauds beginning with the September 18, 1882, issue of the *World*. She also clipped a small piece, date-lined Newport, September 18, 1882, which began, "Acting upon the advice of Mrs. Roebling, Chief Engineer Roebling, of the Brooklyn Bridge, declined this evening to say anything in reference to the charges in today's World." A public admission that a man had acted upon the advice of a woman was indeed rare at the time.

[104]EWR to William Marshall, n.d., RPI.

[105]*World*, September 8, 1882, 1:4; and *Daily Graphic*, September 7, 1882, EWR Scrapbook.

[106]*NYT,* September 12, 1882, 8:1.

[107]Accounts of the meeting at which the vote was taken appeared in the *Star*, September 12, 1882, 3:1; and the *World*, September 12, 1882, 8:1.

[108]*Eagle*, September 22, 1882, EWR Scrapbook.

[109]Ibid.

[110]*NYT*, July 26, 1926, 14:7. Hamilton Schuyler quotes this letter in *The Roeblings* (Princeton, New Jersey: Princeton University Press, 1931), p. 244. According to David McCullough, Schuyler was "the one reliable source of family history." *The Great Bridge* (40th Anniversary Edition; New York: Simon and Schuster, 2012), p. 573. David B. Steinman, the consulting engineer for the restoration of the bridge in the mid-20th century and a key proponent of placing a plaque on the bridge recognizing the contributions of not only John A. Roebling and Washington Roebling but Emily as well, repeated the assertion that Emily addressed the ASCE in his book *The Builders of the Bridge: The Story of John Roebling and His Son* (New York: Harcourt Brace & Co., 1945), p. 404. McCullough includes Steinman's book in the bibliography of *The Great Bridge* but adds in parentheses that Steinman "was long considered the authority on John A. Roebling. His book, however, was based on superficial research

and contains many inaccuracies." *The Great Bridge*, p. 573.

Erica Wagner rebuts the assertion that Emily appeared before the ASCE. Noting that "well into the twenty-first century the rumor persists that she was really behind the Brooklyn Bridge," Wagner points out that the American Society of Civil Engineers Web site had "until very recently" credited a speech made by Emily to the ASCE for preventing Washington Roebling's removal as Chief Engineer. (*Chief Engineer*, p. 252.) Wagner is quick to note that "there is no record of such a speech" (Ibid.) and cites an email to that effect from the ASCE. Wagner also notes that *American National Biography Online* contends that Abram Hewitt referred to Emily as "the real brains behind the bridge" but that no record of this exists. (*Chief Engineer*, p. 252.) Yet, neither the *ANB* entry on Emily nor the draft that the author of the piece submitted to *ANB* contains this quote. Rather, there is one sentence mentioning Hewitt's speech at the dedication of the bridge in which he "openly spoke about her behind-the-scenes role." "Emily Warren Roebling," *American National Biography Online* (April 2014).

[111]A lengthy obituary of Kunz appeared in *The New York Times*, June 30, 1932, p. 23.

[112]*NYT*, Aug. 2, 1921, p.1.

[113]EWR Biography of WAR, Rensselaer Polytechnic Institute archives.

[114]GFK to WAR, Aug. 28, 1903, Smithsonian Institution Archives: Kunz-Roebling Correspondence, No. 7152 Box 1, Folder 21.

[115]Washington A. Roebling Family Letters, 1992.020, Vol. II, p. 793, Brooklyn Historical Society.

[116]*Smithsonian*, Feb. 18, 1926.

[117]Ibid.

[118]A biographical profile in the finding aids of the Kunz Papers at the New-York Historical Society states: "Through his

auspices, the Roebling Collection of father and son went to the U.S. National Museum in Washington."

[119]https://www.asce.org/about-civil-engineering/history-and -heritage/notable-civil-engineers

[120]Historic photograph tells stories of asce past, civil engineering source, Nov. 4, 2021, https://www.asce.org/publications-and-news/civil-engineering-source/article/2021/11/04/ historic-photograph-tells-stories-of-asce https://www.asce. org/about-civil-engineering/history-and-heritage

[121]https://www.asce.org/career-growth/awards-and-honors/ roebling-award

[122]*Union*, May 16, 1883, 1:3.

[123]New York and Brooklyn Bridge Proceedings, February 12, 1883, pp. 745-47.

[124]Draft of WAR letter, May 5, 1883, RPI.

[125]EWR to Mrs. William G. Wilson, May 17, 1883, New-York Historical Society.

[126]An original invitation, RPI.

[127]Ibid., Brooklyn Historical Society.

[128]Hewitt, Abram S. *Address Delivered by Abram S. Hewitt on the Occasion of the Opening of the New York and Brooklyn Bridge, May 24th, 1883* (New York: John Polhemus, Printer, 1883), pp. 11-12. Hewitt's speech and other information about the opening day ceremonies are included in Conant, W.C., and Montgomery Schuyler, *The Brooklyn Bridge: A History of the Bridge* (New York: Harper & Brothers, 1883), a work consisting of articles that had been published in *Harper's Magazine* in May 1883.

[129]EWR to JAR II, August 26, 1895.

[130]*Eagle*, May 25, 1883, 4:7.

[131]Ibid.

[132]Ibid.

[133]Ibid. Interestingly, although the New York and Brooklyn papers gave considerable space to Emily, the *Trenton Times* did not mention her in its coverage of the opening day festivities,

May 25, 1883, 1:1. David McCullough, in his masterful book *The Great Bridge: The Epic Story of the Building of the Brooklyn Bridge* (New York: Simon and Schuster, 1972, and 40th Anniversary Edition, 2012) devotes a chapter to Emily Roebling. Referring to the rumors about her, he states: "She did not, however, secretly take over as engineer of the bridge, as some accounts suggest and as was the gossip at the time." (*The Great Bridge*, 40th anniversary edition, p. 421.) In "The Great Bridge and the American Imagination," an article in *The New York Times Magazine*, March 27, 1983, p. 29, in which McCullough again noted the rumors that Emily was in charge of the bridge project, he summed up her role by stating that she was her husband's "nurse, companion, protector, confidante and private secretary. She was the intermediary between him and the engineering staff. She was also his emissary, first to the directors of the Bridge Company and then to the trustees of the New York and Brooklyn Bridge."

According to McCullough: "She was as indispensable to him as he was to the bridge. … He was like a blindfolded man playing – and winning – several games of chess at once." Given her very noticeable presence at the construction site, rumors that Washington Roebling was mentally incapacitated circulated and "that a woman was building this monument to 19th century daring. *The New York Times* stated categorically that she was the chief engineer." (Ibid.)

In her outstanding biography, *Chief Engineer: Washington Roebling: The Man Who Built the Brooklyn Bridge*, Erica Wagner addresses the issue of Emily's role. She quotes a letter written by Washington Roebling in 1912 in response to an inquiry from the *Times*. Describing Emily's role, Washington stated that "her services as amanuensis became invaluable to me and this led to other duties" including "interviewing people … smoothing over difficulties." (*Chief Engineer*, New York: Bloomsbury, 2017, p. 201.) He praised "her remarkable talent as a peacemaker" with the trustees and her thorough knowledge of the work and the plans carried conviction to the heart of each new member." (Ibid., p. 202.) Washington Roebling ended the letter by stating: "Being assisted in these ways for fourteen long years with the various phases of the work she earned a well-deserved recognition as well as my everlasting gratitude." (Ibid.)

In 1917, on his 80th birthday, Washington Roebling also commented on Emily's role in an interview with an *Eagle* reporter who traveled to Roebling's Trenton home. The resulting article, "Brooklyn Bridge as Firm as Gibraltar Says Colonel Washington Roebling, Its Builder," noted Emily's role in the bridge project. "His first wife, an unusually talented woman," declared the reporter, adding that she "was the active superintendent of construction and saw to it that the plans of the bridge made by her husband's father were fully carried out and Colonel Roebling aided her with his advice." (*Eagle*, May 27, 1917, p. 17.)

[134] *Tribune*, May 25, 1883, 3:2.

[135] *World*, May 25, 1883, 2:4.

[136] *NYT*, May 25, 1883, 2:5.

[137] *Tribune*, May 25, 1883, 3:2.

[138] *World*, May 25, 1883, 2:4.

[139] Ibid.

[140] *Sun*, May 25, 1883, 3:1.

[141] *Union*, May 25, 1883, 1:3.

[142] *Union*, Ibid.

[143] Indeed, like his father, he might not have lived to see the bridge open. In many ways, both the longevity of the Chief Engineer and that of his project were directly attributable to Emily. Years later, he would admit: "[w]e should have common sense in eating, drinking, working, playing, choosing a wife. A good wife is a great help in living many years." *Trenton Evening Times*, June 13, 1921, 3:4.

[144] EWR to JAR II, March 20, 1898. Following the death of Henry C. Murphy in December 1882, William C. Kingsley

presided over the bridge board of trustees. Although he retained the title of vice president, Emily may have feared that he would push her husband into the shadows before the bridge opened. Perhaps more important was Kingsley's work as a contractor. Had Washington Roebling been forced to step down following the second onset of caisson disease, Emily feared Kingsley, using the Roebling design for the bridge, would have built the span.

[145]*NYT*, June 1, 1883, 1:1.

[146]Letter to trustees, May 5, 1883.

[147]*NYT*, June 1, 1883.

[148]*World*, June 1, 1883, 2:3.

[149]Ibid.

[150]*NYT*, June 5, 1883, 8:1. During its first six months of operation, the bridge was crossed by 4,250,000 people on foot. For the entire year 1884, 3,931,000 pedestrians walked across it. In 1888, the figure was down to 1,785,533. Yet for the period 1883-88, the combined rail and pedestrian total was 129,153,182. *Brooklyn Daily Eagle Almanac: 1889*, Vol. IV, p. 59.

[151]*NYT*, June 6, 1883, 8:1.

[152]Ibid., June 5, 1883, 3:2.

[153]Ibid., May 31, 1883, 2:1.

[154]EWR to WAR, May 31, 1896. *NYT* coverage of the Russian stampede, June 2, 1896, p. 5.

[155]*NYT*, July 10, 1883.

[156]*Eagle*, Nov. 21, 1883, p. 4.

[157]Ibid.

[158]EWR to JAR II, March 10, 1895.

[159]Ibid.

[160]Ibid. Robert C. Roebling, Ferdinand Roebling's grandson, explained this incident in a letter of May 21, 1982, to the author. He observed:

Ferd handled the sales and set aside funds for expansion and rainy-day dividends. He set up what the mill called stores in

the principal ports on the coasts and Mississippi so that buy-
ers could get quick delivery wherever, in logging camps, mines,
tram car lines (San Francisco), etc. No doubt he was on the
West Coast promoting Roebling wire rope.

My guess is that some reporter said, "Hey, you're the bridge
builder," and Ferdie didn't bother to deny it, probably figuring
it was excellent cheap advertising for the JAR stores in Los Angeles, San Francisco, Seattle, Portland.

[161]EWR to JAR II, March 26, 1895.

[162]Ibid., January 12, 1896.

[163]Ibid., February 27, 1896.

[164]Ibid., August 14, 1898.

[165]Ibid., August 31, 1898.

[166]NYT, December 4, 1898, 5:1.

[167]EWR to JAR II, December 4, 1898.

[168]Ibid.

[169]Ibid.

[170]WAR to C.C. Martin, December 5, 1898, WAR Letterbook, pp.
596-98; and EWR to JAR II, December 7, 1898. Further evidence
of the Colonel's interest in the safety of the bridge is the fact that
the Washington Roebling Papers at Rutgers University contain
pertinent newspaper articles that he clipped on the subject.

[171]EWR to JAR II, December 7, 1898.

[172]WAR to JAR II, January 4, 1900, WAR Letterbook, p. 603.

[173]Ibid., p. 605.

[174]Ibid.

[175]EWR to JAR II, December 10, 1899.

[176]Ibid.

[177]EWR to JAR II, December 3, 1899.

[178]Ibid., December 17, 1899.

[179]NYT, April 10, 1901, 5:2. According to Robert C. Roebling, in
a letter of May 21, 1982, to the author:
Uncle Wash had no intention of coming out of retirement.
Charlie [WAR's brother] was crazy to have the job and Wash

told Buck that Charlie could and would do it, adding that Wash himself would keep an eye on Charlie, consult with him, and advise him. Thus started the JAR Sons Co. Bridge Department which did a thriving business over the years, contracting for cables alone, or entire structures. … Charles was in [the] hospital when the first ropes for the foot bridge were towed across and hoisted to the tower tops. It was for this reason that Uncle Wash rode the barge across the river supervising the initial phase of parallel wire cable stringing.

[180]EWR to JAR II, April 10, 1901. Other articles about the Roebling cables for Buck's bridge appeared in the *NYT*, December 16, 1900, 14:3; February 17, 1901, 20:7; and April 12, 1901, 2:4.
[181]There was enough apprehension about the overcrowding at the Manhattan entrance to the bridge to warrant a grand jury investigation of conditions that were "at certain hours hazardous to the health as well as the moral sensibilities of women." *NYT*, May 3, 1901, 6:1. Other articles detailing the problem and possible solutions appeared in the *NYT*, May 16, 1901, 5:2; and July 25, 1901, 2:4. Following the cable break, the grand jury extended its investigation, which culminated in a report censuring the commissioner of bridges and the bridge engineers and recommending periodic inspections of the bridge. *NYT*, December 21, 1901, 16:3.
[182]*NYT*, July 25, 1901, 1:7.
[183]EWR to JAR II, June 12, 1901.
[184]Ibid.
[185]Ibid., July 31, 1901.
[186]Ibid.
[187]Ibid., February 5, 1899.
[188]*Troy Daily Times*, February 3, 1899, 2:1.

CHAPTER 3
MASTER

The Troy Interlude

In the years following the completion of the Brooklyn Bridge, Emily Warren Roebling was able to devote herself to all sorts of activities, both serious and social, but her family continued to receive the lion's share of attention. As the Colonel had been the focal point of her life during the bridge years, their son assumed that position in the mid-1880s. This explains the decision to move the family to Troy when John enrolled in Rensselaer Polytechnic Institute in 1884. Undoubtedly it was Emily's idea and the Colonel merely acquiesced. At any rate, the Roeblings moved into a house in the fashionable Washington Park area of the city, a neighborhood inhabited by Troy industrialists and their families, and for a time the Colonel "led a quiet life, free from all care and responsibilities."[1] Unlike his wife, however, he did not remain in the Hudson River community for the entire four years his son attended school there. For part of that time he lived alone in Trenton, tending to the business of the Mill.[2] His health had improved sufficiently to permit him to play a more active role in the family enterprise. By the spring of 1888, although he was not completely well, he was supervising the construction of the Niagara Falls Suspension Bridge.

His wife did not participate in the project, however. She stayed behind in Troy to cope with an entirely new set of problems brought about by her son's poor health. The young man's weak heart caused his mother untold worry. Fearing the effect it would have upon her husband, Emily didn't tell him at first about John's condition. But a month before the boy was to graduate from RPI, she wrote to her husband telling him of their son's recent problems. The letter shocked Washington Roebling and made him temporarily put aside his own cares and complaints about the difficulties he was encountering building his latest bridge. Writing to John, he admitted that his wife's letter "made me feel ashamed of having shown any discontent with my lot when I thought of the fortitude and courage with which she bears her cares and anxieties."[3] Concerning his son's health, he said:

> I was wholly unaware of the fact that you were not in the best of health, strong and robust, until I received her letter. You yourself have never made mention of it in writing to me, and to learn thus of your ill health has made me forget and sink my own little grievances in my solicitude for and constant thought of you.[4]

At the conclusion of his letter, the Colonel said he was "looking forward with pleasure to the thirteenth of June when I count upon being with you again."[5] On that day, John Roebling II received his degree in civil engineering from RPI, where he was president of his class.

Like the opening of the Brooklyn Bridge, John's

commencement was a milestone in the life of Emily Warren Roebling. As she sat in the Music Hall in Troy on the evening of Friday, June 13, 1888, listening to Commodore B.F. Isherwood of the U.S. Navy tell the graduates that the present age of history should be called the "age of engineering," her thoughts may well have reverted to that glorious day five years earlier when the bridge, which would forever symbolize one of engineering's greatest accomplishments, was thrown open to the public. It is not difficult to imagine Emily nodding in agreement when the commodore, speaking of the field she herself had quietly entered, said:

> And although poetry had not sung its praises nor art idealized its powers nor eloquence pronounced its panegyric, yet it is in my estimation worth all that has preceded it, and were mankind compelled to choose, better for them that art were dead, poetry forgotten and eloquence forever dumb, rather than be deprived of the mighty gifts which engineering bestows on the present and promises to vastly increase in a magnificent future.[6]

In John A. Roebling's future were a position at the Mill and marriage to a Trenton woman, Margaret Shippen McIlvaine, daughter of Edward Shippen McIlvaine and Annie Belleville Hunt.[7] Known to her friends as Reta, 21-year-old Margaret McIlvaine became Mrs. John A. Roebling II in June 1889. Emily's reaction to the marriage of her 22-year-old son can only be guessed but it is not unlikely that a mother who tagged along when her child went off to college felt more than a twinge of regret and perhaps jealousy. Yet there was nothing for her to do but graciously acquiesce, even when the newlyweds moved to Arizona.[8]

First Lady of Trenton

From this point forward, Emily would be compelled to find something quite independent of her son to fill her days and provide her with the kind of challenge her brilliant mind needed. For the next few years, she was supervising the design and construction of a Tudor mansion for their permanent residence; in most respects, this was considerably easier than building a mighty suspension bridge.

The site Emily selected for her new home was a large parcel of property along West State Street on the bank of the Delaware River in Trenton, New Jersey. An old homestead, dating from the 18th century, occupied the property at the time the Roeblings purchased it.[9] This structure was demolished to make way for a cream-colored sandstone mansion. Although Washington and Emily moved into their new home in 1892, completing the house, to Mrs. Roebling's exacting standards, would require the better part of the next decade.

Possessing an incredible knowledge of construction to start with, Emily honed her talents as the house rose from its massive foundation. When her new home was at last finished and her son, John, was contemplating building a house of his own in the South, his mother advised him to think small. "I would not care how soon you began this new building if you would not attempt too much," she said. "It will kill you to build a big house if you try to get perfection and carry out all your notions."[10]

Emily certainly knew what she was talking about because she had tried and nearly succeeded in building a veritable dream house, complete with rooms for formal entertaining and more intimate chambers for the family. A noteworthy feature of the home was a stained glass window depicting the Brooklyn Bridge, complete with ships gliding beneath it and puffy white clouds overhead. Located on the main staircase facing the front of the house, it attracted considerable public attention at night, when it was illuminated. As soon as electricity became available, it was installed in the West State Street home. Ecstatic about the new form of lighting, Emily wrote that the house "looked like [a] fairyland," because the electricity made it "brilliant inside and out."[11] She was particularly delighted with the soft glow the new lights imparted to her pink boudoir.

Despite Emily's magnificent surroundings, Trenton was no Shangri-la in the 1890s. Abundant proof of that was offered in February 1893, when burglars invaded the affluent neighborhood where the Roeblings lived. Emily and the Colonel were out for the evening, as were the servants, because, as Mrs. Roebling recalled, "Our house was alone."[12] The family dog, Ponto, whose name meant "bridge" in Esperanto, was home, however, and its presence evidently frightened away the robbers. Charles Roebling, who lived nearby, was not so fortunate. His home was broken into and for days thereafter the wealthy people of Trenton talked of nothing but the robbery. Approximately two months later, on a quiet Sunday evening, the home of the Washington Roeblings' next-door neighbor, Richard Oliphant, was entered through a second-story window. The Oliphants immediately sent for Ponto, whom the Roeblings were delighted to put on the case. The dog sniffed along the fence at the rear of their property but, instead of finding the burglar, it came upon several policemen with lanterns who were doing essentially the same job as Ponto. Since the dog didn't know that, it was ready to pounce on them but the Roeblings arrived just in time. The following day, armed with the excellent description of the intruder provided by Richard Oliphant, the police caught the burglar red-handed. Mrs. Oliphant's bracelets were still in his pockets. [13]

In the meantime Ponto went back to being top dog in the Roebling household. It didn't matter that the big friendly canine flattened the plants in Emily's flowerbeds every day merely by wagging its tail or climbed into her bed after swimming in the muddy water near the power plant on the Delaware River; Ponto was still loved.[14] Its birthday was even celebrated and, when the dog recovered from an illness in the summer of 1893, its mistress suggested to her son, only half jokingly, that the entire family get together to rejoice that the pet was well again. The following month, when Ponto died unexpectedly, Emily was positively distraught,[15] and feared the dog had been done away with "by someone who had designs on the house."[16]

Although their home was not invaded by burglars, the Washington Roeblings became targets less than six months after the Oliphants were robbed. While they were vacationing at the splendid Grand Union Hotel in fashionable Saratoga Springs, New York, a thief ransacked their room. Since this was their first visit to Saratoga, the minute they checked into the hotel and freshened up, they went out for a horsecar ride to see the town. It was while they were out that the burglar entered their room and emptied the contents of their suitcases onto the bed. Evidently looking for cash, the intruder was dismayed to find none and cleared out, taking nothing, before the Roeblings returned.[17]

In the summer of 1894, as the Roeblings were preparing to go away, security-conscious Emily was making regular trips to the Trenton Trust Company to place her portable valuables in safe-deposit boxes because her husband feared not only isolated burglaries, but a full-scale crime wave. His fears proved to be unfounded but perhaps they are understandable in light of the violence and upheaval occurring in America during the turbulent decade of the 1890s. Much of the unrest was associated with the labor movement. The working classes were striving to obtain higher pay, shorter hours and better conditions. The strike was their weapon, aimed straight at the heart of the capitalist entrepreneurial class of which Washington Roebling was an outstanding member. Is it any wonder, then, that he and his wife feared the masses? The Roeblings felt they could trust members of their own socioeconomic group but others, including servants, were suspect.

Aside from the fear that they would walk off with some of the family's belongings, a vague apprehension concerning the servants pervaded most upper-class households. Good servants were hard to find and harder to keep. This explains why Mrs. Roebling was upset when Charles, "the perfect butler," gave his two weeks' notice.[18]

At one point, however, Emily had exactly the kind of household help she needed.[19] Overjoyed with this unusual situation, she declared, "Now that we have a full corps of well-trained servants, we live exactly as if we were wound up by machinery every morning and set for the day."[20] This surely must have pleased the Chief Engineer and his efficient, mathematically oriented wife because they entertained frequently.

Emily ran a tight ship as far as the management of her household was concerned. According to the Trenton *Advertiser*:

> Her beautiful home in this city was built under her own supervision, and it is well ordered and kept almost with the precision of a military post. Mrs. Roebling was very hospitable and some of the largest and most successful entertainments ever given in New Jersey have been in her house, which bears everywhere the stamp of her strong individuality, good taste and practical ideas.[21]

When Emily wasn't hosting luncheons and dinners, she was attending social events. The gatherings she preferred were those given by friends but this in no way deterred her from going to large charity affairs, balls hosted by the governor of New Jersey, and dinners for political figures.[22] In between, she went to luncheons in Trenton and New York, generally given by women Emily knew socially or through her wide-ranging club activities. Frequently, when she traveled to New York, she found time to attend the opera or the theater. A veteran playgoer, Emily viewed the theater as "a great diversion to the minds of simple country folk."[23]

Despite her upbringing in the rural community of Cold Spring, New York, she was a sharp critic. If she did not like a performance, she said so. Although she attended the opera less frequently than the legitimate theater, Mrs. Roebling was a skilled critic of the performances she saw. Wagnerian operas were among her favorites. When the Colonel went to the opera alone, as he sometimes did, he and Emily discussed the performances at length. They also shared their thoughts about lectures that they occasionally attended. Frequently, while staying at seaside resorts during the summer, they availed themselves of whatever cultural opportunities existed in the community or at the hotel.

On her own, Emily went to lectures in Trenton and New York. Her interests, which were wide ranging, extended even to the pineal gland, the subject of a presentation on brain physiology given by a female orator.[24] Mrs. Roebling's quest for knowledge also led her to libraries and bookstores, where she purchased volumes that found their way into a traveling library the Washington Roeblings shared with their son and his in-laws. From her letters to John emerges the impression that Emily was a well-read woman whose taste in literature extended from politics and sociology to the latest novels. Here, too, just as with plays and operas, she had very definite ideas about what she liked and disliked. Because the critics said something was good did not necessarily mean it was so. In the end, Mrs. Roebling was her own judge of everything she read.

When she wasn't stretching her mind by reading or attending the theater, Emily Warren Roebling was attempting to keep her body in good condition. Her efforts were evidently successful. An article about the capacity of the bridge and Washington Roebling's opposition to a two-story railroad on the bridge appearing in *The Brooklyn Daily Eagle* in the fall of 1889 stated: "Mrs. Roebling's many friends in this city will be glad to know that she is the picture of health and quite as handsome and attractive in appearance as when she lived here."[25]

The article concluded with a direct quote from Emily emphasizing her very special relationship with Brooklyn. "I still keep
my account," she said, "at the Brooklyn Bank, and, you know,
'where your treasure is, there will your heart be also.'"[26] But
that wasn't all Emily had to say. After her husband commented
on the pressing issue of the bridge's capacity, pointing out that
a second railroad built above the existing one could "only with
safety be created by doing away with the promenade," and, if
built, "the beauty of the bridge would be destroyed forever by
the cars and smoke vomiting engines," Emily entered the room
where her husband was being interviewed.[27] Turning to him,
she said she was glad he was "opposing the building of that two
story railroad on the bridge."[28] As it was, the approaches to the
bridge, in her opinion, were "ugly and unsightly; the bridge is
only beautiful from the water; put that double decker railroad
there and it will be all ugly."[29]

Aware that she might be quoted by the reporter, Emily
explained: "Now that I have retired from public life I can
allow myself the privilege of talking a little."[30] She then proceeded to explain that "during the early days of the bridge" a
newspaper reporter had asked her to provide facts about the
bridge but when her remarks appeared in the paper "my facts
were all turned around."[31] She told the *Eagle* reporter that
following this incident she "refused to talk to reporters and
this is the first time I have broken my silence. If you ask me
why I do not want to see that two story railroad built I can
only give a woman's reason – because it would not be pretty.
I have always been a stickler for the beauty of the structure,
and I have always been in favor of everything that would add
to its beauty."[32]

One can only imagine how surprised and delighted the *Eagle* reporter must have been as Emily continued to open up. She talked about the bridge trustees, praising Henry C. Murphy as "a wonderful man; he was to my way of thinking a very Napoleon among men. The way he used to run things at the bridge always excited my admiration."[33] Murphy had a similarly high opinion of Emily for, as the *Eagle* reporter noted: "It must be said about the old bridge officers that Henry C. Murphy and Mrs. Washington A. Roebling ran the bridge. Mr. Murphy always referred to Mrs. Roebling as a wonderful woman, and during the building of the structure constantly sought her advice and followed her suggestions. From the window of her home upon Columbia Heights Mrs. Roebling for many long and weary months during her husband's illness, watched the progress of the great work and really directed most of it." [34]

Toward the end of the very lengthy *Eagle* article, Emily opined on the bridge trustees. She confided to the reporter:

> Just between you and me and as a great secret I will tell you that the Bridge trustees never did amount to much in the old days. Half of the time they really did not know what they were voting for. That cable on the roadway I was always in favor of. I remember on one occasion telling Mr. Murphy that it would be a great thing for an old woman like me to ride across the bridge on surface cars and so avoid the climb up the stairs at both ends of the structure.[35]

At 46 Emily was hardly an old woman. A superb horse-woman in her youth, she enjoyed riding well into middle age, but in the mid-1890s regretfully admitted, "Horses are not much use now that the streets are full of trolley cars."[36]

Indoor exercise at the Roebling mansion consisted of bowling. Guests, female as well as male, joined their hostess in her private bowling alley. Adjacent to the lanes was a sort of family room with a billiard table, comfortable chairs, an Oriental rug and a painting of the Brooklyn Bridge on an easel. Even when she was engaging in a bit of recreation, Emily could not get away from the Roeblings' greatest project. As far as the actual bowling was concerned, she thought it "frivolous an occupation" to devote time to on a regular basis but occasionally she enjoyed the sport and took it in her stride when guests surpassed her "best record."[37] She felt essentially the same way about the card games to which the Colonel was addicted. Dinner and overnight guests were invariably subjected, some quite willingly, to endless rounds of cards.

A little more to Emily's liking was the Colonel's generally solitary habit of searching for wildflowers to include in his collection of botanical specimens. There were times when Mrs. Roebling herself was pressed into service to assist the Colonel. The fact that she wasn't exactly in the mood or, on one occasion, had a bad knee didn't seem to matter. From the bridge years, she had been well accustomed to doing her husband's legwork. This was merely a continuation of the service to which, despite his improved health, he had grown accustomed. Emily complained to John that the Colonel "led me through cat-briers and swamps but says I cannot hold a candle to Reta on such trips."[38] Like her father-in-law, John's wife, Reta, had an avocational interest in botany. When she and her husband were visiting, she accompanied the Colonel on his botanical treasure hunts.

Reta also shared her father-on-law's interest in minerals. The fine array of stones Washington Roebling eventually put together would one day go to the Smithsonian but, in the meantime, he thoroughly enjoyed collecting the specimens and showing them off. Noted mineralogists descended upon Trenton to view the Colonel's growing collection. This greatly pleased him as it did his wife, who in 1893 told their son: "Your father had two mineralogists here yesterday. One told him his collection was the finest in America so he felt quite happy."[39]

Something that made Emily less than ecstatic was another of her husband's hobbies, his pet water snake! The Colonel was so attached to the reptile that he even took it along when they went up to New York for protracted stays at the Waldorf-Astoria. During one of these visits, the snake disappeared only to return unexpectedly. Emily told her son: "[The] Colonel received him with such joy and enthusiasm … Neither you nor I can ever hope to receive such a welcome!"[40] Washington Roebling immediately sent to Trenton for worms for his long-lost friend. So pleased was he to get the snake back that the Colonel went out of his way to pamper the reptile, even to the point of buying it a Christmas tree.[41] "It is a small Norfolk pine," Mrs. Roebling noted. "The snake divides his time between stretching himself on the top branches and lying in the earth of the pot where the tree is planted."[42] After the holidays, the snake was placed in a glass vase partially filled with water. Emily dutifully reported to her son that they had only recently discovered that the Colonel's pet was a water snake. Since John had evidently raised the issue of whether the snake was poisonous, his mother assured him that the matter was now settled and that the reptile was perfectly harmless. The next big discovery was the sex of the snake. Emily joked, "We think the snake is a female, because it likes to look at itself in the looking glass."[43]

Female or not, the reptile had the habit of climbing up on a dressing table in the Colonel's room and gazing in the mirror while sticking out its tongue.[44] Finding this perfectly charming, the Colonel was upset when, during his wife's absence in Washington, the snake was either crushed underfoot or caught in a door. Emily described her husband as "mournful" because he was convinced his pet was going to die. She, on the other hand, was more optimistic, saying, "it is hard to kill a snake even when you try to do so."[45] As usual she was right. In less than two weeks the snake shed its skin and displayed no marks from its recent accident.[46] Although Washington Roebling was delighted, he ultimately concluded that the best place for the snake was not his bedroom but their greenhouse. So the reptile was entrusted to the care of the gardener, who, presumably, was less enthusiastic about it than was the Colonel.[47]

What may have prompted Washington Roebling to send the snake into early retirement was an incident that had occurred nearly six months before. Emily was flat on her back in their suite at the Waldorf-Astoria recovering from either illness or exhaustion. From her letters to John, it is impossible to ascertain the nature of her problem but, whatever it was, she was well enough to receive visitors, three women from the George Washington Memorial Association, of which she was a member. For an hour the women entertained her and she enjoyed it immensely. Then, without warning, "The Colonel walked in with a scared-looking white face, and evidently in a high state of nervous excitement."[48] Although he had previously met two of the women, he did not acknowledge them. Instead, he told all three visitors "that talking to women would be the death of me, that they must be careful ... and that I was really about half-dead."[49] The stunned visitors quickly departed, leaving Emily wondering "that he should be so worried over me."[50] As soon as they had left, the Colonel made known the real reason for ushering the women out so unceremoniously. The snake had bitten him and he was convinced that he had been poisoned. As usual, despite the fact that she herself was not feeling well, Emily had to take over. She ordered her husband to "take a big drink of whiskey" and fixed him some ammonia to hold his injured finger in.[51] His finger did not swell and, much to his surprise, the Colonel made a complete recovery.

Emily Warren Roebling was used to such episodes. They were a routine part of her life, something she had grown to expect though by no means cherish. From her extremely insightful letters to John, a picture emerges of a devoted wife who stood by her husband, no matter what, but one who, periodically, had to get away from him. Ironically, the need for a respite from the Colonel often masqueraded as a desire to flee the mansion she had so painstakingly built. Her letters were sometimes sprinkled with references to her dissatisfaction with Trenton. Typical of her comments was: "I am getting very weary of Trenton. It is with the greatest effort I interest myself in anything here. I feel that I am buried alive."[52]

Some of Emily's dissatisfaction with Trenton was

attributable to the laying of trolley tracks on West State Street. She regarded poles for the trolley "as a disfigurement of the public street ... and made up her mind that no pole should be erected in front of her home. When the trolley company's employees dug a hole in her pavement she went out and planted herself in the hole until she could summon one of her servants to relieve her."[53] The trolley company prevailed in the end, contributing to Emily's disenchantment.

In essence, Emily had a love-hate relationship with Trenton and with the home she had built there. "I have an odd feeling about this house. When I am here everything looks so pretty and comfortable I want to stay, but when I get back to New York I am glad I am there, as I find so much to interest me every hour."[54] Mrs. Roebling's active mind required the intellectual stimulation only a great city could provide. Consequently, she prevailed upon the Colonel to move into the Waldorf-Astoria Hotel for the 1898-99 winter season. When the house on West State Street was closed in the fall, Emily frankly wondered if they would ever return. Like the husband she had faithfully assisted for years, the house was an object of affection though, at times, a downright nuisance. Yet through it all, Emily, the master builder, was a consummate lover, devoted to home and mate, and she had every reason to be proud of what she had achieved, vis-à-vis building the house and rebuilding her husband. It surely seemed that she was capable of accomplishing anything she set her mind to, even if it meant battling with her brother-in-law, Ferdinand, over the Roebling Mill.

Emily's experience with the bridge provided the sort of practical background that enabled her to deal swiftly and effectively with a host of problems relating to the family company of which her husband was vice president. As far as Mrs. Washington A. Roebling was concerned, the main difficulty she encountered with the firm was its president, Ferdinand Roebling. In the spring of 1893, she complained to John, "Because I checked your Uncle Ferd in his wasteful extravagance and gross mismanagement of the business he hates me."[55] The real culprit, Emily felt, was Ferdinand's wife, Marjorie, "with her ugly way and uglier manners."[56] During the winter of 1892-93, Margy had done her best to bar Emily from Trenton society. Her efforts were not entirely successful but, even if they had been, Emily would not have been overly concerned, since she had her own circle of friends who were impervious to the gossip being circulated about her.

Then, too, there was the tolerably good relationship she enjoyed with Charles Roebling, another of her husband's brothers. When Emily's son, John A. Roebling II, who had previously been associated with the company, expressed an interest in resuming his position in the Mill, his mother immediately spoke with Charles. He was receptive to the idea, provided his sister-in-law acted as an unsalaried ombudsman. As Emily told her son, "Charles says that you and he will get on well enough if I will make the Colonel behave himself and I have undertaken to see that he does."[57] Realizing how cumbersome a job this would be, Emily added, "I think I have a large contract on hand and should have quite as large a salary for my services as you think you should have."[58] John expected generous compensation for his willingness to return to the Mill but his practical-minded mother advised him to "make yourself of value" before demanding a big salary.[59] She also reminded him that, had he stayed at the Mill in the first place, he would have been firmly established and could have demanded the sort of compensation he judged commensurate with his background. Perhaps discouraged by his mother's words of wisdom, John decided to forget the whole thing. This was not at all to Emily's liking, but there was precious little she could do about it.

As a result of the Panic of 1893, Mrs. Washington Roebling became quite concerned about the general economic climate. Railroads and coal companies were starting to reduce and, in some instances, eliminate dividends. Unemployment and misery were widespread in the United States. The John A. Roebling's Sons Company kept "a good many men" on the payroll but Washington Roebling contended that the firm was not making any money.[60]

Over the next few years the Colonel took a more active role in the business. He went to the company every day and, when his brother Ferdinand took a vacation early in 1896, Washington Roebling was, as Emily put it, "master of all he surveys."[61] Although pleased, she would have been equally delighted to see him extract himself from the business altogether. Late in 1897, when rumors began to circulate about the possibility of pooling all the wire interests in the United States, she expressed the hope that John A. Roebling's Sons Company would sell "if they could get anywhere near the value of the property."[62] Those millions, properly invested, would be able to generate considerable revenue. Emily was so convinced that she wrote to John, "Generation No. 4 will never see a penny out of the business, unless, it is sold to some trust or company."[63] When the plan to pool the country's wire interests fell through, she was extremely disappointed, especially six months later when a royal battle was taking place at the Mill.

The Colonel and Charles were pitted against their brother Ferdinand, accusing him of using dictatorial methods to control the company's finances. They alleged that Ferdinand failed to distribute what they regarded as a fair share of the Mill's current earnings; they also objected to his underhanded way of handling all financial transactions, and the manner in which he invested company funds in various outside ventures prior to adequate consultation with his brothers. Of particular concern to Charles and Washington was that, by commingling vested capital and undistributed profits, Ferdinand made it virtually impossible to determine the worth of the Mill, an important factor in case one of the brothers died and his share in the business was passed on to his heirs.[64] Emily, who had been striving throughout her married life to perpetuate the name and honor of her husband's family, must surely have agonized over the prospect that, should anything happen to her husband, she, her son and grandsons might not receive their fair share of the business. Long after his wife's death, the Colonel would admit that one investment Ferdinand had made, contrary to the wishes of his brothers, yielded a "bonanza" from which they all benefited but in 1898, when Washington Roebling was conferring with the prominent corporation lawyer R.V. Lindabury, it was evident that he feared and despised his brother's actions.[65]

In 1899, there was additional cause for worry. The John A. Roebling's Sons Construction Company was incorporated to undertake the installation of a Roebling-pioneered fireproofing method in buildings under construction. One of the incorporators was Frank H. Croker, son of Richard Croker, the leader of New York City's Tammany Hall Democratic machine.[66] When new specifications for fireproofing municipal buildings in the city were issued, it was evident that they had been drawn in such a way that the Roebling Construction Company was the only firm that could supply and install the materials in accordance with the guidelines.[67] An inconclusive investigation was promptly launched by a committee of the New York State Assembly. "I do not care about the merits of the case," Emily wrote to her son.[68] "I only want to keep [the reputation of] W.A. Roebling … out of compromising business complications."[69]

The Colonel was contemplating getting in touch with a local reporter, whom he knew fairly well, in order to publish the Washington Roebling side of the story. Especially interested in having his views on the Assembly investigation appear in print, the Colonel was ready to "stand or fall by his own convictions."[70] However, Emily opposed his plan. After telling him so, she decided to say nothing further, but the whole affair evidently troubled her because she complained to John, "I have done all I could for the name of Roebling."[71] It was inexplicable to her that her husband wanted to voice his opinion when he wasn't even involved in the company. Since Ferdinand and Charles were, however, perhaps he was acting out of family loyalty but, no matter, it did not set well with his wife. For months she had done her utmost to prevent any hint of scandal from touching her husband, directly or indirectly. When the Crokers, father and son, descended upon the Waldorf while the Roeblings were staying there, Emily made certain that the Colonel did not run into them. Every time the newspapers published something about Washington Roebling's relationship to the construction company, Emily took pen in hand to refute the inaccuracies.

Particularly galling was the charge that the Colonel owned shares of stock in the new construction company. Assuming that her son may have read secondhand versions of New York press accounts, Emily took care to assure him, "Your father does not own a single share."[72] More upsetting was the allegation that Washington Roebling had taken young Croker into his private office to teach him engineering so that they could jointly construct several new East River bridges. Having been his pupil years before, Emily knew how effective her husband could be as an instructor but she was also well aware of the fact that he carefully selected his students. Croker was not among them. The John A. Roebling's Sons Construction Company continued to cause dissension between husband and wife even after it was reorganized in May 1899, under the laws of the state of New York. This time Croker was out and the Roebling brothers, including Eddie and Washington, were in. The Colonel was named president of the reorganized company.[73] This, of course, troubled Emily but she couldn't do anything about it any more than she could control the financial excesses of the Roebling brothers. Early in 1900, she declared in a letter to John: "Your uncle Ferd has just dropped three hundred thousand in the Third Avenue R.R. in New York. How nice it is to be rich enough to throw all your money away where it does no good to you or anyone else."[74] Emily herself was a cautious investor. Yet, in her lifetime, neither her talent for business nor for construction was fully recognized and, as she grew older, she was obliged to find new outlets. Travel was one of them.

World Traveler

Whenever she had had quite enough of Trenton, Emily headed for Philadelphia or New York for shopping, cultural activities and social engagements. There were times, however, when neither of those American metropolises served to divert her from her responsibilities at home. On those occasions, to completely divorce herself from Trenton, she had to go farther afield. The more distance she could put between herself and West State Street, the better, even if it meant risking seasickness to do so. When a full-fledged attack of wanderlust struck, Mrs. Roebling's preferred destination was Europe. Although she had been there shortly after her marriage and again in 1873 and 1884, she longed to return. In her case the wish was definitely the mother of the thought because, twice more in the decade of the 1890s, she managed to crisscross the Atlantic, once in the company of her husband, 1892, and the second time, 1896, alone. Washington Roebling was supposed to accompany his wife but, when he backed out at the last minute, Emily went alone. Soon after she left, the Colonel wrote to John: "I am sitting quietly in Trenton [while your mother] is squirming around England gratifying the ruling passion of all woman – vanity. ... I am once more the prisoner of Chillon."[75]

No doubt Emily quickly learned of her husband's unhappiness; this may explain why she complained of nervousness while staying at the Hotel Savoy in London.[76] On the other hand, her apprehension may have resulted from the realization that she would soon be presented to Queen Victoria, something she had dreamed about for years. As the big day approached, however, Emily frankly wondered if she would be able to curtsy and get up again without becoming entangled in her train.[77] Much to her relief, nothing untoward occurred during the actual ceremony. The Colonel was less than exuberant about his wife meeting the queen of England. He remarked, rather casually, to his son: "Your mother's presentation at the English court is already a thing of the past. … Had I been in London, I would have been obliged to go too, dressed in knee breeches with a small sword and cocked hat – Just think what I missed."[78] Washington Roebling evidently told John a few other things as well because, weeks later, Emily wrote to John, stating: "[The] Colonel says you are singing in Arizona that when grandmother went to London to see the Queen, a little mouse frightened her up on a chair. Now I wish you to know that the largest-sized rat would not have been able to frighten me up on to anything unless it had been the throne when I was in the St. James Palace."[79]

Something else the Colonel missed out on was the coronation of Tsar Nicholas II of Russia and his wife, Tsarina Alexandra. Emily had a perfectly glorious time at the festivities despite her misgivings while en route to Russia. Once she reached Paris, where she stayed for a short time before beginning the eastward trek, she realized how far away from home she was getting and the burdensome responsibilities she had left behind. A slight feeling of nervousness developed and remained with her as Emily and other well-to-do Americans, including Mrs. Potter Palmer, wife of the Chicago merchant and real estate developer, traveled from Paris to Vienna, and from there to Warsaw and Moscow.[80] In Vienna, Emily was supposed to look up prominent Austrian mineralogists for her husband, but she didn't get around to it because the stopover in the Austro-Hungarian capital was only one day. Ten full days to see the sights of Vienna would have been more to Mrs. Roebling's liking. Yet, in the short time she was there, with the assistance of the American consul, she and the other members of the party "managed to get a pretty good idea of that beautiful city."[81]

Warsaw offered few surprises to the American visitor. Emily had been there on the Roeblings' 1884 European trip, and her recollections of the place were so vivid that she even remembered one particular street where she and her husband had watched a fire a dozen years before. Neither the thoroughfare nor the city had changed much in the intervening years. "Warsaw has not been cleaned up any since we were here," she told her son.[82] As proof of this, she cited the city's noxious odors. Having witnessed a herd of swine en route to market, she wrote, "Warsaw pigs smell just like American pigs, the only difference being that in Warsaw you cannot smell them as they are in the minority in the various street odors."[83]

Fortunately, Emily Warren Roebling took everything in stride. She enjoyed the train trip from Vienna to Warsaw since the countryside was beginning to come alive. Fruit trees were in bloom and the peasants were tilling the "beautifully green" fields.[84] The people, as much as the lush countryside, intrigued Emily. As the Orient Express sped past "many queer, peculiar-looking towns with very old cathedrals," Mrs. Roebling took in everything.[85] This portion of the trip was relaxing, but crossing the border between Poland and Russia was not. The party of Americans ran into a customs snag that was complicated by the language barrier. Some of the Americans tried French and broken German to no avail but Emily saved the day. Realizing that a few of the Russian officials understood German, she became the spokeswoman for the party. But it apparently took a while before the foreigners were admitted to Russia because Mrs. Roebling complained of being "so hoarse now I can hardly speak."[86]

When the weary travelers at last reached Moscow, they discovered that, although the owner of the place where they were staying was bilingual, in German and Russian, his wife and the female servants spoke only Russian. Emily quickly mastered 20 essential words in that language in order to inform the maids of the needs of the American visitors, but, still, she complained, saying, "Not for love or money could we find a servant who could speak English and Russian."[87] There was a tiny ray of hope when an American gentleman, a former Philadelphian, residing in Moscow, put his bilingual footman at the disposal of the visitors. The expatriate's generosity may have been due to the fact that Mrs. Roebling, the wife of the Chief Engineer of the Brooklyn Bridge, was among the Americans visiting Moscow. "An engineer of reputation" himself, Mr. Barry had constructed the buildings at the Centennial exposition held in Philadelphia in 1876.[88] Although Washington Roebling's great work was completed after that date, his bridge, like the expo, was a symbol of American achievement. Since Barry was presumably well acquainted with the accomplishments of the Roeblings, father and son, and may have heard about Emily's role as well, it is understandable that he was willing to lend her his footman. The trouble was, though, that English was not one of the servant's languages. He knew only German and Russian. Therefore, whenever any member of the party wanted to go out, Emily had to go along to converse with the footman.

When Emily caught her first glimpse of Nicholas II, on May 26, 1896, she felt rather sorry for him. "He was as pale as marble," she noted. He "looked sad and earnest with an expression on his face I shall never forget." Much more impressed by the young monarch than by his wife, Mrs. Roebling wrote:

> While everyone is raving over the beauty and grace of the [Tsarina] my heart has completely gone over to the [Tsar]. He looks so gentle and lovable with the most beautiful blue eyes I have ever looked into. He looks very frail, is thin ... and wears a sad thoughtful expression as though the weight of his responsibilities are greater than he can endure. The people seem to love him very much.[89]

History would prove Emily right about the tsar's responsibilities.[90] Since she would live to see neither the *Revolution* of 1905 nor the Bolshevik Resolution of 1917, which toppled his regime, Emily's mental image of the tsar would always be that of the 27-year-old who reminded her of her son "in general appearance except his face is not as intellectual."[91]

The observant Mrs. Roebling described the tsarina, Alexandra, whose carriage came along next, as "very fair, young, and timid."[92] She was riding in a coach similar to that of the dowager tsarina, only smaller. A German by birth, the tsarina wore the Prussian court costume, in white with a silver mantle. Although Emily seems to have been a bit disappointed in the young woman's attire, she was quite well pleased with her own appearance. "I wear my cape with the ermine collar and as ermine is a badge of royalty here, you should see the respect we inspire," she told her sister Eliza.[93]

Fully conscious of her position as an upper-class American, Mrs. Roebling was thoroughly convinced that clothes make the person. Hence, on the morning of the big day, Emily rose at 4:30 a.m. to don court dress. By 7 a.m. she and most of the other Americans were inside the Kremlin gates, where they would review the festivities from specially erected seats in the diplomatic stand. The mere thought of sitting outdoors for several hours dressed in an evening gown, with nothing to keep the sun off her face save a tiara and white plumes, was most unappealing. Yet the old stamina was enough to see Emily through. As soon as the invitation arrived, Emily resolved that she could and would survive the heat "if the others could."[94]

She more than held her own. Her active mind was intrigued by everything she saw. "No finer view could have been had of the whole procession," she said after describing the choice seats she and her companions occupied. "We faced the palace and saw the procession … the stairs … were covered with crimson velvet. The march into the church for the coronation … the crowns, scepter, and seal carried on cushions, the necklaces, the mantles of cloth of gold which were put on as soon as they were crowned," all passed before the observant Mrs. Roebling.[95]

When the ceremony ended at 3:30 p.m., Emily was less

weary than her companions. In fact, she was eager to attend what had been billed as a "breakfast" at the royal palace. Since the meal was not served until 4 p.m., this certainly was a misnomer, but that was a minor technicality. The opportunity to follow the newly crowned tsar up the red-carpeted staircase of the palace and into one of several dining rooms made the invited guests forget the time. After drinking to the health of the tsar the Americans drank a toast to the health of Washington Roebling on the occasion of his 59th birthday. Emily communicated this to her far-off husband, adding that his well-wishers had drunk "out of the palace glasses with the [Tsar's] own champagne."[96] The seven different wines served during the repast were apparently the best part of the meal for, though the food was "magnificent," the various dishes "were not always very good."[97] It was, however, served on plates bearing the royal coat of arms. The tsar's champagne was characterized by one of the men at Emily's table as "strong enough to knock your head off"; Mrs. Roebling took but a taste during the toasts.[98] She also passed up the six other wines, mostly Hungarian vintages.

Comparing the tsar's palace with that of Queen Victoria, Mrs. Roebling would later write, "It is well ... I went to the English court first as there is just about as great a difference in state and splendor between the English court and the Russian court as between my own house and St. James Palace."[99] Carrying her analysis one step further, she added, "When we were wandering all over the Kremlin Palace looking at and admiring all the furniture, royalties, and jewels, it made me think of the way Trentonians stray around in my second story when I have a reception."[100]

Since Emily had toured the Russian palace on a previous visit to Europe in 1884, she was already familiar with the layout of the rooms but she admitted, "They looked differently – filled with ladies in court dress and the Russian ladies-in-waiting who were all in scarlet velvet robes embroidered heavily with gold."[101] Despite the opulence of these costumes, Mrs. Roebling was fully convinced that, with the exception of the representatives of various European dynasties, "the American ladies were by far the best-dressed women in the palace."[102] The tsar was attired more elaborately than he had been earlier in the day. Emily told her husband that he "had on his crown and ermine and cloth of gold mantle."[103] The royal family, and for that matter, the guests, looked "tired" after their long day but the indomitable Emily had energy to spare.[104]

There was still much to be seen and done in Moscow and she did not want to miss out on anything, certainly not the fireworks display, which was more magnificent than the fine show celebrating the opening of the Brooklyn Bridge 13 years earlier. According to the observant Mrs. Roebling, the Moscow "illuminations … far surpass anything I have ever seen in that line. They look like set pieces of fireworks that never burn out."[105]

No matter where she journeyed, Emily was reminded of the mighty span that had dominated her young life. Upon returning to Western Europe following the coronation, she headed to France, where she noted that "the big picture of the Brooklyn Bridge which used to be in the Eden Museum is now at the National Museum at [Le] Havre. It was bought by the state and has the post of honor there."[106]

Even on vacation she could not get away from bridges and, for that matter, neither could her husband. During Emily's stay in Europe, he wrote her of his interest in a proposed bridge across the North or Hudson River. "If you had aspirations in the same direction," she told her son, "I should urge him to go in for it, but as it is, I advise him to leave it for Paul [the Roeblings' grandson] to build when he grows up as I do not think there will be any pressing need of it before that time."[107] Her assessment was quite correct. The Hudson would be spanned by the George Washington Bridge, between upper Manhattan and Fort Lee, New Jersey, only in 1931.

John Roebling II had no desire to return to the East Coast to work on a Hudson River crossing, but his father was extremely interested in this project and in the Williamsburg and Manhattan bridges, which in less than a decade would parallel the Brooklyn Bridge across the East River. Due to Washington Roebling's intense curiosity about the plans for the new bridges, he went up to New York in his wife's absence. Although his stated purpose in visiting Manhattan was to enjoy the Fourth of July celebration there, Emily knew otherwise.[108] "It was a sad selection of places to visit on that day," she told John. "But I suppose there was something in New York he wanted to see. He takes the greatest interest in the two new bridges and I am worrying lest he may be persuaded into taking some active part in either one or both of them."[109]

Engineering and construction in general, and bridges in particular, were still of interest to Mrs. Roebling, but they were no longer her overriding concern. Having completed her life's most important work in Brooklyn 13 years before,

Emily was now in semiretirement. For her, it was time to take a well-deserved rest from the cares of the bridge, the Mill and the West State Street mansion. None of these matters was totally banished from her active mind during the European trip in 1896 but, perhaps indicative of her new order of priorities, the souvenirs she purchased had nothing to do with engineering or construction.

Not long after she arrived home following "a most horrible trip having been seasick one day and very uncomfortable the other five," and an official welcome by her coachman, Alfred Pagden, and the Colonel, who "was almost hysterically glad to see me," Emily unpacked an array of souvenirs.[110] For her daughter-in-law there was a wrapper, dressing sacque and silk petticoat from Paris and, for the two grandsons, pictures of the tsar and tsarina, gifts that were about as unrelated to engineering and construction as one could imagine.[111] The souvenir for John was also very remote from his chosen field. It was a dagger similar to those worn by the tsar's Cossack soldiers.[112] Symbolically, the sharp-edged weapon may have represented Emily Warren Roebling's determination to cut the ties with the past and make a new life for herself in the world of women rather than in the male world of engineering. She had taken bold steps in that direction following her European tour in 1892. After the most recent trip, this reborn woman of the world, who had managed to live apart from her husband for three months, would redouble her efforts in the women's sphere, bringing to the many organizations of which she was a member the same kind of dedication that had been in evidence during the bridge years.

Organization (Wo)Man

For three-quarters of her life, Emily Warren Roebling was a veritable stranger to the world of women. Aside from her closeness with her mother and sisters and a handful of female friends, she existed in a largely masculine world, devoting herself to her husband and functioning behind the scenes as silent bridge builder, clerk of the works on the mansion construction project and confidential adviser on matters relating to the John A. Roebling's Sons Company. In the 1890s, however, she emerged as a prominent figure in women's organizations. Had she lived well into the next century, she might have become a leader in the fight for the woman's suffrage amendment. Although death cut short her career as an organization (wo)man, her accomplishments were, nevertheless, considerable.

From a personal standpoint, her service as secretary-treasurer of the New Jersey Board of Lady Managers for the Columbian Exposition of 1893 was one of Emily Warren Roebling's most gratifying undertakings in the world of women. Also rewarding was her work as chair of the committee on statistics for the New Jersey Board. In this capacity she gathered data about women employed outside the home, the type of work they performed and the number of patents obtained by women.[113] To assist her friend Margaret Tufts Yardley, who chaired the literature committee of the New Jersey Board of Lady Managers, Emily wrote the preface to *The New Jersey Scrapbook of Women Writers*.[114]

Despite her commendable achievements in connection with the Columbian Exposition, Emily almost didn't make it to the fair. When the time came for her to depart for

Chicago in late April, she had misgivings about going since her husband was ill. "It troubled me to leave the Colonel half sick and alone in Trenton and I did not want to leave the house," she told John, "but I have worked hard for my present position in the world of women, and here is the place to be this year if I want to hold on to it."[115] Go she did, arriving on the afternoon of April 25. A few days later she was on hand for the opening ceremonies of the exposition.[116]

Mrs. Roebling also participated in the dedication of the New Jersey Building. Despite the socializing that occurred before and after the gala opening of the building, Emily pointed out "a few of us with all of this have done a good deal of work."[117] But there were dividends. Meeting a French duchess, Emily spoke with the distinguished visitor in her native language and, while the duchess did not comment on Mrs. Roebling's proficiency, she "complimented my skill as an engineer!"[118] The exclamation point may indicate Emily's surprise that a foreigner knew of her involvement with the Brooklyn Bridge or it could be a reflection of her inordinate modesty when it came to publicly revealing her behind-the-scenes work on the project.

During the 1890s, Emily made room in her life for many other interests, including the women's club movement, in the process becoming "one of the best-known women in America."[119] Moreover, "the executive ability and intellectuality which enabled her to prove so valuable an assistant and substitute for her husband manifested itself in her club life."[120]

Mrs. Roebling's involvement with women's clubs began in March 1894, when she was elected to Sorosis, a pioneering women's club founded in New York City in 1868.[121] Emily looked forward to traveling up to Manhattan to attend the society's meetings. For her they were "a pleasant little diversion,"[122] affording members an opportunity to listen to papers on a variety of serious topics. In December of 1895, for example, at a gathering of Sorosis that *The New York Times* called "the best meeting of the season, so far," those in attendance were treated to papers on "Travel as a Means of Education," a topic on which Emily was already an expert, "Kindergarten," "College Preparation," "Physical Education" and "University Centers in America."[123] In February 1896, 400 women turned out for a Sorosis gathering at the Waldorf-Astoria. What attracted the women, in such large numbers, was a debate revolving around the question, "Do business pursuits improve women mentally, morally, socially, and physically?"[124] The ayes clearly had it. One speaker, who had previously chaired the Sorosis Committee on Businesswomen, pointed out that, not so many years before, it was difficult to convince people that business pursuits did indeed develop a woman. Nevertheless, she declared: "The businesswoman has come to remain. Not a jot of grace, charm of manner, or dignity has she lost or need she lose. Some of our strongest and loveliest women in and out of Sorosis are, and have been businesswomen."[125]

As Emily Warren Roebling sat in the audience listening to this, she must have felt a certain sense of satisfaction because, as she happily stated in a letter to John, "Those on the affirmative side of the question comfortably annihilated the unfortunates who had the negative."[126] One speaker, a female minister, contended: "Business pursuits are the builders of character. … It all depends on the quality of the pursuit and the enthusiasm of the woman."[127] Given the quality and quantity of her input on the bridge project, doubtless Emily was in full agreement with the speaker. In printing excerpts from several of the most outstanding orations delivered at the Waldorf, the *Times* reported, "The unanimous opinion of Sorosis seemed to be that the businesswoman was a person to be respected."[128]

Advanced though this idea was in 1896, Sorosis was not altogether forward looking and neither was its distinguished member, Mrs. Roebling. Like most white Americans in this period, Emily and many of her fellow members of Sorosis did not believe in equality for African-Americans. Preceding the debate on women in business, the women were entertained by a musical program that included a much-applauded song, "Little Alabama Coon." While it would be unfair to assert beyond a shadow of a doubt that Mrs. Roebling sat there clapping her hands at the end of the rendition, it is safe to say that such a reaction would have been in keeping with her views on minorities. Emily may not have necessarily thought she was better than everyone else but, on the other hand, she had little regard for people who did not measure up to her high standards. Thus, she reported to John in 1893: "We have begun improving our new Quarry Alley property. I am expecting the cholera this summer so I was glad to tear down the two Negro houses and remove the filth which had been accumulating round that corner for years. … There is a prospect of Taylor Alley being made a street which will take down that awful row of Negro cabins."[129] What would happen to the people who resided there, she did not say. Nor, perhaps, did she care because, as late as 1901, she complained to John about entertainments held at the Manchester, Massachusetts, hotel where she and the Colonel were spending their summer vacation because the purpose of these fundraisers was to "help the education of the Negroes of the South."[130] There had been three such entertainments and the Roeblings were tired of contributing.

Yet in comparison with her rather frugal husband, Emily was much more generous. During the summer, she donated money to ease the suffering of infants living in New York City tenements.

A generous contributor to charitable causes, at a Sorosis "Philanthropy Day" gathering she was elected chair of the philanthropy committee.[131] Subsequently elected vice president of Sorosis, she had to wait to make a bid for the presidency of the organization until she had fulfilled a minimum membership requirement. She explained this to John, saying:

> I have never had a chance of being the President of Sorosis because I am not old enough! This reason would console any woman for the loss of the chance of being President of the United States, but this reason is not really as flattering as it looks ... my years ... being numbered, not from the hour of my birth, but from the date of my entrance to Sorosis.[132]

Besides her involvement in Sorosis and in various patriotic and historical organizations, Emily was active in the Federation of Women's Clubs. In 1896, when the New Jersey State Federation of Women's Clubs held a gigantic meeting in the Senate chambers of the Statehouse, Mrs. Roebling made the welcoming address. Three hundred women, mainly from New Jersey, but with a mixture of representatives from state federations up and down the eastern seaboard, turned out to hear addresses on "Forestry Interests of New Jersey," "Traveling Libraries," "Household Economies" and "Women's Place Today."[133] The women also listened to presentations on the future role of the Federation of Women's Clubs. One speaker, whose views paralleled those of Emily Roebling, urged the formation of women's clubs "in every nook and corner of the State. A women's club in a place soon becomes the center for all kinds of improvements. Women should seek other women in [their] search for knowledge."[134]

Describing the day's events to John, his mother wrote, "The popular conundrum in Trenton is still what did they want?"[135] Referring specifically to the fact that none of the speakers, including herself, made a big pitch for suffrage and prohibition, she said, "The wiseacres who are always reading my motives, I think, are beginning to fear that I am going to try to run for President next Fall!"[136] Although the reference to the upcoming national election was made in jest, Emily wasn't joking when she told John, "We did not invite any men to the State House and did not provide seats for them and yet there were fully a hundred there in the afternoon who stood for more than an hour listening to the speeches."[137]

Having moved almost entirely in the sphere of men while the bridge was being built, Emily was beginning to discover the rewards of associating with her own sex. The success of the meeting at the Statehouse was the impetus Trenton women needed to form a women's club. Although some female residents, like Emily, had become extremely interested in women's causes, they had not, until now, been able to organize a full-fledged women's club. After the Statehouse meeting, Mrs. Roebling invited some of the women to be trained in parliamentary procedure. For women to make an impact, singly and through organizations, they would have to run their affairs as men did. Therefore, "how to respond to toasts and how to prepare impromptu speeches" were on the agenda.[138] "We are going to conduct the whole affair," said Emily, "just like men do their large public dinners, and I even have two very good slightly 'off color' historical anecdotes of Washington and Lincoln which I am going to tell. … This is to be my little surprise to the other speakers."[139]

The training in parliamentary procedures and public speaking continued for more than a year, culminating in a festive luncheon at the Roebling mansion in May 1897. The perfume of hundreds of roses filled the house as the women arrived. Adorning the dining room table was a centerpiece consisting of a miniature Maypole with purple and yellow ribbons and dozens of pansies. Following the luncheon, each of the guests was required to rise and respond to a toast by saying something original and witty. This final exam of sorts was preceded several days earlier by a forensic debate on the improbable topic, "Resolved that Women's Clubs are a Foe to Home Life." Emily proudly reported, "One would not believe how well we did – I was surprised that there was so much eloquence in Trenton."[140]

Besides putting her organizational talents to work in Trenton, Emily traveled to other parts of the United States for the Federation of Women's Clubs. According to *The Brooklyn Daily Eagle* she "addressed the club women of Maine on their annual club day, and also delivered a number of addresses at midsummer gatherings in several other New England states. Mrs. Roebling is a member of Sorosis and never fails to score a hit when called on to speak. She is one of the few Sorosisters who know how to make an offhand speech that is the genuine thing."[141]

In the fall of 1897, she made speeches in Nashville, where she found the people most receptive but the "dust awful."[142] Denver, which was the site of the fourth biennial of the Federation in 1898, was more to Emily's liking. Writing from the Brown Palace Hotel, she told John, "I have very handsome rooms and when I get used to the light air, I think I shall like Denver."[143] En route to the West, the delegation was received by President William McKinley in Washington, and then went on to make stops in Cincinnati, St. Louis and Kansas City. "At all of these places we had a great deal of attention," Emily reported.[144] Some of it, though, was less than flattering. "The universal opinion all along our route has been that our five carloads of women were long on brains and short on beauty! An old man at Gypsum City asked where we gathered up so many ugly women. He thought there was not one of the lot who would be allowed to live in Kansas."[145] Her husband, perhaps annoyed by her prolonged absence from Trenton, was in full agreement with the negative comments about the women, but even this, Emily managed to take in stride, saying:

> The group of ladies that went to Denver on the Federation Special have just materialized in the shape of a photograph taken on the steps of the Congressional Library. [The] Colonel says the Kansas man's remarks about us did not … do us justice as they are all so ugly,

each one worse than the other, that just one look at the picture spoiled his appetite for luncheon.[146]

Once in a while, Emily managed to get even with the Colonel for such jibes. After seeing the play, *The Contented Woman*, for example, she teased him about the very advanced plot, which portrayed a man and wife both running for the office of mayor. In the end, the woman wins, an outcome Emily applauded. Yet she admitted to John: "The leading female politician put me sadly in mind of myself several times and when she appeared in a pair of plaid 'gents-pants' she looked very much as I should in a similar garb. I hope you can see this play sometime – it quite meets your views on the advanced woman."[147] Less progressive than his son, Washington Roebling regarded his wife's interest in women's affairs with detachment and, often, downright amusement. This surely must have aggravated Emily and, had it not been for her fine sense of humor, the two would have clashed repeatedly on this subject. Quite serious about her views on women's advancement, Mrs. Roebling, even in lighter moments, got her point across. In one letter to John, she joked about moving to Arizona "now that women can vote out there and see if I cannot run for Governor."[148]

Fundamentally committed to the progress of women, Emily was keenly interested in the work of the International Council of Women established in 1888, "as a federation of existing women's organizations around a broad program of activity."[149] Commenting on the fact that the group "made a greater success of their mission than the Peace Commission at the Hague," the all-male conference considering the question of disarmament, Emily rejoiced.[150] Referring to the women, she said: "Verily the world moves! Think of Queen Victoria shaking hands with Susan B. Anthony and after a cordial conversation with her inviting her to take a cup of tea in Windsor Castle – out of the royal teacups!"[151] Less sensational, but nevertheless important, was something that occurred at a diplomatic dinner Emily attended at the home of Senator R.A. Alger. Among the guests were the Chinese minister and his wife. This diminutive woman had mastered enough English to inform Mrs. Roebling that "she was sorry she had such little feet as she would like to walk around everywhere like we Americans did."[152] Emily reacted by asking: "Are not the whole world of women progressing?"[153]

To an extent, they were. Although they were denied the suffrage in most states, as well as in foreign countries, they were permitted, indeed encouraged, to undertake responsibilities heretofore considered beyond their physical and intellectual capabilities. In the 1890s, some of the barriers were being removed and women were increasingly called upon to accept positions that entailed something more demanding than ceremonial duties. Emily Roebling, for example, was elected to the boards of the Women's Hospital in New York and Evelyn College in Princeton, New Jersey.[154] Founded by the Reverend Joshua Hall McIlvaine in 1887, the college had a brief and stormy history.[155] Although the female students had library privileges at Princeton University and the departments in which they were enrolled were supervised by chairmen of the respective departments in the university, the trustees of Princeton refused to grant regular university degrees to the women.[156] By the fall of 1895, when Emily Roebling was elected president of the board of trustees of Evelyn College, only six months after becoming a board member, the institution was in serious financial difficulty.[157] Since Emily was first and foremost a realist, she undoubtedly came to the conclusion that the college's problems were insurmountable. Thus she resigned from the board early in 1896, telling John, "I have left Evelyn College and you should hear how they weep and wail over my loss!"[158] One year later the college permanently closed its doors.

As she grew older, Emily was less able to deal with controversy, of which she surely had had her share. The efforts of the early years were catching up with her. Bad eyes, hearing problems and general weakness plagued her by the dawn of the new century. Whereas heretofore she was so robust that no undertaking was too great, now she was inclined to heed the advice of her personal physician to refrain from going to Milwaukee for the fifth biennial of the Federation of Women's Clubs in 1900. To her dismay, the doctor "even hinted that I had better drop women's societies altogether."[159]

Later that year, however, she was well enough to attend a meeting of the New York State Federation of Women's Clubs in Albany. A highlight of the gathering was a gubernatorial reception at the Executive Mansion. Governor and Mrs. Theodore Roosevelt extended a warm welcome to all of the women. Mr. Roosevelt "seemed to have some personal remark to make to everyone," Emily told her son.[160]

When I came up in front of him, he said, "Ah Mrs. Roebling, what relation are you to my elector down in New Jersey and what relation is he to the Engineer of the Brooklyn Bridge?" I replied, "Your elector is my husband Washington A. Roebling who built the

Brooklyn Bridge." To which Teddy made answer, "I had no idea I was honored by having so distinguished a man for an elector. How patriotic it was of the *old man* to show such an interest in the Republican Party."[161]

Emily had some fun with Governor Roosevelt's characterization of her husband as an old man but other aspects of the Albany meeting were not to her liking. Perhaps it was her deteriorating health that hardened already existing prejudices, making them almost granitelike, but, whatever the reason, by the time the gathering ended, Emily had resolved to abandon the federation. "I am not broad enough to embrace the colored race in my social life," she stated,[162] "nor to take the platform for suffrage and that is what the Federation of Clubs is coming to so I have made my parting bow to them. We kept the colored delegate from getting the floor by tactics that would have done Tammany Hall credit, but it has got to be met someday. We cannot always dodge it."[163] The same held true for women's suffrage, but Mrs. Roebling simply wasn't well enough to take to the stump to campaign for it.

Before her health deteriorated, Emily enjoyed belonging to patriotic organizations. She joined the Daughters of the American Revolution (DAR) and by February 1899 she was a vice president general of the DAR, a position that necessitated periodic trips to Washington to attend meetings.[164] In 1900, when she was re-elected for another two-year term as vice president general, the DAR began to consider her for the top position in the organization. Having presided, more than once, at meetings that the president could not attend, Emily wondered if she wanted to head the DAR. The gatherings she had chaired were so tumultuous that she felt "just as I have on two or three occasions when I have been trying to control a runaway horse."[165] Within a year, however, she was ready to grasp the reins. The New Jersey Regents unanimously endorsed her for the position of president general of the national organization. Even the Colonel was thrilled about this "great compliment" his wife had received.[166] The nomination and perhaps the prospect of the upcoming election may have been a bit too much for Emily, though. After hosting a magnificent luncheon for the New Jersey Chapter Regents in honor of the State Regent, she succumbed to the grippe, as influenza was often called at that time.

At the beginning of February 1901, however, Emily was well enough to go to Washington for the DAR election. Ever the realist, she confided: "Fighting is on, all along the line. States are all split up on candidates. New Jersey so far is the only state that is working together. I do not expect to win but I shall leave my mark in a good many places."[167] While in Washington, Emily again became ill and had to withdraw her candidacy for the position of president general. The aftermath of the grippe, compounded by a recurring eye problem and general exhaustion, was responsible for her decision to bow out. "It was a pity too," she explained, "for I had put up a finer fight than the Society had ever seen."[168] She hated letting her friends down but concluded that it was "God's will."[169] Resigned though she was to following her doctor's orders to lead a quiet life, Emily complained, "I seem like a ship at sea without a rudder or compass."[170] Perhaps the most telling comment of all was, "I felt like the woman who worked herself to death for her family and requested them to put on her tombstone, 'Don't mourn for me now; don't mourn for me ever for I am going to do nothing forever and ever.'"[171] It's no wonder, since for the past year she had lived, breathed and eaten organization business and now it was all over.

However, Emily Warren Roebling wasn't the kind of person who could remain idle for very long. Her friends knew that and this may explain why some of them voted for her for DAR president general even though she had officially withdrawn from the contest. Her modest explanation of their loyalty was that they wanted to "go on record as opposing the idea that only a woman whose husband held an official position was eligible to the office of president general."[172] No matter what the reason, Emily was glad she was out of the whole thing. She characterized the election proceedings as "disgraceful," an apparent reference to the internal wrangling that accompanied the contest.[173] When it was all over, some of the New Jersey Regents paid her a visit and divulged "all the disgusting details of the late conflict."[174]

Deteriorating health was undoubtedly responsible for Emily's negative reaction to DAR politics because, two years earlier, she had thoroughly enjoyed a hard-fought battle to oust the president of the George Washington Memorial Association. Emerging from the struggle as a second vice president of the organization, Emily admitted: "This taking part in women's petty fights for office amused me. … I am reminded of the keen delight Paul took when he was in New York with me seeing the street ragamuffins fight each other."[175] Like her grandson, Mrs. Roebling enjoyed the role of bystander. Although she had been urged to make a

181

bid for the presidency of the George Washington Memorial Association, she admitted, "I did not want that office, having discovered that Vice-Presidents are creatures of dignity and importance with neither responsibilities nor hard labor attached."[176]

Emily had reached that time of life when she felt no longer suited for the role of chief executive, but she was by no means ready to retire completely from public life. She continued attending meetings of the Colonial Dames, an organization of which she was a member, and occasionally gave public lectures, including a talk in the spring of 1897 at the Young Women's Christian Association in Brooklyn about the coronation of the tsar. Emily gave the lecture at least half a dozen times and on each occasion it was well received. While visiting a friend at Lake Sunapee, New Hampshire, in the summer of 1898, she had a particularly enthusiastic audience of club women. When she finished speaking, the women asked her all sorts of questions. One wanted to know how long she had been a lecturer, and if it paid well. "Another woman asked me if I got to Russia because my husband built the Brooklyn Bridge and then one standing near her said 'What is the Brooklyn Bridge? I never heard of it!' Do you not think it was high time that a missionary visited that benighted region?" asked an incredulous Emily.[177]

Despite an occasional inane question, Mrs. Roebling continued lecturing on her European experiences and later on women's concerns and law. The once-retiring woman who had functioned largely behind the scenes during the bridge years had made her public debut and decided she liked being on center stage. "A certain amount of flattery," she told her son, "… is as necessary to me as oxygen."[178] Receptive audiences provided it in abundance.

One of the most receptive groups Emily ever had the pleasure of appearing before was made up of American soldiers who had volunteered for the Spanish-American War. In the immediate aftermath of that conflict, Mrs. Roebling descended upon Camp Wikoff, on eastern Long Island, in the company of other female volunteers, not to entertain the soldiers with her amusing talks, but rather to assist them in recovering from disease and exhaustion. She felt it was the least she could do out of gratitude that her only child had not ended up like the suffering veterans in the camp at Montauk.

In April 1898, soon after Congress declared war on Spain, despite his precarious health and family responsibilities, John Roebling made the decision to volunteer for service in the First Regiment, U.S. Volunteer Engineers.[179] A Roebling going off to war was not a simple matter. To begin with, John had to transfer his stock in John A. Roebling's Sons Company to his father as well as resign as a director of the firm.[180] The Colonel thought the latter was completely unnecessary but, dutiful man that he was, John wanted to do the right thing. He gave his wife power of attorney permitting her to sign his name and to transact all other business for him in his absence. John communicated all of this, rather matter-of-factly, in a three-page letter to his mother, whom he addressed as "Dear Em." In the last paragraph, he stated that he agreed with his father "that good-byes are to be avoided on general principles."[181] He thus refrained from making an elaborate farewell and in signing the letter, "your affectionate son, John A. Roebling," he apparently wrote "aff son" and had to squeeze in the rest of the word *affectionate* by slanting the additional letters to the right and allowing them to fall beneath the line.[182]

Emily reacted with equanimity to her only child's decision to go off to war. Yet, given her inordinate affection for him, it is truly amazing that she did not attempt to dissuade him. On the other hand, coming from a family where the military tradition was held in high esteem, she really had no choice but to applaud his self-sacrificing dedication. Then, too, by this time in her life, Emily Warren Roebling had endured an infinite number of trials. This, she may have viewed as just one more, and not a difficult one at that because the conflict ended before John was sent to the front. John himself, however, regretted the abrupt end of the war, but his mother promised to help him "get a commission to fight the Kaiser, which I think will be our next war."[183]

Although her prediction was positively brilliant, conflict with Germany was nearly 20 years away. In the meantime, America would have to grow into the oversize boots it acquired by leaping into war with Spain. An internal struggle would be waged between imperialists and anti-imperialists over the Treaty of Paris of 1898. Another domestic conflict surfaced simultaneously. It centered on the question of whether to bring home the military personnel sent to Cuba and, if so, what to do with them after they returned. The fear was that the men would bring tropical diseases with them. For this reason, some experts favored leaving them abroad until the illnesses ran their course. Others, however, including Assistant Secretary of the Navy Theodore Roosevelt, who had resigned his subcabinet position to lead the Rough Riders, a volunteer cavalry unit famous for its bravado, demanded that the veterans be repatriated as quickly as possible. If isolation was required, surely there had to be someplace on the vast East Coast where a temporary military camp could be created far enough away from the civilian population to prevent the spread of disease. Montauk Point, Long Island, was an ideal location for such a camp.

After Theodore Roosevelt suggested this spot, the government, with uncharacteristic speed, took steps to transform that picturesque, windswept pile of sand at the tip of the South Fork into an ad hoc military base called Camp Wikoff. By the first week in August, only a month after the war ended, enough of the camp was in place to permit the landing of 600 men from the Sixth United States Cavalry. They were the advance guard of the repatriated soldiers who would soon be as numerous as sea gulls at the usually deserted Montauk Point. Emily Warren Roebling read of the cavalrymen's arrival with great interest because she planned to journey to Montauk, in the company of other female volunteers, to help out among the sick and wounded.[184]

Soon after she arrived, Emily prevailed upon the authorities at the camp to allow her to send in a cook to prepare meals for some of the ill men and she personally dispatched two nurses, whose salaries she paid, to assist one of the surgeons.[185] When she wasn't reorganizing the kitchen, Mrs. Roebling was down at Quarantine, with the secretary of the Women's National War Relief Association, assembling clothes for the soldiers, some of whom had nothing to wear but nightshirts. With the efficiency that characterized all of her undertakings, Emily got the men outfitted in short order.

Still, she lamented, the job could have been done faster, "only nothing could be procured or sent by express on Saturday afternoon."[186]

Emily and the other women refused to wait any longer than they had to for anything that might make life more bearable for the men confined to Camp Wikoff. Appalled to find typhoid patients sleeping on the damp ground, without tents or blankets, the women saw to it that tents were erected, not on the sandy soil, which was still wet from a rainstorm, but on wooden platforms. With the women acting as foremen, a job Emily had been well accustomed to at the bridge, the construction work proceeded apace. Once the platforms were ready and the tents set up, the women provided clean sheets and fluffy pillows for the cots of ill soldiers. Bottled water and milk were also brought to the camp. These wholesome, refreshing liquids were made available to all the men and, for those who were merely weak and emaciated but not suffering from any disease, the women provided fruit, jams and other edibles plus underwear and shoes.

The poor condition of the nondiseased soldiers prompted Emily to write to John that she wished he was there at Montauk with her "to see a picture of war and its attendant misery with the glory left out."[187]

A few days after her initial visit to Camp Wikoff, Emily returned to Montauk to render further assistance to the soldiers. After an overnight stay at East Hampton, she set out for the camp early the next morning. Knowing there was a quarantine in effect, which prevented outsiders from entering the camp via the railroad station, the spunky and determined Mrs. Roebling took herself around to the rear of the camp, where she presented her pass and was allowed in.

In view of her visits to her brother and fiancé in military camps during the Civil War, it is not surprising that Mrs. Roebling adapted to life behind the lines. Whenever and wherever there was a task to be done, the resourceful Emily made the necessary adjustments. A doer as well as a thinker, she immediately put her superb organizational skills to use. She scurried about the so-called healthy, that is, nonquarantine, areas of the camp, supervising the nurses dispatched by the Women's National War Relief Association. Proudly, she told her son that these female medical personnel were on the job a full five days before the military authorities "would accept the female nurses sent down by the Red Cross – but now that the women are established, I think the male nurses will be fired out – as they demand more comforts than the women do."[188]

When President William McKinley paid a visit to Camp Wikoff in September, he commented enthusiastically on the achievements of the women. Emily, who was there to greet him, wrote to her son: "I had the honor of a long talk with President McKinley … last Saturday. … I fail to find in any paper that he praised anything he found there except the women."[189]

One of those women, Reubena Hyde Walworth, daughter of the president of the Women's National War Relief Association, made the ultimate sacrifice. A Vassar graduate and teacher who had volunteered as a nurse at Montauk, Miss Walworth died of typhoid. Of the young woman's passing, *The New York Times* said, "Her death ended one of the most cruel sieges of suffering that a woman was ever called on to undergo for the sake of her country's service."[190] Writing in the same newspaper, Charles Hanson Towne, poet, lyricist, novelist and later editor of the periodicals *Smart Set*, *Harper's Bazaar* and *McClure's Magazine*, paid tribute to Miss Walworth, saying:

> No storm of praise will be bestowed on her
> Sweet nurse – yea, angel – gentle minister
> And yet she served her flag – not as a man
> But better still, as only women can![191]

In a letter to John, Emily Roebling noted that Miss Walworth "was buried wrapped in an American flag. Had a military funeral and escort of soldiers."[192]

In the aftermath of the great tragedy suffered by the leader of the Women's National War Relief Association, Mrs. Roebling, the treasurer of the association, assisted with the preparation of a final report on the organization's war-related activities.

Even before the report of the Women's National War Relief Association was forthcoming, the work of individual members, including Emily Warren Roebling, was receiving public recognition. The New Jersey Legislature passed a resolution commending Emily for her fine work.[193] But Mrs. Roebling's job wasn't over. The following summer, when the reports of the Women's National War Relief Association were printed, Emily helped distribute them to libraries, historical societies and government officials.[194]

Once the summary of the Women's National War Relief Association's contributions had been distributed, Emily was able to close the books on the Spanish-American War and turn her attention to something she had longed to do for many years, namely, undertake the study of law.

Law Student

In 1899, Emily enrolled in New York University's Woman's Law Class. Designed for businesswomen whose careers would benefit from knowledge of the law and for any other woman interested in gaining greater insight into the American legal system, the Woman's Law Class was begun in 1890.[195] It was the brainchild of Dr. Emily Kempin, a Swiss attorney, who, with the backing of the Woman's Legal Education Society, convinced Vice Chancellor Henry M. MacCracken of New York University to launch a unique experiment in legal education.[196] Dr. Kempin taught the first class and other female attorneys, along with male members of the faculty of the New York University School of Law, subsequently became instructors.

By the time Emily Warren Roebling enrolled in the course, 500 women had attended, and 300 had passed an examination entitling them to a university certificate.[197] Although the curriculum, which included straight law of contracts, real property and domestic relations, was hardly watered down, the course did not constitute the equivalent of full-time legal studies. In the 1890s, the regular law program at NYU was two years, whereas the Woman's Law Class consisted of only one semester of instruction. The top student in the Woman's Law Class was awarded a full scholarship, with a monetary value of $200, to the New York University School of Law and a number of winners took advantage of the opportunity to pursue a law degree, knowing that they would be able to practice in the State of New York.

Ever since 1886, when women were admitted to the bar in New York, well-educated women began taking an interest in law. To be sure, for some, it was merely an intellectual avocation and women in this category generally audited the Woman's Law Class. Others, however, plugged away and sat for the final examination. As might be expected, Emily was in the latter group. Well accustomed to giving her all to any project she undertook, Emily, despite illnesses that caused her to miss some classes, completed the course. She spent two weeks in seclusion boning up for the most rigorous final examination thus far in the history of the program because she yearned to win "the right to wear the cap and gown of the Law University."[198]

Shortly before the course ended, Professor Isaac Franklin Russell challenged the class with a number of exceedingly difficult questions. The entire student body of nearly 50 women found them complex but somehow muddled through. Although the course in which the women were enrolled was nonprofessional in nature, Professor Russell refused to lower his standards because "desultory reading, self-imposed tasks, and ill-directed studies cannot exhibit results at all comparable with those produced by an academic regimen which appoints its hours, measures its duties, plans its curriculum, and tests its progress."[199] The learned professor believed in a rigorous curriculum and considerable work outside the classroom but on campus he encouraged, among the female students, "oral disputation and friendly wrangling, without the bitterness of real antagonism."[200] Such methods guaranteed that "the mere accumulations of fact-knowledge are thus supplemented by comparison and reflection, and thereby enhanced [its] value, and an impression is made on the mind of the student all the more vivid and permanent for the concrete environment with which it is associated."[201] Professor Russell was also proud of the fact that his class was a heterogeneous group in which "the most wifely and motherly of women meet here with the most advanced and aggressive of those who assert woman's demand for rights still denied."[202] In addition to homebodies and women's rights advocates the class included, at one time or another since its inception, women from different socio-economic groups and levels of education. "The most cultured and scholarlike, proudly wearing the honors of the university, dispute freely with those who have no degrees to parade; women of fortune sit next to bread winners in the class room while almost every race, creed and language has its representation in our little commonwealth of learning, where humble and obscure mingle with the celebrated and the great."[203]

Although Emily Warren Roebling clearly belonged to the last group, she was not about to sit back and indulge herself. Instead, she worked night and day to get ready for the final exam. In so doing, she compared herself to the tramp who was thrown off the train so many times while trying to make his way from New York to San Francisco that he harbored hopes of reaching his destination only "if his trousers held out."[204] Emily's weak spot was her eyes. If they held out, she told her son, "I shall get my diploma from the Chancellor."[205] Toward the end, it was an uphill fight because, besides increasingly weak eyesight, Emily had to contend with a fire in the Waldorf-Astoria, where she and her husband were staying while she completed her legal studies.

Taking a brief respite from the books, Mrs. Roebling was stepping out for the afternoon but, as she opened the door of their suite, she was nearly overcome by a thick cloud of black smoke. Hotel officials contended that the fire had broken out when servants were burning rubbish in the basement. The Roeblings did a little detective work on their own and discovered that faulty wiring had caused a window frame and curtains in a first-floor room directly beneath their suite to go up in flames. Even before Emily and Washington had ascertained the real cause of the blaze, she lost not a second in returning to their suite to alert her husband to the danger and bring him downstairs. The fire was contained, apparently without damaging the Roebling suite, because five days later Emily wrote to her son from the Waldorf saying, "Of course this building is fireproof, but you could be choked by smoke all the same."[206]

In the same letter she proudly announced that she had passed the law examination with high honors. "I am 'terrible' proud of myself," she told John, "and strange to say, [the] Colonel is both pleased and amused, and has accepted Professor Russell's invitation to sit on the platform with the Faculty of the Law School when they give us our diplomas."[207] Perhaps Washington Roebling found humor in the fact that his wife had taken her legal studies so seriously. When she enrolled at NYU, he may have thought she would merely audit the Woman's Law Class, rather than spend her time cramming to pass a stiff examination. After all, there was really no reason for a well-to-do woman in her 50s to push herself. When they were both considerably younger and he needed her help at the bridge, it was perfectly all right for

Emily to undertake intellectually and physically demanding tasks. Back then her study of mathematics and engineering had been pursued to aid her husband. The law course, in contrast, was all her own doing. Perhaps, it was a survival technique because, as she confided to John, it wasn't that her love for the Colonel had grown cold, rather it was the case of the emotional and intellectual maturation of an extremely gifted woman. In middle age Emily wanted to strike out on her own. Enrolling in the Woman's Law Class was one way of doing that.

At 8 o'clock on the night of Thursday, March 30, 1899, Emily Warren Roebling donned cap and gown and proudly walked down the aisle of the Concert Hall at Madison Square Garden. The second of several such buildings bearing that name, the Garden of the 1890s, designed by McKim, Mead and White, was an ornate structure complete with a tower crowned by Augustus St. Gaudens' statue of Diana. On the night of her commencement, Mrs. Roebling was as regal as the sculptured goddess as she strode confidently to the platform to read an essay on "A Wife's Disabilities," which had won her an award of $50.[208] This first prize money in the essay contest was considerable in view of the fact that the scholarship for the full two-year law program at NYU awarded to the top graduate of the Woman's Law Class amounted to $200.

Emily Warren Roebling received extensive press coverage, as practically all of the major dailies on both sides of the East River plus Trenton, New Jersey, carried articles about her successful completion of the Woman's Law Class.[209] The *Herald* printed a major article about the commencement and, while it listed the names of all the graduates, a picture of a scholarly but most attractive-looking Emily Warren Roebling accompanied the article.[210] In her picture, Emily appears younger than her 55 years. Her loosely curled hair is parted in the center and pulled back into a small top knot. No jewelry is visible to detract from the seriousness of the portrait. Her high-collared, lace-trimmed shirtwaist concealed a somewhat fleshy chin. The face is lined but not excessively despite her years of work and worry. Most impressive of all is the subject's gaze. Her eyes, which appear to be quite dark, possess a bit of Mona Lisa-like inscrutability. One wonders whether she is deep in thought or on the verge of making an important pronouncement.

If the artist's rendering of Mrs. Roebling had been done the night of the commencement, the odds would favor the latter interpretation. That evening, in the midst of a profusion of flowers brought in to decorate a hall where music rather than delicate perfume normally filled the air, Emily read an abbreviated version of her prize-winning essay. A stunned audience listened as she called for the elimination of laws discriminating against wives and widows. Under common law, Emily explained, "The sacred rite of marriage conferred upon her the honor of ranking in legal responsibility with idiots and slaves."[211] Single women, she pointed out, were not encumbered in this way, but the desire of fathers to protect property left to their female offspring from grasping sons-in-law led to statutes that, in effect, prohibited married daughters from obtaining what was rightfully theirs. Compounding the problem was the fact that husbands were not legally bound to leave their wives any of their personal property. To correct this injustice, Emily recommended that "the statutes should be so changed that the property, real and personal, belongs equally to man and wife and can only be distributed and divided on the death of the last one of the parties in the marriage contract."[212]

Referring consciously or unconsciously to her own experience, the eloquent graduate then asked with regard to the married woman: "Does she not contribute largely to his success or failure in life? Must she not bear poverty and reverse of fortune with her husband when they come, and shall she not lawfully share in all the profits of his success and prosperity?"[213] The carefully thought out response to this rhetorical question was that the law had to be changed to protect widows because, despite the generosity of many husbands, there were some who denied their wives what common law termed their *paraphernalia*, namely, clothing and other personal possessions.[214]

Just as she was angered by the inheritance laws, Emily was totally infuriated by the inequitable treatment of men and women in criminal cases. She told the audience that, if a husband killed his wife, in a fit of passion, he would be treated as if he had killed, not his wife, but a total stranger. In the reverse situation, "no matter what the provocation, it was a much more atrocious deed."[215] The murderess "not only transgressed the laws of humanity and conjugal affection, but by her wicked act threw aside all submission to her husband's authority, and was guilty, not of murder, but treason, just as if she had killed the king."[216] On making this statement, Mrs. Roebling was careful to emphasize the word *authority*. Her voice reverberated throughout the hall, sending a chill through the audience. When her essay was printed in *The*

Albany Law Journal, the word *authority* was italicized at the request of the author.

Besides tackling the extreme case of conjugal murder, Emily explored the question of lesser crimes in both her speech and the printed version of the essay. She pointed out that, in the past, women were routinely sentenced to death for larceny, bigamy and manslaughter, even if this was their first offense. Since men could get off with lighter punishment, generally a short prison sentence or a nonlife-threatening mutilation such as branding of the hand, the law was tilted in their favor. Of course a husband was held responsible for his wife's wrongdoing but, as he was legally able to keep her in line by hitting her with "a stick as large as his finger, but not larger than his thumb," as many times and with as much force as he could muster, Emily felt that a man "had the power in his own hands of preventing her [from] getting him into legal difficulties."[217]

How many congratulatory handshakes, kisses and pats on the back the courageous Emily received for the oral version of her prize-winning essay is unknown but, most assuredly, her husband was not among those expressing approval. Following the ceremony, the Colonel approached Professor Russell and, after cordially expressing his gratitude to him for having taught Emily a great deal about the law, he added, "I never heard her essay until tonight and I do not agree with one word she has said."[218] Much to Emily's dismay, the professor concurred but tried to soften the blow by saying how much he had enjoyed having a "faithful student" like Mrs. Roebling in his class.[219] "Our pupils," Professor Russell told Colonel Roebling, "are allowed to advance any theory they like, if their legal reasoning is all right. We leave them the entire responsibility of their essays."[220] Emily concluded that the controversial subject matter of her essay, plus the interpretation of the topic, had been all her own doing anyway and that male advisers, whether at home or on campus, were really unimportant.

The determined Mrs. Roebling was immensely proud of her accomplishment and longed to spend the $50 award on a silver pitcher to commemorate her success. Yet, in keeping with her position as the wife of a multimillionaire, she felt compelled to donate the prize money to the Woman's Legal Education Society's endowment fund. It is not difficult to imagine her frugal husband deriving a sort of perverse pleasure from the fact that his wife had to part with the money. He may have also been secretly pleased, or at least amused, a year and a half after Emily received her certificate from New York University to learn that mice had gotten into boxes stored under the windows in the Roeblings' Trenton mansion. The hungry little creatures didn't much care what they nibbled on, but the woman of the house certainly did. She was positively distraught to discover that papers relating to organizations in which she was active had been gnawed, together with her parchment from NYU. "[The] Colonel says I will not now be able to practice law, but I hope to get Professor Russell to give me a new one," she told John.[221]

In reality, Emily Warren Roebling had not practiced, and would not be practicing, law. That wasn't the purpose of the Woman's Law Class. The vast knowledge of legal matters acquired in the course, however, combined with extensive reading, gave her considerable insight into the law and served to perpetuate her interest in the subject after she completed her studies. She did research on the Magna Carta, refusing to be satisfied with the explanations of that document found in *The Encyclopedia* and *Blackstone's Commentaries*, the two sources to which her former instructor, Professor Russell, referred her. The project seems to have been undertaken at the request of John Roebling, whose road-building and land-acquisition activities in North Carolina sometimes immersed him in legal matters. Although she did not practice law, Emily was always willing to give legal advice, especially to her son.

Emily's legal interests were wide-ranging. In an undated note written sometime after she had completed the Woman's Law Class, she asked John to send her any books he might have on the sociological view of sovereignty. Another letter, written from New Haven, Connecticut, described a recent legal case involving property taxes. That Emily kept up with such things while traveling, in this case returning from a summer vacation at Narragansett Pier, Rhode Island, is proof of her genuine interest in law. The plaintiff in the case to which she referred was John D. Rockefeller Sr., who contended that his property at Pocantico Hills in Westchester County, New York, should be taxed as it had been before extensive improvements had been made. To assess his land at the price for which neighboring properties were then selling he alleged was unjust because, if he had not undertaken the far-reaching work already completed on his property, the rest of the land in the community would not have appreciated in value. The court agreed and Emily evidently applauded its decision because she told John that the judge "wound up by saying the rich have rights – as well as the poor and they should be respected by the law of the land."[222]

In the same letter, she spoke about a recent decision in *Colonial Dames of America v. The National Society of Colonial Dames*. Both organizations had used the name Colonial Dames for years until the Colonial Dames of America sued, claiming that it had originated the title. The judge ruled that, since the organization had not heretofore invoked its claim, it could not prevent the other society from using the name. This was essentially the conclusion Emily herself, a member of the New Jersey Society of Colonial Dames of America, had come to weeks before. The judge, however, modified his decision a bit by requiring each group to pay its own costs. Emily did not actually think the matter would be laid to rest as a result of the judicial decision. An appeal was a distinct possibility. She relished the prospect, telling John, "I give warning to all my friends and family that nothing but a surgical operation, which keeps me motionless, will prevent my attending every session of the trial."[223]

Besides being an interested observer of legal matters, Mrs. Roebling took to the stump to enlighten the public about the value of female lawyers. Six months after emerging from the Woman's Law Class, she mesmerized the population of Wellsville, Ohio, an oil town, which gave Emily the feeling of having "dropped in on the last century, instead of being on the threshold of the new one."[224] Homes of the community's well-to-do citizens were comfortable enough. They were all "heated and lighted by natural gas," but the people, though educated, were, in the opinion of the distinguished visitor, "so far behind the world's civilization in their dress, and home adornments."[225] Unsophisticated or not, the people of Wellsville turned out en masse to greet Mrs. Roebling. She was feted at a City Hall reception, attended by men, women and children, and her remarks about women lawyers were better received by male than female listeners.[226]

On another occasion, Emily was greeted at New York's City Hall by Mayor William L. Strong. In the company of other invited female guests, Mrs. Roebling had tea with the mayor. She wrote afterward, "I cannot say that his Honor made much of an impression on me."[227] Other political figures had a greater effect upon her. Among them were President William McKinley, whose first inauguration she attended, and the mastermind of McKinley's electoral success in 1896, Mark Hanna. While visiting New York City in 1897, Emily sat next to Hanna at a dinner and charmed him with a repertoire of amusing political stories; by the end of the evening, he declared that, if women were ever named to the National Committee of the Republican Party, she would be the first one appointed. Despite her somewhat muted enthusiasm for Mr. Hanna, observing that "he is different from any man I have ever met, rather egotistical but very entertaining," Emily started to lose faith in the man he had almost single-handedly put in the White House.[228] "This is a world of change and I have deserted the Republican Party and have become down on Billy McKinley! *Town Topics* calls him a big 'jelly fish' but I am not as hard as that yet," she declared in 1900.[229] The publication to which Emily was referring was a gossip-filled high society newspaper published by William d'Alton Mann. Enticement and innuendo were very much a part of Mann's style, but he didn't stop there. Sometimes he even published untruths. Indeed, he became so expert at it that certain society people paid him to keep their names and doings out of *Town Topics*. Emily Warren Roebling was not among them. Ironically, the most sensational thing Colonel Mann could have said about her had already been revealed by Abram Hewitt. Yet the publicity she received at the time the bridge opened notwithstanding, Emily remained the silent builder. Despite all of her attainments, including the recent honors in law at NYU, she was still home and family oriented, and would be so for the rest of her life.

Endnotes

[1] *The New York Times*, January 3, 1887, 8:2. Additional information may be found in the *Troy Daily Times*, March 2, 1903; and Troy City Directories, 1885-87, in the collection of the Rensselaer County Historical Society.

[2] WAR memo, n.d.; WAR Letterbook, p. 593.

[3] WAR to JAR II, May 30, 1888, WAR Letterbook, p. 516.

[4] Ibid.

[5] Ibid.

[6] *Troy Daily Times*, June 14, 1888, 3:3.

[7] Daughters of the American Revolution, *Lineage Book* (Washington, D.C.: Daughters of the American Revolution, 1896), p. 340.

[8] Interestingly, John chose for his bride a woman who was quite similar to his mother. His bride had graduated ahead of her classmates at Trenton High School. Once married, she applied her considerable intelligence to helping her husband as his mother had once aided his father. In later years, Mrs. John A. Roebling II managed the family estate at Bernardsville, New Jersey, and served as her husband's chief assistant in the chemistry laboratory he set up on the property. What was said of Mrs. John A. Roebling II in an editorial in *The Bernardsville News*, October 30, 1930, 4:1, at the time of her death, could have been applied to her mother-in-law, namely, "that her many good works were accomplished so quietly that many of her benefactions will probably never be known."

[9] *True American*, March 2, 1903.

[10] EWR to JAR II, July 17, 1900. WAR's nephew, Karl Roebling, credited Emily with the design of the Trenton mansion and said that she "knew what she wanted for an impressive house." Karl Roebling, *The Age of Individuality: America's Kinship with the Brooklyn Bridge* (Fern Park, Florida: Paragon Press, 1983), p. 31.

[11]EWR to JAR II, October 21, 1893.
[12]Ibid., February 17, 1893.
[13]Ibid., April 13, 1893.
[14]Ibid., June 14, 1893.
[15]Ibid., July 26, 1893.
[16]Ibid., September 24, 1893.
[17]Ibid., September 10, 1893.
[18]Ibid., November 18, 1900.
[19]Ibid., February 15, 1894.
[20]Ibid.
[21]*Advertiser*, Trenton, March 1, 1903.
[22]EWR to JAR II, July 26, 1893.
[23]Ibid., February 27, 1901.
[24]Ibid., May 15, 1899.
[25]*The Brooklyn Daily Eagle*, Oct. 1, 1889, p. 6.
[26]Ibid.
[27]Ibid.
[28]Ibid.
[29]Ibid.
[30]Ibid.
[31]Ibid.
[32]Ibid
[33]Ibid.
[34]Ibid.
[35]Ibid.
[36]EWR to JAR II, July 16, 1894.
[37]Ibid., January 20, 1895.
[38]Ibid., May 1, 1901.
[39]Ibid., February 17, 1893.
[40]Ibid., October 20, 1898.
[41]Ibid, December 21, 1898.
[42]Ibid.
[43]Ibid., January 8, 1899.
[44]Ibid., January 12, 1899.

[45]Ibid., February 28, 1899.

[46]Ibid., March 10, 1899.

[47]Ibid., May 3, 1899.

[48]Ibid., December 4, 1898.

[49]Ibid.

[50]Ibid.

[51]Ibid.

[52]Ibid., May 14, 1894.

[53]*True American*, March 2, 1903.

[54]EWR to JAR II, September 21, 1898.

[55]Ibid., April 25, 1893.

[56]Ibid.

[57]Ibid., May 4, 1893.

[58]Ibid.

[59]Ibid.

[60]Ibid., December 30, 1893.

[61]Ibid., February 20, 1896.

[62]Ibid., December 17, 1897.

[63]Ibid.

[64]WAR to R.V. Lindabury, July 20, 1898, WAR Letterbook, pp. 590-91.

[65]WAR to JAR II, March 29, 1917.

[66]*NYT*, January 10, 1899, 1:6.

[67]*Trenton Times*, April 8, 1899, 1:1.

[68]EWR to JAR II, April 9, 1899.

[69]Ibid.

[70]Ibid.

[71]Ibid.

[72]Ibid.

[73]*World*, April 9, 1899, 1:7; *Trenton Times*, April 5, 1899, 1:5; and *NYT*, April 25, 1899, 1:1

[74]EWR to JAR II, March 1, 1900.

[75]WAR to JAR II, April 26, 1896.

[76]EWR to JAR II, April 30, 1896.

[77]Ibid.
[78]WAR to JAR II, May 11, 1896.
[79]EWR to JAR II, June 6, 1896.
[80]Ibid., April 30, 1896. Potter Palmer's biography may be found in *Dictionary of American Biography*, VII, pp. 190-91; and Bertha Honorè Palmer's in *DAB*, VII, pp. 176-77, and *Notable American Women*, III, p. 70.
[81]EWR to JAR II, May 17, 1896.
[82]Ibid., May 18, 1896.
[83]Ibid.
[84]Ibid., May 17, 1896.
[85]Ibid.
[86]Ibid.
[87]Ibid., May 18, 1896.
[88]Ibid., May 22, 1896.
[89]EWR to WAR, May 31, 1896.
[90]Emily's observations of the tsar were similar to those made by a *NYT* reporter who said, "The [Tsar] reveals himself as a pallid and nervous figure overwhelmed by either illness or settled depression." *NYT*, May 24, 1896, 1:2. Other articles about the coronation appeared in the paper on May 26, 1896, 1:1; May 27, 1896, 1:7; and *Trenton Evening Times*, May 25, 1896, 4:3.
[91]EWR to WAR, May 31, 1896.
[92]Ibid.
[93]EWR to Eliza Hook, May 22, 1896.
[94]EWR to JAR II, May 26, 1896.
[95]Ibid.
[96]EWR to WAR, May 31, 1896.
[97]Ibid.
[98]Ibid.
[99]Ibid., June 6, 1896.
[100]Ibid.
[101]Ibid.
[102]Ibid.

[103]Ibid., May 31, 1896.

[104]Ibid.

[105]Ibid. Following her European trip, Emily, accompanied by her husband, traveled to Brooklyn, where they stayed at the Hotel St. George. While there, Emily addressed a huge audience in the Young Women's Christian Association's Memorial Hall at Flatbush Avenue and Schermerhorn Street. Her lecture was titled "An American Woman at the Coronation of [Tsar] Nicholas II." All proceeds from the sale of tickets were donated to the Brooklyn Home for Consumptives. As Emily read her lecture, the audience gazed at numerous pictures that "in rapid succession were thrown upon the screen." (*Eagle*, April 30, 1897, p. 11) The pictures of the tsar's palace "were very beautiful and furnished an excellent idea of the magnificence of Russian court life." (Ibid.) So, too, did the inclusion of details about the tsarina's jewels and her coronation robe, which Emily indicated was estimated to have cost $200,000. Emily regaled her listeners with information about the royal vehicles, including the tsarina's glass-sided carriage and the different color horses of each regiment in a three-mile-long military procession. The *Eagle's* account of the lecture noted that Mrs. Roebling "did not see the actual coronation" because only six Americans were admitted to the cathedral for the ceremony but her detailed lecture indicated that she had been an eyewitness to the other events of coronation week. (Ibid.)

[106]EWR to JAR II, July 13, 1896.

[107]Ibid., July 27, 1896.

[108]WAR to JAR II, circa mid-June 1896, WAR Letterbook, p. 570.

[109]EWR to JAR II, July 27, 1896.

[110]Ibid., August 13, 1896, and WAR to JAR II, August 17, 1896. Her husband insisted that it took Emily awhile to get over the trip. "Your mother still talks of Kings, Queens, [Tsars], etc. in her sleep," the Colonel told John, adding, "in another week she

will get down to commoners and ultimately I hope to our low level." WAR to JAR II, August 17, 1896.

[111]EWR to JAR II, August 13, 1896.

[112]Ibid., September 5, 1896.

[113]Ibid., March 18, 1893.

[114]Margaret Tufts Yardley, *The New Jersey Scrapbook of Women Writers*, Vol. I (Newark, New Jersey: Advertiser Printing House, 1893), pp. v-viii.

[115]EWR to JAR II, April 25, 1893.

[116]Descriptions of opening day and of the fair's numerous and varied exhibits can be found in the *NYT*, April 30, 1893, 20:1; and May 3, 1893, 5:1.

[117]Description of New Jersey Building: Benjamin Truman, *History of the World's Fair, Being a Complete and Authentic Description of the Columbian Exposition from its Inception* (Philadelphia: H.W. Kelley, 1893), p. 471.

[118]EWR to JAR II, May 4, 1893.

[119]*Herald*, March 1, 1903, 1:2.

[120]*Eagle*, March 1, 1903, 5:2.

[121]Jennie C. Croly, *History of the Woman's Club Movement in America* (New York, H.G. Allen & Co., 1898), p. 18; and Karen J. Blair, *The Clubwoman as Feminist: True Womanhood Redefined*, 1868-1914 (New York: Holmes & Meier Publishers, 1980), p. 15.

[122]The Colonel accompanied his wife to one Sorosis dinner but did not enjoy himself. He told his son: "The dinner at Sorosis nearly finished me as the window at my back was open and my dress suit was very thin – Of course the female rhinoceri (of whom a large herd surrounded me) did not mind in the least, they being protected by a thick coating of vanity." WAR to JAR II, n.d., circa winter 1896-97.

[123]*NYT*, December 3, 1895, 7:2.

[124]Ibid., February 4, 1896, 8:1.

[125]EWR to JAR II, n.d., circa winter 1896-97.

[126]Ibid., February 7, 1896. Emily's talent in this area was noted in the journal of the Daughters of the American Revolution, which observed:

It is unusual to find such executive ability so well developed in a woman who has not acquired them in the effort to support herself. She is firm and decided, with opinions on almost every subject, which opinions she expresses with great frankness. To her natural talents for organizing are joined tact, energy, unselfishness and good nature, and this combination of traits has made her popular with the thousands of women who have met her in the many societies with which she is associated. ("Mrs. Washington Augustus Roebling," *American Monthly Magazine*, Vol. 17, July-December 1900, 246-250.)

[127]*NYT*, February 4, 1896, 8:1.

[128]Ibid.

[129]EWR to JAR II, March 18, 1893.

[130]Ibid., August 11, 1901.

[131]Ibid., September 20, 1896. A year later, Sorosis members gathered in the ballroom of the Waldorf for a discussion of philanthropy. On this occasion Emily posed the question of the day, "By what means can the condition of the poor in large cities be practically improved?" (*NYT*, Oct. 5, 1897, p. 7) She proceeded to say that "we must see what we can do in helping the people by bettering the condition of the tenements." (Ibid.) But she also observed:

It is a fallacy that the rich are growing richer and the poor are growing poorer. The rich are growing richer, but the poor are also growing richer. The wealth is flowing into this country, and the rich are not taking it away from the poor. (Ibid.)

[132]EWR to JAR II, March 5, 1899.

[133]*NYT*, March 21, 1896, 8:2.

[134]*Trenton Times*, March 20, 1896, 1:4.

[135]EWR to JAR II, March 2, 1896.

[136]Ibid.

[137]Ibid.

[138]Ibid., May 1, 1897.

[139]Ibid.

[140]Ibid.

[141]*Eagle*, Sept. 17, 1898, p. 15.

[142]EWR to JAR II, October 15, 1897.

[143]Ibid., June 20, 1898.

[144]Ibid.

[145]Ibid.

[146]Ibid., July 29, 1898.

[147]Ibid., February 16, 1897.

[148]Ibid., February 27, 1895.

[149]Eleanor Flexner, *Century of Struggle* (New York: Atheneum, 1970), p. 218.

[150]EWR to JAR II, July 16, 1897.

[151]Ibid.

[152]Ibid., February 28, 1899.

[153]Ibid.

[154]Ibid., March 19, 1899.

[155]The most comprehensive account of the history of Evelyn College can be found in a doctoral dissertation done at Ohio State University. Francis P. Healy, "A History of Evelyn College for Women in Princeton, New Jersey, 1887 to 1897." Ohio State University, 1976. Other sources include Adaline W. Sterling, "Women's Colleges – Evelyn College," *Harper's Bazaar*, November 17, 1888. College catalogues and annual reports have been preserved in the Princeton University Archives.

[156]Alice McIlvaine to M. Halsey Thomas, May 14, 1939. Princeton University Archives.

[157]EWR to JAR II, October 6, 1895.

[158]Ibid., February 7, 1896.

[159]Ibid., May 29, 1900.

[160]Ibid., November 18, 1900.

[161]Ibid.

[162]Ibid.

[163]Ibid.

[164]Ibid., February 28, 1899.

[165]Ibid., March 1, 1900.

[166]Ibid., February 5, 1901.

[167]Ibid.

[168]Ibid., February 14, 1901. In an article published in its journal the previous year, the Daughters of the American Revolution acknowledged Emily's role in the Brooklyn Bridge project, stating:

> When Mr. Roebling, the engineer of the noble structure, nearly lost his life in the bridge caisson at the bottom of the East River, the success of the undertaking hung trembling in the balance. His wife, Emily Warren Roebling, bravely assumed the responsibility of keeping things going just as they were for a few days … .[T]he work assumed for a few days was not laid down until the bridge was completed – eleven years. ("Mrs. Washington Augustus Roebling," *American Monthly Magazine*, Vol. 17, July-December 1900, 246-250.)

[169]Ibid., February 14, 1901.

[170]Ibid.

[171]Ibid.

[172]Ibid., February 25, 1901. Mrs. Charles N. Fairbanks, wife of Senator Fairbanks of Indiana, was elected president general. *True American*, March 2, 1903.

[173]EWR to JAR II, March 3, 1901.

[174]Ibid. and *Trenton Times*, February 22, 1901, 1:6.

[175]EWR to JAR II, December 13, 1899.

[176]Ibid., December 17, 1899.

[177]Ibid., July 17, 1898.

[178]Ibid.
[179]JAR II to Ferdinand W. Roebling, August 7, 1898.
[180]Ibid., April 21, 1898.
[181]JAR II to EWR, April 21, 1898.
[182]Ibid.
[183]EWR to JAR II, July 18, 1898.
[184]Several months earlier, Emily represented the Women's National War Relief Association at the Women's Club Biennial in Denver. An article in the *Denver Evening Post* began by stating: "Mrs. Roebling was introduced to the public by the remarks made by Abram S. Hewitt at the opening ceremonies of the Brooklyn Bridge." The article proceeded to quote part of the speech before getting to the reason for Emily's appearance in Denver, which was to enlist "the women of Denver … in the noble work being carried on by the Association for the relief of the sick and wounded soldiers and sailors in the United States." (*Denver Evening Post*, June 19, 1898, p. 14) For a complete description of the work performed by the women at Montauk, see *Women's National War Relief Association Report: March 1898, to January 1899* (New York: Board of Directors, WNWRA, 1899), pp. 71-83.
[185]*Women's National War Relief Association Report*, p. 75.
[186]EWR to JAR II, August 14, 1898.
[187]Ibid.
[188]Ibid., August 19, 1898.
[189]Ibid., September 10, 1898.
[190]*NYT*, October 19, 1898, 12:1.
[191]Ibid., October 20, 1898, 6:7.
[192]EWR to JAR II, October 25, 1898.
[193]Ibid., February 2, 1899.
[194]Ibid., July 29, 1899.
[195]*For the Better Protection of Their Rights. A History of the First Fifty Years of the Woman's Legal Education Society and the Woman's Law Class at New York University* (New York: New

York University Press, 1940), p. 17.

[196]One of the founding members of the Woman's Legal Education Society was Mrs. Abram S. Hewitt, the wife of Emily Roebling's old admirer. Another was the celebrated physician Dr. Mary Putnam Jacobi, *For the Better Protection of Their Rights,* p. 17.

[197]New York University Catalogue for 1895-96, pp. 217-18.

[198]EWR to JAR II, February 18, 1897.

[199]*The Albany Law Journal,* March 8, 1899.

[200]Ibid.

[201]Ibid.

[202]Ibid.

[203]*Eagle,* March 31, 1899, p. 5.

[204]EWR to JAR II, March 10, 1899.

[205]Ibid.

[206]Ibid., March 26, 1899.

[207]Ibid.

[208]*For the Better Protection of Their Rights,* p. 47.

[209]EWR to JAR II, March 31, 1899.

[210]*Herald* clipping, New York University Law Library file on Woman's Law Class.

[211]*The Albany Law Journal,* April 15, 1899, p.342.

[212]Ibid.

[213]Ibid.

[214]Ibid., p. 343.

[215]Ibid.

[216]Ibid.

[217]Ibid., p. 342.

[218]EWR to JAR II, April 9, 1899. Something else that Washington Roebling would disagree with years later was the idea of women serving as jurors. Two decades after Emily's death and a year after women gained the right to vote, he "predicted that in a short time women would not care to continue to vote and

he thought women were too emotional and nervous to make satisfactory jurors." *NYT*, May 27, 1921, p.7.

[219]Ibid., EWR to JAR II, April 9, 1899.
[220]Ibid.
[221]Ibid., November 18, 1900.
[222]Ibid., September 6, 1899.
[223]Ibid.
[224]Ibid., October 22, 1899.
[225]Ibid.
[226]Ibid.
[227]Ibid., December 21, 1897.
[228]Ibid., October 19, 1897.
[229]Ibid., January 7, 1900.

CHAPTER 4
LEGEND

The Family Circle

Uppermost on Emily Warren Roebling's list of priorities were her husband, son and two grandsons, Siegfried, born in 1891, and Paul, born in 1893. For much of their married life, John Roebling II and his wife, Reta, lived a considerable distance from Trenton. Residing first in Oracle, Arizona, and then in Asheville, North Carolina, they remained in touch with John's parents through letters. Indeed, had John not decided to leave his position at the Mill, we would know scarcely anything about his mother. It is through her letters to him, which he carefully preserved, that one can ascertain not only the extent of Emily's involvement in the bridge project but the depth of her attachment to John, whom she sorely missed, and her boundless affection for Paul, who, as a toddler, lived with Emily and the Colonel while his mother was ill.

Something else that comes through in Emily's letters is her tendency to be overbearing, as, for example, when she informed John, in a letter accompanying money he requested to cover unexpected bills, "What you call grinding poverty, that is, having to think beforehand how to spend your money to the best advantage, I call simply good management."[1] When John complained about his meager allowance, Emily scolded him, saying, "The starvation fund allotted for your maintenance is the interest of all the money well invested which your grandfather left your father when he died except the interest in the Mill which you despise and never intend having anything to do with."[2] Although he had severed his ties with the family business, John could not cut the umbilical cord linking him with his mother. Indeed, that golden cord made of $1,000 bills was, to a certain extent, Emily's way of holding on to her only child. "You cannot be entirely independent of me if you are dependent upon me for all your needs," she reminded him.[3] "Your expenses are likely to increase each year; there certainly is but little chance of their decreasing – I feel that if you had an independent fortune you would drift entirely away from me and until you had spent all you had, we should be strangers to any common interest."[4] In reality, John was dependent upon his father as well as his mother. She, in turn, was dependent upon her husband, which led her to tell their son: "People like you and I who live on what someone chooses to give us, are always poor! I have tried to impress on you the fact that no one can be entirely independent of those they are entirely dependent upon."[5]

In the Roebling family, differences of opinion about money occurred frequently but they never seriously disrupted the fundamental harmony characterizing the relationship of Emily and Washington. Since the burden of keeping up the mansion fell on Emily, who paid all the bills from her investment income, there were times when she was overwhelmed by responsibility, but that was something she had gotten used to long before during the Brooklyn period. Although she bore her burden well, with the advancing years, the weight of it, though considerably lighter than previously, seemed to bear down upon her more heavily. At first she made light of it, telling John, for example, on her wedding anniversary: "Your father has been married 31 years today. I twice that time."[6] John immediately got the message and composed an amusing poem to mark the occasion. It positively delighted his mother and helped make her numerous and complex responsibilities a little easier to handle.[7] There were, however, many days when Emily wondered how much more she could take. As she advanced into late middle age and thought about the three decades she had been married to Washington Roebling, she did not necessarily have doubts about having married him. No, that was never the case, for the Roeblings had been passionately in love in their youth, but the thought that she may have married too young seems to have crossed her middle-aged mind.

Telling John about the recent marriage of someone he had known in Trenton, she remarked about the bride's tender years.[8] The woman was 21, the same age Emily was at the time of her wedding to the Colonel. In 1865, when she recited the marriage vows, that seemed to be the perfect age for a woman to wed. At 52, Emily thought otherwise, but it didn't really matter much because she was committed for a lifetime. In marking their 31st anniversary, Emily noted that she and the Colonel "feel we are rapidly approaching the golden wedding day."[9] With John and his family so far away, the Roeblings were compelled to focus more attention on each other and spend considerable time alone. Often this is good for a marriage but, in their case, the opposite seems to have been true. Total togetherness was fine during the Brooklyn years when they had a common objective but, once the bridge was completed and Washington Roebling began to recover from the effects of the bends, they fell into a pattern typical of many couples married for several decades.

What comes through very clearly in Emily's letters is that, after years of catering to the Colonel and listening to his almost daily complaints about his health, she became hardened. Now this in no way implies that the faithful wife who saw her husband through the many crises of the bridge years was totally indifferent to his complaints. That certainly was not the case. Neither of the Roeblings seems to have stopped loving the other for one minute but, to insure their individual survival, each had to establish different priorities over the years. For the Colonel, it was his health that became the overriding concern. For Emily, it was her husband and the great Roebling bridge during the early years and her involvement in various women's causes in the middle years. In a sense, the organizations she joined and the affiliations she had with other women constituted a safety valve. Without them, she would probably have been less able to render assistance to her husband, a man who always needed some help, or thought he did.

A careful review of Emily's letters to her son reveals that, despite the pronouncements of the doctors that he had largely recovered from the effects of caisson disease, Washington Roebling had numerous ailments. Some, like the fever, which was diagnosed as malaria, were quite real. Others, including the fairly regular attacks of indigestion that plagued him, may have been caused by nervousness. In contrast with the young Army officer who made light of danger during the Civil War, the mature Washington Roebling was an extremely apprehensive man. He always expected the worst and, if possible, tried to prepare for it. This attitude sometimes placed him in more danger than would otherwise have been the case. While traveling in the South in 1895, for example, he panicked when sparks from the locomotive set fire to the railroad car in which he and Emily were riding. According to Mrs. Roebling: "People acted very badly – the men as usual much worse than the women. I was afraid," she told John, "your father would try to jump off. He has a mania for jumping off electric cars, just because they do not stop at the exact point where he wants to get off."[10]

Fortunately, the Roeblings were rescued before the Colonel did anything rash, but the train incident clearly indicates his extreme nervousness. Having been confronted with the stark realization of his own mortality at a rather young age, when he was afflicted with the bends, he spent the rest of his life trying to keep the grim reaper away as long as possible. Thus, whenever he came down with the grippe, bronchitis or a severe attack of indigestion, with symptoms resembling those of a coronary, the Colonel thought the end was at hand. One would think that, by sheer force of will and the exercise of his considerable intellectual ability, he would have been able to overcome this tendency to suspect the worst immediately, but he could not. The intellect actually had very little to do with this.

When he was not feeling well, it was Washington Roebling's emotions, not his intellect, that dominated him and led him to dominate Emily. On numerous occasions she postponed or canceled trips to be at the side of her ailing husband. If he appeared to be in good health and she went away, with his blessing, more often than not she returned to find he had taken to his bed. Confronted by this all too familiar scene after returning from the wedding of a close friend's daughter where "I enjoyed myself very much and saw all my old Brooklyn friends," an exasperated Mrs. Roebling declared, "I am getting very, very weary, and feel like trying a new life."[11] A few days later, Emily told John: "Your father has taken one of his cantankerous spells again, and dies hourly but he still manages to eat and sleep like other people. To save Dr. Clark from going wild, I have sent for Dr. Weir to tell us there is nothing the matter."[12] Emily went on to recount how she and a family friend nearly came to blows over whether to send for still a third doctor. "I told him," Emily advised John, "I thought we had better try a first-class veterinary next."[13] Dr. Weir, who journeyed down from New York to examine the Colonel, ended up telling his patient that "there is absolutely nothing in the world the matter with him. That it is about time he tried to live like other people, and stop thinking about himself."[14]

Through all of the upsets relating to the Colonel's real and imagined illnesses, Emily remained devoted because, as she told her son, "If you take him as he is, there are enough good qualities in him to make a grand noble man, with many of nature's finest traits, and enough talents of doubtful value left over to make two or three ordinary bad men."[15]

Emily's Farewell

Ironically, although it was Washington Roebling who was always ailing, Emily predeceased him. She died following a protracted period of declining health characterized by general weakness and vision failure, the latter a problem of several years' duration. Several months before Emily's death, a distraught Washington Roebling wrote to his son, saying, "Your mother reports herself just the same – no improvement – nurse says she is better – whom shall I believe."[16] So concerned was Washington Roebling that he summoned Dr. Weir to have a look at Emily. The results were less than satisfactory. Unable to find any evidence of serious ulceration of the stomach, the consulting physician could not account for Mrs. Roebling's inability to tolerate food. "He suggests washing out of the stomach provided she can stand it which is doubtful," the Colonel told John. "In the meantime she is losing strength daily."[17] Emily was so weak that two people were required to hold her up while moving her from one bed to another. The same attendants made a practice of rubbing her arms and legs with olive oil. This alleviated some of the pain in her legs but she, nevertheless, remained weak.

Ever the realist, Emily rejected the platitudes of those who insisted she was getting better. No one could fool her. She sensed that she was growing weaker by the day. Yet despite her waning energy, Mrs. Roebling managed, in January 1903, to write a preface for *The Journal of the Reverend Silas Constant*, a book by a clergyman who lived in northern Westchester County, New York, in the late 18th century. For years Emily had labored to prepare the hand-written diary for publication. When the task was at last completed, she said of the minister's journal:

> It is a simple record of twenty years of patient toil in the service of the Master, and has a pathetic interest, quite apart from its value genealogically. The weary miles he rode in snow and heat ... sometimes so ill he could scarcely sit on his horse, and his gentle summing up of his own shortcomings, at the beginning of each year, bring his goodness and unselfishness so vividly before us.[18]

The same might be said of Emily Warren Roebling as she approached the end of her life. Like Silas Constant, who had been a help and source of consolation to his parishioners in northern Westchester, Emily had been a faithful helpmate of her husband. For him the realization that the end was coming was an unwelcome thought but one he had to accept. Already, in mid-December, Washington Roebling wrote to his son, saying, "After Christmas you must come up to see your mother once more."[19]

The fact that he underlined the word *once* clearly reveals that he entertained absolutely no hope for his wife's recovery. The Colonel's tendency to suspect the worst immediately notwithstanding, this time his fears, based upon Dr. Weir's frank diagnosis, were well founded. His ailing spouse was less inclined than her husband, however, to accept the inevitable. In February, she decided to go to Sharon Springs, New York, west of Albany, because she hoped the medicinal properties of the water at the old spa would extend her lease on life. Realizing the futility of this arduous journey, Washington Roebling told his son: "[Y]ou can take the contract of moving her. I certainly shall not. She gets an additional night nurse this week. No. 191 is now called the Roebling Hospital."[20]

Two weeks after the Colonel wrote these words, his wife died in the Trenton mansion he had ironically dubbed the Roebling Hospital. The family physician, Dr. William A. Clark, who for years had been at Emily's side during crises involving the Colonel, attempted to dispel rumors that Mrs. Roebling had died of internal cancer. His explanation for her demise was heart failure brought on by progressive muscular weakness. According to Dr. Clark, Mrs. Roebling succumbed because of overwork, which had exhausted her vitality. This condition, he explained, was widespread among individuals who "displayed unusual mental or physical activity."[21] In a lengthy obituary that described Emily as "a bright, witty conversationalist and a woman whose intellectual gifts were undeniable," *The Brooklyn Daily Eagle* concurred with Dr. Clark.[22] After pointing out that Emily "superintended the detail work, connected with the building of the bridge during her husband's illness," the paper went on to say: "The work done by Mrs. Roebling at this time was far too great for any woman and her health has never been the same since."[23]

The eye condition, which had developed several years earlier, was viewed as a forerunner of the muscular illness that led to her death. Washington Roebling attributed his wife's death to "progressive muscular atrophy" resulting from a seemingly small accident she was involved in while visiting Atlanta in 1900.[24] He was convinced that the motorcycle that struck her in the spine was the source of the problem.

No matter what the true origins of her decline were, Emily was compelled to remain at home for five months prior to her death. Throughout that time, her indomitable spirit gave her doctors a bit of fleeting hope that their diagnoses were incorrect. Indeed, it was not until the day before she actually died that the physicians gave up all hope of recovery. On the morning of Saturday, February 28, 1903, she lapsed into a coma and passed away at approximately five in the afternoon. With her at the time were her sister, Mrs. E.H. Hook, her husband, daughter-in-law, grandchildren and her beloved son John. Despite the physical and emotional distance that at times had separated them over the years, John told a reporter from Trenton's *Daily True American*, "Of all the compliments which have been paid my mother during her life, kindly insert a last tribute from me – she was a kind and loving mother."[25]

In the immediate aftermath of Emily's death, obituaries appeared in newspapers all over the United States and in Germany. The European edition of the *New York Herald* began its coverage by pointing out that Emily had been the first woman to cross the Brooklyn Bridge and that she had "assisted in its building." The *Herald Dispatch*, published in Utica, New York, proclaimed, "Mrs. Roebling Dead: Gained Prominence in Helping Husband Direct Building of Brooklyn Bridge" while Philadelphia's *North American* announced Emily's death by stating in the headline of the obituary that she was "Famous as One of the Builders of the Brooklyn Bridge." The Baltimore *Sun* credited Emily with "finishing the work after her husband became incapacitated." The Milwaukee *Journal* concurred, stating that Emily "became famous for the part she took in finishing the work." Elaborating, the paper made reference to Washington Roebling's illness, stating, "It was then that his brilliant wife sprang into prominence. She carried on the building of the bridge by communicating to the workmen on the bridge what her husband had planned in bed." According to the Buffalo *Express*: "She shared with her husband and her father-in-law the honor of having directed the construction of the Brooklyn Bridge." After referring to Washington Roebling's health, the paper went on to say: "His wife then assumed charge of the work under his direction." Chicago's *Record Herald* went a step farther with the headline it used for the obituary: "Mrs. Washington A. Roebling, Who Achieved Fame as a Civil Engineer."[26]

Interestingly, while the obituaries paid tribute to Emily for her role in the bridge project, they devoted considerably more space to her achievements as an active member of numerous women's organizations, popular lecturer, and law student. A careful reading of these articles, which are preserved, together with letters of condolence from around the world, in a large scrapbook kept by Emily's grandson Siegfried, indicates that Emily was well known in her own right because of her many activities and accomplishments. She was, according to the obituary published in the *North American*, "A Woman of Affairs."[27]

While the press was touting Emily's very busy life and her achievements in a number of different fields, Washington Roebling's thoughts at this time were as elusive as the man himself had been during the construction of the Brooklyn Bridge. About the only clue we have to his true sentiments was a notation in pencil included in an envelope bearing the words, "Undated Notes, Clippings, etc., found among W.A.R.'s Papers After His Death." In his own hand the Colonel copied what he believed to be Mark Twain's epitaph on his wife's tombstone. Although the poem was actually the epitaph on the tomb of Mark Twain's daughter, Washington Roebling apparently chose the following words because they expressed his innermost feelings about his own dear Emily:

Warm Summer Sun shine kindly here

Warm Summer Wind blow softly here

Green Sod above, lie light, lie light

Good night, Dear heart, good night, good night.[28]

Though he was prepared for his wife's death, her actual passing presumably shocked the Colonel and may help explain why an old friend of his wife's, rather than any of the Roeblings, selected the casket. While friends and neighbors filled the ground floor rooms of the West State Street mansion, the Roebling family listened to the funeral service from upstairs. They heard the Reverend Dr. John Dixon of the First Presbyterian Church, from his makeshift pulpit on the lower landing of the grand staircase with its stained glass window of the Brooklyn Bridge in the background, praise "the splendor of her genius."[29] Elaborating further, Dr. Dixon said, "Nature highly gifted her, and to a liberal education she added the charm of a winning manner."[30] His most significant comment was, "Through a most strange and sad misfortune an opportunity was given her to show the greatness of her genius as she aided in the accomplishment of the stupendous piece of work which is such a great credit to the great city nearby."[31]

It is not known whether Washington Roebling shed any tears as he listened to Dr. Dixon. Nor is there any way of telling how he reacted to his wife's request to be buried "immediately beside her mother," in Cold Spring, New York.[32] Whatever his thoughts were, he complied with Emily's wish.

As for Washington Roebling, his sister-in-law, Eliza Hook, recommended that he be buried, alone, in Trenton, "in a magnificent monument" provided for in her brother-in-law's will. Her real motivation for suggesting this is unclear, but the Colonel evidently took it as a compliment, telling John that "Aunty Hook didn't want him to be hidden and forgotten in a foreign land as it were."[33] Washington and Eliza saw eye to eye on a number of things including the realization that "death absolutely wipes out everything," but they seemed to have reached this conclusion in entirely different ways.[34]

Mrs. Hook arrived at it after discovering that the gate to the rural cemetery where her sister was buried was open, permitting cows, pigs and cattle to stroll about. The mere thought of animals trampling the grave of the remarkable Emily Warren Roebling affected Eliza so deeply that she "returned from the grave in a disconsolate frame of mind."[35] For Washington Roebling, the realization that death destroyed everything stemmed not from seeing the true condition of the cemetery where his wife was buried, but from a deep-seated belief. "The puny efforts of the individual compared with eternity," he told John, "are as nothing – we might as well never have lived – and why we do live no one knows."[36] One wonders how the Colonel could have written those words had he stopped but for a moment to realize that, had Emily Warren not lived and married Washington Roebling, the great bridge over the East River would not have been a Roebling bridge. But instead of reflecting upon his own and his wife's remarkable achievement, he spoke his mind with characteristic force.

The period following the loss of his wife was "a year of sorrow, trouble, turmoil, personal misery, and unhappiness," prompting Washington Roebling to write in German on the anniversary of her death:

Ne'er hast without a struggle
Thou gained in life the beauteous.
Must not the diamond's lustre
Be wrested from its cover?
And would'st thou twine a garland,
Each flower must be plucked.[37]

The poetry was not original. It was taken from F. Bodenstedt, but the sentiments contained in these lines echoed the Colonel's feelings as he stopped to contemplate the brilliant jewel that had been prematurely snatched from him. Though certain that there was life after Emily, Washington Roebling seriously questioned whether that life was worth living but, having had the benefit of nearly 40 years of his wife's guiding hand and spirited approach to life, he knew he could not give up. To do so would have been a betrayal of the woman who had devoted her mental, physical and emotional strength to making the Roebling name world famous. In life she had never, not even for one small moment, let him down. In death she deserved nothing less than the widower's firm resolve to preserve what she had built.[38]

The Roeblings Without Emily

Emily's passing necessitated readjustment and compromise on the part of the Roebling men. There were numerous financial details to be taken care of and, with John so far away, the bulk of this work fell to his father. The son, however, was the sole beneficiary of his mother's estate, which totaled more than $475,000. Under the terms of a will made in 1896, Emily left an impressive collection of jewelry, real estate and stocks in railroads, communications and sugar-refining companies to her only child to be equally divided between his two children following his death.[39] She gave John almost complete freedom to sell anything he deemed advisable to divest himself of, particularly real estate she owned in Brooklyn.

Accustomed to having his mother handle his finances, John was inclined to have the Trenton Trust Company collect his dividends and take charge of his affairs, but his father would not hear of it. The Colonel insisted that he learn to manage things himself "in a common-sense and businesslike manner – and without lawyers."[40] Moreover, he impressed upon his son, "It was your mother's special desire that these trust securities should remain in New Jersey under jurisdiction of a N.J. court where they cannot possibly be alienated or disposed of at some future time and whereby your own children are assured against actual want in their later days."[41]

With characteristic frugality, Washington Roebling managed to wind up his late wife's estate for legal fees totaling a mere $50. But he spent a hundred times that amount to endow a bed in Emily's memory at Roosevelt Hospital in Manhattan. The idea for this lasting tribute was not the Colonel's, but rather Dr. Weir's for, as Washington Roebling told his son, "Weir got me in a corner and before I could escape I had given $5,000."[42]

After Emily's estate had been settled, the Colonel decided to get his own affairs in order. He began by asking his only child what he would specifically like to inherit. John responded by saying that his father's books, papers, sword and family records were "the things I care most about."[43] He also requested the Colonel to do exactly the opposite of what Emily had done in her will, namely "in the clause bequeathing the property to the children, do not leave it simply to Siegfried and Paul by name, but let it read to the children of my son John A. Roebling."[44] The wisdom of this request was evident three years hence, in 1908, when a third son, Donald, was born.

The baby's arrival was not the only surprise the Roeblings had that year. In March, the Colonel wrote to John asking if he would be shocked "if I were to marry a 'Merry Widow' of 40."[45] He hastened to add, "She would not cost any more than Victor [his manservant] and be more companionable."[46] The relative costs of a manservant and wife aside, in planning to take Cornelia Witsell Farrow of Charleston, South Carolina, for his bride, the Colonel was determined to make sure that the charming woman he had met at a party given by mutual friends would not be a financial drain. He intended to have her sign antenuptial agreements but John dissuaded him. Although he had not yet met his father's fiancée, the young man was happy for the Colonel and advised in a letter written from his Palm Beach, Florida, vacation retreat: "You speak of prospective 'antenuptial agreements'! Why have any? A woman worthy to be your wife is entitled to all the rights of her high position; anything less would be unjust."[47]

The second Mrs. Washington Augustus Roebling was tall and thin, with shiny brown tresses.[48] An outgoing amiable woman, she had "a strong Southern accent," which was understandable in view of the fact that she was born in Walterboro, South Carolina.[49] Although she had a teenage son from her first marriage, the Colonel was careful to assure his own son that "I am fair and no wrong will come to you or yours."[50] In the same letter, he offered John all the photographs that were still on display in the Trenton mansion. "Her mobile face would never photograph well," Washington said of his first wife, adding, "The painted miniature on my table is mine, and stays there."[51]

Both bride and groom apparently knew exactly what they were getting into but they didn't know for how long the commitment would last. On that subject the Colonel reasoned, "A second marriage late in life cannot be judged by the standard of the first because its motives are usually quite different, and if it should not prove happy, death soon remedies all troubles."[52] Although Washington Roebling was in his 71st year, at 40 the bride was hardly "late in life." Indeed, she was practically the same age Emily had been when the Brooklyn Bridge was finished. Her youth was a decided advantage because, for the next 18 years, until the Colonel's death, she had to take charge of the house Emily had built and function as companion, nurse, confidante and mainstay of the man who came along with the mansion. All the while Washington Roebling complained about the high cost of keeping the West State Street house open. "This house should never have been built," he insisted.[53] "It only keeps me poor. Vanity costs more than any other folly."[54] Presumably he was referring to his first wife's vanity, which caused the mansion to be built, and Cornelia's vanity in presiding over the house and acting as a gracious hostess.[55]

Complain though he did about money, the Colonel took his new bride to New York, where they stayed at the Waldorf, traveled over the Brooklyn Bridge, attended a performance of the aptly titled play, *Spendthrift*, and otherwise tore around town shopping. "Cornelia is exhausted trying to keep up with me," declared the Colonel.[56] Her ability to keep pace with him improved somewhat after he bought her a brand-new "Peerless" automobile in which she traveled around Trenton and occasionally made trips elsewhere. Whenever her husband needed her, however, she was at his side.

This was especially important after the Colonel assumed the presidency of the John A. Roebling's Sons Company in 1921, following the death of his nephew, Karl G. Roebling, at the age of 48. Karl had been the chief executive officer of the firm.[57] Charles Roebling, the Colonel's younger brother, died in 1918, and Ferdinand passed away in 1917, three years after the death of his wife of 50 years.[58] Washington Roebling lived on until 1926, going regularly to the Mill on the trolley Emily had so despised from the day the tracks were laid in front of her mansion. Each morning when he boarded the trolley in front of his home, he was accompanied by his Airedale, Billy Sunday. Man and dog roamed around the Mill supervising such innovations as the conversion of the plant from steam to electricity.[59] The Colonel remined active until several months before his death, at the age of 89, on July 21, 1926.[60] With him when he died were Cornelia, his son and daughter-in-law, who nearly 20 years before had moved back to New Jersey from North Carolina, and his grandson Siegfried. Each of these individuals, plus grandson Donald and stepson John B. Farrow, was included in Washington Roebling's will, as were the Roebling servants, executives of the company, several Trenton hospitals and RPI. Grandson Paul had died of influenza in 1918.

Thanks to John, the Colonel's fabulous mineral collection soon found its way to the Smithsonian. John's gift to the museum was accompanied by an endowment of $150,000.[61] This act of generosity helped establish John Roebling's reputation as a philanthropist. Indeed, at the time of his death in 1952, he was better known as a philanthropist than as an engineer. An obituary in *The New York Times* explained that "a heart ailment in his youth prevented Mr. Roebling from participating fully in the engineering activities that made the name of John A. Roebling's Sons widely known in the steel wire and cable manufacturing and engineering fields."[62] Nevertheless, he lived to the ripe old age of 84, passing away at his Bernardsville, New Jersey, estate, Boulderwood, after an illness of four weeks.[63] His wife Reta died of a stroke in 1930.[64] The following year, John married Helen Price of New York; he was in his 60s at the time and the bride, who had been born in Shropshire, England, was in her 30s. The second Mrs. John Roebling outlived her husband by 17 years, about the same length of time Cornelia Farrow outlived Washington Roebling.[65]

The younger generation of Roeblings were not so long-lived. Emily's favorite grandson, Paul, died of influenza following a two-day illness in 1918, at the age of 25, leaving an estate of over half a million dollars.[66] His older brother, Siegfried, remained a bachelor until he was almost 40. Then he took as his bride a Matawan, New Jersey, woman, Mildred K. Kunath, who was in her early 20s.[67] The marriage ended in divorce several years later, whereupon Siegfried married Mary Gindhart of Moorestown, New Jersey.[68] When he died of a heart attack three years later on New Year's Day, while on the West Coast to attend the Rose Bowl, he was vice president of the John A. Roebling's Sons Company and a director of the Trenton Trust Company. He was 45 years old at the time. [69]

In 1959 Emily's third grandchild, the one she never knew, Donald Roebling, also passed away at a comparatively young age, 50, following a lengthy illness.[70] During his lifetime he gained fame as the inventor of an amphibious tank known as the Alligator, which was used by the Marines in World War II landing operations. Roebling created the prototype of the Alligator as a hurricane rescue vehicle in the machine shop on his estate in Clearwater, Florida, and tested the device in his swimming pool. More than a decade before the United States entered World War II, the vehicle was used in rescue operations on Lake Okeechobee during a hurricane. In the late 1930s Roebling's invention was featured in a piece in *Look* magazine. With the onset of the war the rescue vehicle's potential for landing Marines on beaches became evident because it could climb over barriers. Initially less than enthusiastic about the Roebling LVT (Landing Vehicle Tracked), the government warmed to the idea of a vehicle that could deposit men on a beach rather than having them swim or wade ashore while being strafed by enemy gunfire. During the war this amphibious tank was manufactured in Dunedin, Florida. Dunedin was also the home of an amphibious tractor detachment where training was provided in the use of what was by then widely known as the Alligator.

In recognition of the role played by Roebling's invention (which he turned over to the government without compensation) in saving lives during the war, President Harry Truman conferred the Medal of Merit on Donald Roebling in 1948. In the ensuing decades the Roebling LVT evolved with newer, speedier versions used in future conflicts but the World War II Alligator was not forgotten. In 2005 Stephen Spielberg used a working model on loan from the Armed Forces Museum in Alton, Florida, in *Flags of Our Fathers*, a film about the battle of Iwo Jima. Instead of being filmed in the Pacific, where the monthlong battle that claimed 30,000 American and Japanese lives took place, the film was made in Iceland, where the black sand beaches are similar to those on the island battleground. In 2015 another Roebling LVT manufactured during World War II was welcomed home to Dunedin. Following an intensive worldwide search, the Dunedin LVT Preservation Group purchased a vehicle from a Midwest collector. Accompanied by a sheriff's escort, the LVT was transported on a tractor trailer to its new home at Dunedin's Veterans of Foreign Wars post.[71]

Just as his amphibious tank continued to make news long after World War II, Donald Roebling's Clearwater estate attracted press coverage. The centerpiece of the estate was an Elizabethan Tudor mansion constructed between 1929 and 1935 in the Harbor Oaks enclave developed on bluffs affording views of Clearwater Harbor. In 1988 Harbor Oaks was listed on the National Register of Historic Places. The Roebling mansion, which had its own separate designation on the National Register, was compared with the Brooklyn Bridge for its sturdiness. Steel girders were used in its construction along with two-foot-thick concrete.[72] The floors were two- to four-foot-thick concrete. Donald Roebling, who, at 6 feet 2 inches tall and weighing 325 pounds, was a big man, evidently wanted something solid. He also wanted a beautiful home not unlike the Trenton mansion his grandmother had built. Donald's 17,000-square-foot home had 40 rooms, including 10 bedrooms, 12 bathrooms, an elevator and a tunnel connecting the house with the swimming pool. Other special features were a great hall with a sandstone fireplace and marble floors and a dining room chandelier measuring 6 feet in diameter. During World War II a wing of the house was occupied by Secret Service agents who provided security for Roebling.

Donald Roebling enjoyed the house until 1954, when he downsized to a 6,500-square-foot ranch house in Clearwater, where he was well known for his philanthropic generosity. Following his death in 1959, his third wife, Joy Gilmore Roebling, continued to live in the house until her death in 1977. The house was then sold and, in the years that followed, it had several different owners. This was also the case with the Harbor Oaks mansion. In 1995 the house was sold by its then owner, a co-founder of the Home Shopping Network, to a local couple. The new owners had an abiding interest in historic preservation as had Donald Roebling, as evidenced by the fact that, years earlier, he had brought the famous stained glass window of the Brooklyn Bridge, which had adorned the staircase of his grandparents' home, to Harbor Oaks.[73] The window met an unfortunate end when it was sent to an expert in stained glass for cleaning. The expert disassembled the window in the course of the work but died before reassembling the pieces, which were eventually discarded.[74] The Trenton mansion Emily Roebling had built was demolished in 1946 to make way for expanded parking facilities for the New Jersey Statehouse. Today, a plaza, the New Jersey State Library and the New Jersey State Museum occupy the site.

Although the magnificent window depicting the Roeblings' greatest triumph was spirited away from the house Emily had built and the house itself fell to the wrecking ball, the great bridge remained long after she died and long after her husband went to join her in Cold Spring in a tree-shaded grave marked by a large cross of Westerly granite with an epitaph referring to Emily as:

GIFTED

NOBLE

TRUE

This fitting inscription is not the only posthumous tribute to Emily Warren Roebling. Another is affixed to the east tower of the Brooklyn Bridge. It is a bronze plaque placed there by the Brooklyn Engineers Club on May 24, 1953, the 70th anniversary of the opening of the bridge.

The idea for this commemoration of Emily's role in the building of the bridge began percolating in the mid-1940s. In March 1946 George Currie, in his popular Brooklyn column in *The Brooklyn Daily Eagle*, observed: "Unsung by the many ecstatic troubadours of the Brooklyn Bridge … is Mrs. Emily Warren Roebling, devoted wife to the bosom of Col. Washington A. Roebling. She it was who 'booted' the bridge home to its opening on May 24, 1883."[75] Currie then went on to quote a letter from Theodore Belzner, a trustee of the Brooklyn Engineers Club. According to Belzner:

Mrs. Roebling, who had studied the mathematics of bridge building – stresses and strains, cable construction, specifications, etc. – visited the construction every day. She brought her husband's directions and reported back to him from out of her extraordinary intelligence. She became a bridge engineer the hard way.

Resurrecting the intriguing story of Emily's appearance before the American Society of Civil Engineers, Belzner continued:

She did better than that. In an era when a woman appearing before men to tell them what should be done was regarded as something almost unholy, she braved the American Society of Civil Engineers to argue her case. I need not say this was unprecedented, at the time. Her eloquent plea to let the project continue as was, according to the plan, won her a unanimous endorsement. And it occasioned the defeat of Seth Low's campaign to oust Colonel Roebling.[76]

A few months later Belzner, in a letter to the editor of *The Brooklyn Daily Eagle*, quoted Abram Hewitt's praise of Emily Roebling on the opening day of the Brooklyn Bridge and then added his own observation, stating: "In my judgment the Brooklyn Bridge is a memorial to Mrs. Emily Warren Roebling as to her husband, and his father John A. Roebling."[77]

Theodore Belzner wasn't the only one promoting the idea of a memorial to Emily. Brooklyn clergymen, civic organizations and Dr. David Steinman, author of *The Builders of the Bridge* and the consulting engineer overseeing the modernization of the bridge, and the Brooklyn Engineers Club all supported the idea. Toward the end of 1946 *The Brooklyn Daily Eagle* reported that the Brooklyn Engineers had begun a drive for a memorial to Emily Warren Roebling. This initiative was spearheaded by a committee composed of three trustees of the club and chaired by Belzner.

George Currie lent his support to the effort by urging Brooklyn Borough President John Cashmore to get on board. Reminding the borough president that "so many of your predecessors never thought of this," Currie went on to say:

But wouldn't it be smart to make up for their derelictions? And the ladies might not mind if you did something for Emily Roebling, the faithful little wife who, her husband upon a bed of pain, made herself into a bridge engineer and lived to become the first woman ever to read a paper before the American Society of Civil Engineers.[78]

In another column, Currie elaborated further on Emily's contribution, stating:

She worked on the great dream at a time when woman's place was most definitely in the home. It wasn't nice for perfect ladies to tell men what to do and I gather that she had her troubles and probably, a few cries, when she came home to sit at the side of her stricken husband ... to receive his orders for the next day. That she lived to be greeted with cheers as the first woman ever to address the American Society of Civil Engineers is eloquent testimony to her brave but wise defiance of the conventions and the talent she discovered she really had.[79]

Several years passed before the effort to memorialize Emily's role in the bridge project came to fruition and, during that time, Theodore Belzner, in a letter published in

The Brooklyn Daily Eagle, responded to a request for more information about Emily Roebling. He reiterated some of what he had said earlier about her mastery of various aspects of engineering, thereby "making herself a competent engineer."[80] Adding to his comments about Emily's appearance before the American Society of Civil Engineers, he asserted that she "obtained the unwavering support of the society" and that this "won the public's confidence."[81]

The efforts of the committee Belzner chaired culminated in the dedication of a tablet on May 24, 1953. In attendance at the dedication to hear Dr. David Steinman refer to Emily as "the devoted heroic woman who was one of the immortal Builders of the Bridge" were Emily's great-grandson Paul Roebling and John Roebling II's wife.[82] How pleased they must have been with the inscription on the bronze plaque, which reads:

The Builders of the Bridge

Dedicated to the Memory of

Emily Warren Roebling

1843 – 1903

whose faith and courage helped her stricken husband

Col. Washington A. Roebling, C.E.

1837 – 1926

complete the construction of this bridge

from the plans of his father

John A. Roebling, C.E.

1806 – 1869

who gave his life to the bridge

"BACK OF EVERY GREAT WORK WE CAN

FIND THE SELF-SACRIFICING DEVOTION

OF A WOMAN."[83]

The plaque was refurbished in 1983 to mark the centennial of the bridge. In anticipation of the span's 100th anniversary, film producer Ken Burns highlighted Emily's role in a 1982 documentary. Emily also figured prominently in the sound and light show that debuted at the Brooklyn Bridge on May 24, 1983. Viewing the show and the spectacular fireworks display that evening were members of the Roebling family who had gathered for a reunion at Brooklyn's River Café, adjacent to the bridge. Among those in attendance were Paul Roebling and his son, Kristian, at the time the only living direct descendants of Washington and Emily. "It's rather awesome," Kristian said of the occasion.[84]

Also in attendance was Mary Roebling, the widow of Emily and Washington Roebling's grandson Siegfried and mother of Paul. Mary had succeeded Siegfried as president of the Trenton Trust Company in 1937. She was 30 years of age at the time and was the first woman to hold such a position. She was also the first woman governor of the New York Stock Exchange and president and chair of the Women's Bank, N.A., of Denver, the first nationally chartered bank established by women. In 1984 Mary Roebling retired as chair of the National State Bank of Elizabeth, New Jersey. The institution had $1.2 billion in assets at that time and Mary was regarded as the country's leading female banker. She died in 1994 at age 89. Her son, Paul, an award-winning Broadway actor who also appeared in films and on television and had voice roles in Ken Burns' documentaries, predeceased his mother by a few months. He was 60 and had been predeceased by his wife, actress Olga Bellin, in 1987. They were survived by their son, Kristian, a derivatives trader, music producer and signed recording artist with Captured Tracks records.

In 2009 Kristian Roebling entered the political fray over a proposed 17-story apartment building less than 100 feet from the Brooklyn Bridge at its closest point. Although the building would not obstruct the view of the bridge from the apartment he shared with his wife and two children, Kristian was concerned about the structure's proximity to the bridge as well as its height. The project, initially called Dock Street, Dumbo, but renamed 60 Water Street, nevertheless proceeded despite legal challenges.

This wasn't the only controversial project in the vicinity of the bridge. Similar concerns were voiced about the last two apartment buildings proposed for Brooklyn Bridge Park, a popular waterfront oasis built on piers in the East River. Soon after plans for the towers were unveiled in 2014, the People for Green Space Foundation contended that the buildings planned for Pier 6 were unnecessary because other projects would yield sufficient revenue to maintain the park. Construction on one of those projects, Pierhouse, consisting of a hotel and condominiums, had been halted by an injunction that was lifted in June 2015 following a court ruling against the Save the Views Now group. This was vindication for the Brooklyn Bridge Park Corporation because, from its inception in 2002, the park was dependent upon revenues from residential and commercial development.[85]

In addition to recurring maintenance expenses, the Brooklyn Bridge Park Corporation incurred additional costs for rebuilding a pedestrian bridge linking Brooklyn Heights to Brooklyn Bridge Park. This structure was known as Squibb

Park Bridge for its starting point in a small park by that name in the section of Brooklyn Heights known as Columbia Heights, where Emily and Washington Roebling had lived during the construction of the Brooklyn Bridge. The pedestrian bridge was designed to bounce a wee bit but, when the movement became more pronounced, the $4.1 million structure was closed in August 2015. It had been open for a little more than two years. The Brooklyn Bridge Park Corporation sued the company that had designed the bridge and in 2016 engaged a new engineering firm to remedy the problems. One of the planned fixes involved the span's suspension cables. Given the cable issue the Roeblings had to deal with during the construction of the Brooklyn Bridge, one wonders what Emily would have thought of the plan to stabilize the little suspension bridge linking the parks or, for that matter, what her reaction would be to all of the changes along the 1.3 miles of the East River comprising Brooklyn Bridge Park. One would like to think that she would be delighted with the carousel, theater, marina and the Brooklyn Historical Society's museum, which opened in 2017 in Empire Stores, a 19th-century commodities warehouse. She undoubtedly would be pleased with the new entrance to the bridge from the Brooklyn side as well. In 2017 the City of New York moved ahead with plans to create a pedestrian- and cyclist-friendly portal flanked by trees and wildflowers. Above all, Emily would be gratified that, as it neared its 135th birthday, the bridge had become an iconic symbol and that she herself had garnered more recognition during the bridge's second century.

Endnotes

[1]EWR to JAR II, June 17, 1894.

[2]Ibid.

[3]Ibid.

[4]Ibid.

[5]Ibid., July 12, 1894.

[6]Ibid., January 18, 1896.

[7]Ibid., February 7, 1896.

[8]Ibid., December 29, 1896.

[9]Ibid., January 18, 1896.

[10]Ibid., October 31, 1895.

[11]Ibid., May 16, 1894.

[12]Ibid., May 20, 1894.

[13]Ibid.

[14]Ibid., May 24, 1894.

[15]Ibid., July 18, 1898.

[16]WAR to JAR II, December 9, 1902, WAR Letterbook, p. 609.

[17]Ibid., December 18, 1902, p. 610.

[18]Emily Warren Roebling, ed., *The Journal of the Reverend Silas Constant* (Philadelphia: J.B. Lippincott Company, 1903), p. vi.

[19]WAR to JAR II, December 18, 1902, WAR Letterbook, p. 610.

[20]Ibid., February 12, 1903, p. 612.

[21]*Eagle*, March 1, 1903, 5:2.

[22]Ibid.

[23]Ibid.

[24]Note on the back of EWR's letter to WAR, October 1902.

[25]*Daily True American*, March 2, 1903, 5:4. Obituaries: *Sun*, March 1, 1903, 4:5; *Herald*, March 1, 1903, II, 3:5; *Eagle*, March 1, 1903, 5:2; and *The New York Times*, March 1, 1903, 7:7.

[26]*New York Herald*, European edition, March 2, 1903; *Herald Dispatch*, Utica, New York, March 2, 1903; *North American*, Philadelphia, March 1, 1903; *Sun*, Baltimore, March 2, 1903; *Journal*, Milwaukee, March 2, 1903; *Express*, Buffalo, March 2,

1903; *Record Herald*, Chicago, March 2, 1903. Siegfried Roebling Scrapbook, Special Collections and University Archives, Alexander Library, Rutgers University, New Brunswick, New Jersey.

[27]*North American*, Philadelphia, March 1, 1903.

[28]WAR Letterbook, p. 613.

[29]*Weekly State Gazette*, March 5, 1903, 3:1.

[30]Ibid.

[31]Ibid.

[32]*Trenton Times*, March 2, 1903, 1:1.

[33]WAR to JAR II, May 30, 1903, WAR Letterbook, p. 618.

[34]Ibid.

[35]Ibid., pp. 618-19.

[36]Ibid.

[37]Letterbook notation, February 28, 1904, p. 645.

[38]At the time Emily died, *The Presbyterian* published an article titled, "One Woman's Self-Sacrifice," detailing her contributions. The piece begins with the following quotation: "She died, as many a woman has died, silently crowning the deed done by a man, and in her finer immortality can perhaps smile at being forgotten, since it is not by him." "Romance of Dollard," *The Presbyterian*, March 11, 1903, Vol. 73, No. 10, p. 1.

[39]Will of EWR, April 9, 1896, Superior Court of New Jersey, Trenton, Somerset County, Book I, Fol. 166. Some of Emily's jewelry went to her sister Mrs. Hook who, upon inheriting money later on, returned the jewelry, minus pieces valued at $20,000 lost in a burglary, to the Colonel. He, in turn, gave them to his daughter-in-law, as trustee, who was instructed to bestow Emily's diamond dog collar on the wife of the first grandson to marry. WAR to RMR, October 18, 1918.

[40]WAR to JAR II, June 16, 1903, WAR Letterbook, p. 619.

[41]Ibid., p. 620.

[42]Ibid., May 17, 1903.

[43]JAR II to WAR, August 19, 1905, WAR Letterbook, p. 673.

[44]Ibid.

[45]WAR to JAR II, March 7, 1908, WAR Letterbook, p. 690.

[46]Ibid.

[47]JAR II to WAR, March 10, 1908.

[48]The "simple and unostentatious" wedding ceremony took place at the estate of friends of the bride in the Berkshires. *Trenton Times*, April 21, 1908, 1:5.

[49]WAR to JAR II, March 21, 1908, WAR Letterbook, p. 693.

[50]Ibid.

[51]Ibid.

[52]Ibid., p. 692.

[53]Ibid., April 27, 1909, p. 698.

[54]Ibid.

[55]Hamilton Schuyler, *The Roeblings: A Century of Engineers, Bridge-Builders, and Industrialists* (Princeton, New Jersey: Princeton University Press, 1931), p. 270; WAR to JAR II, October 25, 1908, WAR Letterbook, p. 695. Writing to his daughter-in-law about Cornelia's quest for new servants, the Colonel said hid dog Billy Sunday was "almost mad trying to make friends with so many new cooks." WAR to RMR, October 14, 1918, WAR Letterbook, p. 804.

[56]WAR to JAR II, August 28, 1910, WAR Letterbook, p. 705.

[57]Karl Roebling obituary: *NYT*, May 30, 1921, 9:5.

[58]Charles Roebling obituary: *Trenton Evening Times*, October 15, 1918; Ferdinand Roebling obituary: *Trenton Evening Times*, March 16, 1917, 1:4.

[59]Schuyler, *The Roeblings*, p. 267.

[60]*NYT*, July 22, 1926, 19:1. Other Roebling obituaries: *Troy Daily Times*, July 22, 1926, 10:3; *Troy Record*, July 22, 1926, 22:6; and *Trenton Evening Times*, July 21, 1926, 1:6.

[61]*NYT*, January 3, 1927, 18:8.

[62]John was also a chemist. He put his master's degree in Chemistry to good use in the extensive laboratory on the grounds of his Bernardsville, New Jersey, estate. Another of his interests

was meteorology. He undertook research on long-range weather forecasting and its potential for increasing the world food supply. *The Bernardsville News*, February 27, 1952, 4:2.

[63]*NYT*, February 3, 1952, 85:1; other obituaries: *The Bernardsville News*, February 7, 1952, 4:2; and *Trenton Evening Times*, February 4, 1952, 4:3.

[64]*NYT*, October 13, 1930, 25:1; other obituaries: *Trenton Evening Times*, October 24, 1930, 3:1; *The Bernardsville News*, October 30, 1930, 1:3.

[65]Helen Price Roebling obituary: *NYT*, April 29, 1969, p. 45; and *The Bernardsville News*, May 1, 1969, 1:3; and Cornelia Roebling obituary: *NYT*, May 3, 1942, 53:2.

[66]Not long before his death, Paul was elected a trustee of the John A. Roebling's Sons Co., then a $40 million corporation. WAR to RMR, January 14, 1918. Roebling Company Correspondence, Rutgers University. Paul's obituary in *The Bernardsville News*, December 19, 1918, 5:2, noted that he was visiting his parents when he was stricken and that his home was in Asheville, North Carolina, where he had "extensive real estate interests." The article failed to mention his late grandmother but it did point out that Paul was the grandson of "Colonel Washington Roebling, who built the Brooklyn Bridge, regarded at the time of its construction as the greatest engineering feat America ever had seen." A death notice appeared in *The Trenton Times*, December 17, 1918, 3:1. Paul Roebling Will, June 23, 1917, Superior Court of New Jersey, Somerset County, Book V, p. 375.

[67]*NYT*, May 3, 1929, 25:1.

[68]*NYT*, August 5, 1933, 12:6.

[69]*NYT*, January 2, 1936, 20:5; *Trenton Evening Times*, January 2, 1936, 1:4.

[70]Donald Roebling's obituary appeared in *NYT*, Aug. 30, 1959, p. 82.

[71]Information about the amphibious tank appeared in the *Sarasota Herald-Tribune*, Aug. 17, 2006, p. B54.

[72]A description of the house appeared in the *St. Petersburg Times*, Dec. 1, 1995, North Pinellas Section, p. 1.

[73]*NYT*, June 16, 1936, p. 29.

[74]Conversation with Kristian Roebling, May 29, 2018.

[75]*The Brooklyn Daily Eagle*, March 13, 1946, p. 3.

[76]Ibid.

[77]Ibid., June 19, 1946, p. 10.

[78]Ibid., Jan. 2, 1947, p. 3.

[79]Ibid., Jan. 8, 1947, p. 3.

[80]Ibid., June 22, 1952, p. 19.

[81]Ibid.

[82]David B. Steinman, "Tribute to a Woman," reprint of speech, Clipping Files, Trenton Free Library.

[83]Account of ceremony in *The Bernardsville News*, June 4, 1953, Clipping Files, Bernardsville Library. Additional information about the plaque: *Trenton Sunday Times Advocate*, May 3, 1953, 1:1. Twenty years earlier, on the 50th anniversary of the bridge, *The New York Times* printed a letter to the editor from May Parker Eggleston detailing Emily's role in the bridge project and ending with the observation, "It would seem fitting that Mrs. Roebling's devotion and work be commemorated on this anniversary." *NYT*, May 23, 1933, 18:7. The bridge was included in the National Register of Historic Places in 1964.

[84]*NYT*, May 25, 1983, p. B4:1.

[85]The story of Brooklyn Bridge Park is recounted in Joanne Witty and Henrik Krogius, *Brooklyn Bridge Park: A Dying Waterfront Transformed* (New York: Fordham University Press Empire State Editions, 2016) and Nancy Webster and David Shirley, *A History of Brooklyn Bridge Park: How a Community Reclaimed and Transformed New York City's Waterfront* (New York: Columbia University Press, 2016).

CHAPTER 5
EWR SUPERSTAR

All-Around Renown:
The Centennial as Catalyst for Emily's Stardom

Like Hollywood elites whose career trajectories from obscurity to stardom began with their discovery, Emily Warren Roebling embarked upon the path leading to national and international recognition in earnest with the Centennial of the bridge in 1983, and the pace accelerated in the early 21st century.

Beginning with the 1983 centennial, she received numerous public accolades. A resolution of the New York State Assembly, introduced in 1983 by Assemblyman Daniel B. Walsh, majority leader, recognized her achievements, while Lenore Segan, arts consultant to Mr. Walsh, coordinated a visual exhibition titled "A Dedication to Emily Warren Roebling." This exhibition, which marked the 140th anniversary of Mrs. Roebling's birth, opened in Manhattan in September 1983.

A traveling exhibition on American women assembled

by the National Women's Hall of Fame also included Emily Warren Roebling. In 1983, the National Women's Hall of Fame and Citicorp jointly created an Emily award to be presented to a female recipient for outstanding accomplishments in the areas of business, science or technology. The Association of Business and Professional Women in Construction began making an annual Emily Roebling award in 1982, and the Society of Women Engineers featured Emily in its periodical, *U.S. Woman Engineer*, and provided interpretive and other support for the exhibition that the Smithsonian Institution created to honor the Brooklyn Bridge's centennial.

In a lighter vein, a musical titled *The Brooklyn Bridge* was produced in New York City late in 1983. Emily was the real star of the play. Her portrait, painted during the 1896 trip to Europe, was the star of a 1995 exhibition at the Brooklyn Museum. Called "Grand Reserves," the exhibit featured "hitherto unknown canvases" that had been relegated to storage.[1] Among them was Charles-Émile-Auguste Carolus-Duran's portrait of Emily "painted with tremendous verve" and portraying her "as a woman of intelligence and good humor, whose beauty radiates from her character (assisted by a fabulous yellow silk gown)."[2] The Carolus-Duran painting emerged again, along with a portrait of Washington Roebling, as part of a reinstallation of the Brooklyn Museum's American collection in 2016. In the meantime, Emily was again portrayed on the stage in a play called *The Chief Engineer*, which was performed in Bath, Maine, in 2007. In 2014 Emily figured prominently in a musical, *The Bridge*, at the Brooklyn Historical Society. That same year, the film industry was abuzz with excitement over the announcement that Daniel Radcliffe, star of the Harry Potter movies, would play Washington Roebling, alongside Brie Larson as Emily, in a film titled *The Brooklyn Bridge*.

A different sort of excitement was evident in 2018, the 135th anniversary of the opening of the Brooklyn Bridge. Emily was featured in a *New York Times* Women's History Month series on overlooked women. The series was conceived by *Times* gender editor Jessica Bennett, who wrote the lengthy article on Emily.[3]

Emily Warren Roebling Way:
The Street Sign Dedication

Two months later, as the result of New York City Councilman Stephen Levin's co-sponsorship of a bill to co-name the street where the Roeblings lived "Emily Warren Roebling Way," a ceremony was held on May 29. On this occasion, Councilman Levin noted that "Though her circumstances are unique, Emily fought to prove that talents and ability are not the exclusive domain of one gender. Her story, one of determination, ambition and intellect, is one we are fortunate to have. But there are countless other overlooked stories we will never know. The same way Emily fought for equality in the 19th century, we must continue to fight today. This commemoration is one symbolic step to show we will continue the work Emily Warren Roebling started."[4] In addition to Councilman Levin, the ceremony included remarks by other government officials as well as representatives of historical and civic organizations. Kristian Roebling, Emily's great-great grandson, summed up the importance of the co-naming, saying that it had added to "history recognizing her really profound contribution both to the building of the bridge and to the advancement of women in America in general."[5]

August and Chace, the two young sons of Kristian and Meg Roebling, pulled the cord revealing the new street sign honoring their great-great-great grandmother.

The Roebling Museum

In the early 21st century, Brooklyn wasn't the only place where Emily was garnering recognition. She was featured in an exhibit at the Roebling Museum, which opened in 2009 in Roebling, New Jersey, in the former main gatehouse of the John A. Roebling's Sons Company. A sprawling complex on the Delaware River employing 10,000 workers, the factory was 12 miles from the Roebling plant in Trenton, where 12,000 people were employed. Construction of a model industrial community in Roebling began in 1905 and a dozen years later a visitor noted the "hundreds of modern houses, clubhouses, churches, theaters, stores, etc."[6] And that wasn't all. According to the visitor:

> The men have their baseball team in the Delaware Valley League, football teams, basketball teams, athletic games, boat racing on the river and swimming and water sports. Everything is done for the comfort and happiness of the men and their families. … There are no saloons and can be none on the thousands of acres owned by the company. The town is unique and has been a great success from the start.[7]

A century later Roebling's historic charm was still evident. This, in itself, was a great achievement considering the challenges the community faced in the second half of the

20th century following the acquisition of John A. Roebling's Sons Co. by the Colorado Fuel and Iron Company in 1952 and the closing of the plant in the early 1980s. By then the factory grounds had been declared a Superfund toxic waste site. Remediation took years but was eventually completed and Roebling was listed on the National Register of Historic Places. The museum occupying the one structure remaining from the John A. Roebling's Sons Company became a focal point of the community. Besides featuring lectures, exhibits and special programs, including educational outreach initiatives designed to acquaint young people with opportunities in Science, Technology, Engineering and Mathematics (STEM) and Science, Technology, Engineering, Art and Mathematics (STEAM) fields, the museum collects and preserves documents and material cultural artifacts relating to the company, the community and the Roebling family.[8]

The Emily Warren Roebling School (P.S. 8): Ribbon Cutting and a Hip-Hop Tribute

In Brooklyn, STEM and STEAM were evident at P.S. 8. The school, as noted on its Web site, "is a learning community dedicated to creativity, academic excellence and intellectual curiosity, with the aim of developing life-long learning and engaged citizens."[9] In 2022, P.S. 8 was renamed for Emily Warren Roebling. Following a ribbon-cutting ceremony on May 24 to mark the day the bridge had been opened to the public in 1883, students walked to the Brooklyn tower of the span. Reminiscent of Emily's trip across the bridge carrying a symbol of victory, a live rooster, students at the head of the line made do with a toy rooster. The enthusiasm so evident among the students was echoed in "Once Upon a Bridge," a hip-hop story of Emily's life, created by P.S.8's Raising the Bar after-school club. With guidance from a faculty mentor, students learned about multiple aspects of production ranging from writing to recording and performing. The end result was a delightful original production honoring the new namesake of their school.[10]

Emily Warren Roebling Plaza

In comparison with the lightheartedness evident at the P.S. 8 renaming ceremony, the dedication of the final component of Brooklyn Bridge Park five months earlier had been a very different sort of event and not just because of the chilly weather. Despite the cold air, there was cause for celebration because the opening of a plaza fittingly named for Emily Warren Roebling completed the 1.3-mile park linking Jay Street north of the Manhattan Bridge with Atlantic Avenue to the south. The sizable plaza is a hardscaped area "designed with concrete pavers that echo the pattern and engineering of the Bridge above."[11] It also affords visitors a fabulous view of the bridge from beneath. Speaking at the dedication ceremony New York City Mayor Bill de Blasio stated: "The completion of Brooklyn Bridge Park with the addition of this iconic new space beneath the Brooklyn Bridge ... is a tremendous accomplishment for the borough (of Brooklyn) and the City. Just over 10 years ago, this was an abandoned waterfront, and today it's an 85-acre urban oasis enjoyed by millions of people."[12] Vicki Been, deputy mayor for housing and economic development, echoed the mayor's views on the significance of the completion of the park and then directed her attention to Emily, saying, "As we celebrate the final phase of Brooklyn Bridge Park, we honor the legacy of lead engineer Emily Warren Roebling, a New Yorker who made history as the woman who brought the construction of the Brooklyn Bridge to completion."[13]

City Parks Commissioner Gabrielle Fialkoff also praised Emily "for bringing the construction of the Brooklyn Bridge to the finish line" while State Senator Brian Kavanagh called her "a driving force behind the construction of the Brooklyn Bridge ... an astounding achievement in its time, that played a major role in uniting New York as one of the world's great cities."[14] Assemblymember Jo Anne Simon saw the plaza as "long-overdue homage to Emily Warren Roebling," who "was ahead of her time, a persistent woman whose vital role in building the iconic Brooklyn Bridge we enshrine with the beautiful Emily Warren Roebling Plaza. She was intelligent and savvy, an advocate for equal rights, and had an attitude for navigating New York politics!"[15] The remarks of the officials who spoke at the dedication provided some new insights, e.g., the use of the term lead engineer, but Kristian Roebling's brief observation that the opening of the plaza recognized "the groundbreaking efforts of my ancestor, Emily," really summed things up.[16]

Ahead of Her Time

Emily Warren Roebling Plaza is a fitting tribute to a remarkable woman and very timely given the efforts to diminish women in the first quarter of the 21st century. To push back on this, an estimated half a million women participated in the January 21, 2017, Women's March on Washington and millions more marched in other American cities and abroad to demonstrate their opposition to the administration of new U.S. President Donald Trump and to demand equality for women and other marginalized groups. Marches are one way for American women to demonstrate their opposition to government leaders as well as legislative and judicial actions that they perceive as threatening to women. So, too, is running for office and voting for candidates who support women's rights. Turning back the clock to the 19th century when Emily Warren Roebling was born just five years before the Seneca Falls Convention, a time when women lacked basic rights, is not an option today. In the 19th century, women persevered in their quest for the vote. It proved to be a long struggle that extended from the Seneca Falls meeting in 1848 to the ratification of the 19th Amendment to the U.S. Constitution in 1920. In the 20th century, women campaigned for an Equal Rights Amendment that eluded them because ratification by the requisite number of states fell short but today there is renewed interest in reviving the quest for such an amendment.

Emily did not live long enough to vote nor to support the Equal Rights Amendment but she would have supported it. Her prize-winning essay, "A Wife's Disabilities," which is discussed in Chapter 3, clearly states her position on the need for legislative reform to grant women rights they were denied. During her lifetime, middle- and upper-class women were constrained by the cult of domesticity, which deemed that women's sphere was the home while men's was the outside world. In Emily's case, this is rather ironic because she moved about freely, interacting with engineers in the field, contractors, members of the bridge board of trustees and politicians in her successful efforts to ensure that the Brooklyn Bridge would remain a Roebling project and that the family name would be long remembered. Although knowledge of the work she did to accomplish this was largely unknown in her lifetime, her importance was gradually recognized. Yet it took considerable time for a woman born nearly 200 years ago to become a heroine and inspiration for young women aspiring to careers in engineering and for anyone dealing with overwhelming challenges in the 21st century.

Just as the Brooklyn Bridge is recognized the world over as an iconic symbol of New York and America, Emily Warren Roebling, long beloved in Brooklyn and New Jersey, has achieved recognition nationally and internationally. Feted in song, children's books, articles and works on engineering, Emily has emerged as an important figure in American history. In recent years, publications have increasingly referred to her as an engineer but other terms are used as well. The Encyclopaedia Britannica categorizes her as a "socialite, and businesswoman" in that order.[17] The New-York Historical Society referred to her as an "engineer and activist."[18] Titles that appear in other sources include secretary, assistant to the chief engineer, assistant engineer, first female engineer, lead engineer, secret engineer, surrogate chief engineer, builder and constructor. Those who believe Emily should be called an engineer can argue that, in her day, opportunities for earning an engineering degree, even for men, were limited. The designers and builders of the Erie Canal lacked degrees but succeeded in creating a badly needed component of New York State's transportation infrastructure.

One might also argue that, if Emily were alive today and applied for admission to schools offering degrees in civil engineering, she could earn life experience credit. Regardless of whether this is an option at Rensselaer Polytechnic Institute, where Emily's husband and son earned their degrees, Emily was inducted into RPI's Alumni Hall of Fame in 1998. RPI listed Emily as a manager and stated that she was "among the first women leaders in the management of technology" and credits her with "a thorough grasp of the engineering" in her written and in-person interaction with contractors.[19] But was she an engineer or do some of the other terms used on the RPI site and elsewhere define her role more accurately? One response to this question was forthcoming in the fall of 2018 during the question-and-answer portion of a program featuring a lecture on Emily Warren Roebling at the headquarters of the New York State Power Authority. One of the more than 100 members of the Authority's Women in Power association raised the question of whether Emily should be accorded the title of engineer. At the urging of her fellow engineers in attendance, a straw vote was taken. The outcome was a resounding victory for Emily, whom the engineers regarded as one of their own.

Conferral of a posthumous honorary degree in civil engineering could resolve the issue of what to call Emily once and for all.[20] In the final analysis, however, when one views Emily's contribution to the Brooklyn Bridge project, it's important to remember that she built upon the foundation of her father-in-law and husband to ensure that the bridge would be completed and that the name Roebling would thereafter be linked with the majestic span. Emily took complete credit for this, telling her son 15 years after the bridge opened, "... but for me the Brooklyn Bridge would never have had the name of 'Roebling' in any way connected with it!"[21]

With the passage of time, both Emily and the bridge were accorded the recognition they deserved. The bridge was designated a National Historical Monument in 1964, 81 years after it was completed. Emily had to wait longer to be suitably recognized for her role in the project that culminated in the completion of what at the time was the world's longest single-span suspension bridge and the first suspension bridge to use steel wire cables. But by 2023, the 140th anniversary of the bridge's completion and the 180th anniversary of Emily's birth, she had emerged from the shadows of obscurity and become a recognized historical superstar.

Endnotes

[1]*NYT*, March 3, 1995, p. C11.

[2]Ibid.

[3]*NYT*, March 8, 2018; https://www.nytimes.com/interactive/2018/obituaries/overlooked-emily-warren-roebling.html; http://gothamist.com/2018/05/30/emily_roebling_way.php#-photo-1;http://womenatthecenter.nyhistory.org/emily-warren-roebling/; https://bklyner.com/brooklyn-heights-emily-warren-roebling/; https://www.brooklynpaper.com/stories/41/22/dtg-emily-roebling-way-co-naming-2018-06-01-bk.html.

[4]"Finally Emily Roebling Has a Street Named After Her," Gothamist,https://gothamist.com/arts-entertainment/finally-emily-roebling-https:/

[5]http://brooklynheightsblog.com/archives/86403

[6]*Eagle*, May 27, 1917, p. 17.

[7]Ibid.

[8]Roebling, New Jersey's, challenges and recovery are recounted in *The Philadelphia Inquirer*, Dec. 12, 2004, Section: Neighbors Gloucester, p. I07, and June 22, 2005, Section: South Jersey, p. B1. In 2015, elsewhere in New Jersey, the former Roebling Steel Factory complex in Trenton was slated for redevelopment as a mixed-use complex.

[9] : https://ps8brooklyn.org/

[10]https://www.youtube.com/watch?v=DVOu

[11]"A Plaza Under Brooklyn Bridge Honors the Woman Who Built It," *Brooklyn Daily Eagle*, Dec. 9, 2021.

[12]Ibid.

[13]Ibid.

[14]Ibid.

[15]Ibid.

[16]Ibid.

[17]https://www.britannica.com/biography/Emily-Warren-Roebling

[18]https://wams.nyhistory.org/industry-and-empire/labor-and-industry/emily-warren-roebling/

[19]https://www.rpi.edu/about/alumni/inductees/roebling1.html

[20]Emily's inclusion in the National Women's Hall of Fame and the Hall of Fame for Great Americans would be fitting as well.

[21]EWR to JARII, March 20, 1898. In her book, *Chief Engineer*, Erica Wagner states that Emily "was invaluable to her husband; whether it is fair to call her an engineer is another question." (Wagner, *Chief Engineer*, p. 205.) Following the publication of *Chief Engineer*, Wagner took issue with a reviewer's statement that Emily "was in charge of completing the great bridge." According to Wagner, evidence was lacking "to support the claim." (*NYT*, Aug. 27, 2017, Book Review, p. 6.) Referring to Emily during a podcast in 2020, Erica Wagner stated: "I don't think that the Brooklyn Bridge would be standing were it not for her. She was absolutely integral to its construction." "In Her Words: Equal Pay Day," *The New York Times* (online), March 31, 2020.

PHOTO GALLERY

The Warren house in Cold Spring as it looked in 2018. *Photo by Jeff Canning*

Young Emily Warren. *Courtesy of Rensselaer Polytechnic Institute Archives*

Washington Augustus Roebling at his Brooklyn home. *Courtesy of Paul Roebling*

Emily Warren Roebling. *Courtesy of Special Collections and University Archives, Rutgers University Libraries*

John A. Roebling II.
*Courtesy of Special
Collections and University Archives, Rutgers
University Libraries*

Paul Roebling, son of John
A. Roebling II. *Courtesy of
Special Collections and
University Archives, Rutgers
University Libraries*

The front of the Roebling Mansion in Trenton, viewed from West State Street. *Courtesy of Special Collections and University Archives, Rutgers University Libraries*

The rear of the mansion, viewed from the bank of the Delaware River. *Courtesy of Special Collections and University Archives, Rutgers University Libraries*

The famous Brooklyn Bridge window with the mistress of the house on the mansion's grand staircase. *Courtesy of Special Collections and University Archives, Rutgers University Libraries*

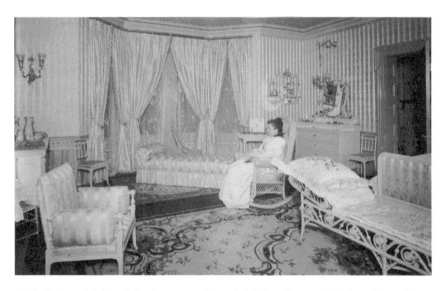

Emily in her pink boudoir. *Courtesy of Special Collections and University Archives, Rutgers University Libraries*

Emily in mid-life. Courtesy of Special Collections and University Archives, Rutgers University Libraries

The proud graduate of the Woman's Law Class. *Courtesy of the Collection of the New-York Historical Society, image 59518*

The graves of Emily and Washington Roebling in the Cold Spring Cemetery. *Photo by Jeff Canning*

The grounds of the Roebling Museum (background) in the former mill in Roebling, New Jersey, include equipment that was used in the manufacture of wire. Below, the entrance to the museum. *Photos by William Roger Clark*

Columbia Heights, the street where the Roeblings lived while the bridge was under construction, was co-named Emily Warren Roebling Way in an outdoor ceremony on May 29, 2018. *Photo by Jeff Canning*

Emily Warren Roebling seated in front row left at the annual convention of the American Society of Civil Engineers in 1888. *Courtesy of the Library of Congress*

George Frederick Kunz, vice president of Tiffany and Company, collaborated with Washington Roebling on mineralogical research and documented Emily Warren Roebling's presentation to the American Society of Civil Engineers. *Courtesy of the U.S. Geological Survey/Library of Congress.*

BIBLIOGRAPHY

Manuscript Sources

Both Rensselaer Polytechnic Institute and Rutgers University have sizable collections of Roebling material. Of special importance at RPI are Emily Roebling's two enormous scrapbooks of newspaper clippings covering the period from April 1876 to October 1882. Emily's unpublished biographical sketch of her husband, letterbooks and illustrations of the Roeblings and the Brooklyn Bridge are also included in the collection.

Although somewhat smaller than the RPI collection, the holdings at Rutgers University's Alexander Library are significant. In addition to Washington Roebling's correspondence, which includes letters written to Emily during the Civil War, Emily Roebling's voluminous correspondence with her son is found here. The collection also includes photographs of the Roeblings and their Trenton home.

The Brooklyn Historical Society in Brooklyn has a fine collection of notes, letters, engineering computations, reports, speeches and inventories pertaining to the building of the bridge plus the scrapbook of William C. Kingsley, letters of Henry Murphy and invitations to the opening day ceremonies and to the reception at the Roebling home.

The archives of Georgetown Visitation Convent in Washington, D.C., contain Emily Warren's academic and financial records.

Books and Periodicals

Albany Law Journal, The. March 8, 1899, and April 15, 1899.

Barnes, A.C. *The New York and Brooklyn Bridge* (pamphlet). Brooklyn: 1883.

Betancourt, Marian. *Heroes of New York Harbor: Tales From the City's Port.* Guilford, Connecticut: Globe Pequot, 2017.

Billington, David P. T*he Tower and the Bridge: The New Art of Structural Engineering.* Princeton, New Jersey: Princeton University Press, 2022. ebook. ISBN: 9780691236933069123693. OCLC: 1303082550.

Blair, Karen J. *The Clubwoman as Feminist: True Womanhood Redefined, 1868-1914.* New York: Holmes & Meier Publishers Inc., 1980.

Blake, William J. T*he History of Putnam County, New York.* New York: Baker and Charles Scribner's Sons, 1849.

Borden, Sandra L. "Obituaries and the Good Life." *Journal of Media Ethics,* Oct.-Dec. 2022, Vol. 37, Issue 4, pp. 252-265.

"The Bridge Builders' Triumph." *Munsey's* (1902), pp. 717-24.

Brooklyn Bridge 1883-1933. New York: Department of Plant and Structures, City of New York, 1933.

Brooklyn Bridge: Its History and Romance, The. Brooklyn: A.W.F. Leslie Publishing Co., 1883.

Brooklyn Museum, The. *The Great East River Bridge, 1883-1983.* New York: Abrams, 1983.

Burg, David F. *Chicago's White City of 1893.* Lexington, Kentucky: University Press of Kentucky, 1976.

Burks, Dennis. "Bridging over Troubled Waters: Components of Building over Safety Obstacles." *Professional Safety,* March 2021, Vol. 66, Issue 3, pp. 54-55.

Byrne, Edward. "Brooklyn Bridge: A Half Century of Service." *Civil Engineering* (June 1933), pp. 299-303.

Chronological Narrative of the Brooklyn Bridge. New York: Department of Public Works, City of New York, 1933.

Collingwood, Francis. "Progress of Work at the East River Bridge." *American Society of Civil Engineers Transactions*, IX (April 1880), pp. 170-72.

Conant, William C. "The Brooklyn Bridge." *Harper's New Monthly Magazine*, No. 396 (May 1883), pp. 925-46.

Conant, W.C., and Schuyler, Montgomery. *The Brooklyn Bridge: A History of the Bridge.* New York: Harper & Brothers, 1883.

Croly, Jennie C. *History of the Woman's Club Movement in America.* New York: H.G. Allen & Co., c.1898.

Daughters of the American Revolution. *Lineage Book.* Washington, D.C.: Daughters of the American Revolution, 1896.

Dim, Joan Marans, and Holzer, Harold. *New York's Golden Age of Bridges.* New York: Fordham University Press, 2022. eBook. ISBN: 9780823253081 0823253082. OCLC Number: 1302165819.

Dogancay, Burhan. *Bridge of Dreams: The Rebirth of the Brooklyn Bridge.* New York: Hudson Hills Press, 1999.

East River Bridge. Laws and Engineering Reports: 1868-1884. New York: New York Bridge Company, 1884.

Farrington, Edwin F. *Concise Description of the East River Bridge. Two Lectures at Cooper Union: 1880.* New York: C.D. Wynkoop, Printer, 1881.

Fernow, Berthold. *New York in the Revolution.* New Orleans: Polyanthos, 1976.

Flexner, Eleanor. *Century of Struggle.* New York: Atheneum Publishers, 1970.

Flynn, Katherine. "Human-Centered Design." *Architect*, Feb. 2020, Vol. 109, Issue 2, p. 49.

For the Better Protection of Their Rights. A History of the First Fifty Years of the Woman's Legal Education Society and the Woman's Law Class at New York University. New York: New York University Press, 1940.

Great East River Bridge, The, 1883-1983. New York: Brooklyn Museum, 1983.

Green, S.W. *A Complete History of the New York and Brooklyn Bridge.* New York: S.W. Green's Son, Publisher, 1883.

-------- *Complete History of the New York and Brooklyn Bridge: From Its Conception in 1866 to Its Completion in 1883.* (Classic reprint.) London: Forgotten Books, 2022.

Haw, Richard. *The Brooklyn Bridge: A Cultural History.* New Brunswick, New Jersey: Rutgers University Press, 2005.

-------- *Engineering America: The Life and Times of John A. Roebling.* New York: Oxford University Press, 2020. eBook. ISBN: 0190663928 9780190092870 0190092874 9780190663926 9780190663919 019066391X. OCLC Number: 1111637037.

Hayner, Rutherford. *Troy and Rensselaer County, New York: A History.* 3 vols. New York: Lewis Historical Publishing Company, 1905.

Hewitt, Abram. *Address Delivered by Abram S. Hewitt on the Occasion of the Opening of the New York and Brooklyn Bridge, May 24th, 1883.* New York: John Polhemus, Printer, 1883.

Hopkins, Jerry. "Brooklyn's Grand Old Bridge." *Coronet*, 49 (November 1960), pp. 197-98.

Howard, Henry W.B. *History of the City of Brooklyn.* Brooklyn: Daily Eagle, 1893.

Hyman, Stanley Edgar. "Profiles: This Alluring Roadway." *The New Yorker*, May 17, 1952, pp. 39-84.

"In Memoriam: Mrs. Emily Warren Roebling." *Georgetown Visitation Convent Annual Alumnae Bulletin* (1903), pp. 24-26.

Jordan, David M. *Happiness is Not My Companion: The Life of General G.K. Warren.* Bloomington, Indiana: Indiana University Press, 2001.

Lancaster, Clay. *Old Brooklyn Heights: New York's First Suburb.* New York: Dover Publications Inc., 1979.

Latimer, Margaret W., and Hindle, Brooke. *Bridge to the Future: A Centennial Celebration of the Brooklyn Bridge.* New York: New York Academy of Sciences, 1984.

Marks, Patricia. "What Builders These Mortals Be: Puck's View of the Brooklyn Bridge." *American Periodicals*, 2019, Vol. 29, Issue 1, pp. 43-62.

Matthews, Alva. "Emily W. Roebling, One of the Builders of the Bridge," *Women in Engineering: Pioneers and Trailblazers*, ed. Margaret E. Layne. Reston, Virginia: American Society of Civil Engineers, 2011.

Mayakovsky, Vladimir. *Brooklyn Bridge*. Toronto: Dromadaire, 1985.

McCullough, David. *The Great Bridge*. New York: Simon & Schuster, 1972.

-------- *The Great Bridge: The Epic Story of the Building of the Brooklyn Bridge*. 40th anniversary edition. New York: Simon and Schuster, 2012.

-------- "The Great Bridge and the American Imagination." *The New York Times Magazine*, March 27, 1983, p. 28.

-------- "The Roeblings: Their Great Bridge Fulfilled a Dream." *Smithsonian*, 20, No. 7, pp. 71-83.

Mensch, Barbara G., and Perrone, Fernanda. *In the Shadow of Genius: The Brooklyn Bridge and Its Creators*. New York: Fordham University Press, 2018.

Meredith, Virginia C.; Henrotin, Ellen M.; and Bates, Clary D. Soty. "Woman's Part at the World's Fair." *Review of Reviews*, 7 (1893), pp. 417-23.

Mumford, John Kimberly. *Outspinning the Spider: The Story of Wire and Wire Rope*. New York: Robert L. Stellson Co., 1921.

"One Woman's Self-Sacrifice." *The Presbyterian*, 73, No. 10 (1903), p. 1.

"Opening of Modernized Brooklyn Bridge." *The Municipal Engineers Journal*, Vol. 40 (1954), pp. 60-62.

Pelletreau, William S. *History of Putnam County, New York*. Philadelphia: W.W. Preston, 1886.

"Progress of the Great Suspension Bridge Between New York and Brooklyn." *Scientific American*, May 21, 1881, pp. 1, 322.

Rensselaer County Historical Society. *City of Troy 1816-1966*. Troy, New York: 1966.

Rhodes, Lynwood Mark. "How They Built the Brooklyn Bridge." *American Legion Magazine*, March 1970, pp. 16-19 & ff.

Richman, Jeffrey I., Haw, Richard, and Wagner, Erica. *Building the Brooklyn Bridge 1869-1883: An Illustrated History with Images in 3D*. New York: Bauer and Dean Publishers Inc., 2021.

Rodin, Richard. *The Brooklyn Bridge: The Official Illustrated History*. New York: Brooklyn Bridge Centennial Corp., 1983.

Roebling, Emily Warren. *Richard Warren of the Mayflower and Some of His Descendants*. Boston: David Clapp & Son, 1901.

--------, ed. *The Journal of the Reverend Silas Constant*. Philadelphia: J.B. Lippincott Company, 1903.

Roebling, Karl. *The Age of Individuality: America's Kinship with the Brooklyn Bridge*. Fern Park, Florida: Paragon Press, 1983.

Sayenga, Donald, ed. *Washington Roebling's Father: A Memoir of John A. Roebling*. Reston, Virginia: American Society of Civil Engineers, 2009.

Scelfo, Julie. *The Women Who Made New York*. New York: Seal Press, Hachette Book Group, 2019.

Schuyler, Hamilton. *The Roeblings: A Century of Engineers, Bridge-Builders, and Industrialists*. Princeton, New Jersey: Princeton University Press, 1931.

Schuyler, Montgomery. "The Bridge as Monument." *Harper's Weekly* (May 27, 1883).

-------- (1843-1914). *American Architecture: Studies*. eBook Project. Gutenberg, 2019. OCLC Number: 1339570076.

Shapiro, Mary. *A Picture History of the Brooklyn Bridge*. New York: Dover, 1983.

Smith, Diane Monroe. *Washington Roebling's Civil War: From the Bloody Battlefield at Gettysburg to the Brooklyn Bridge*. Guilford, Connecticut: Stackpole Books, 2019.

Society of Old Brooklynites. Dedication, Washington A. Roebling Memorial Program, May 24, 1983.

Steinman, David B. *Builders of the Bridge: The Story of John Roebling and His Son*. New York: Harcourt, Brace, Jovanovich, 1945.

-------- "Engineers Pay Tribute to the Woman Who Helped Build the Brooklyn Bridge." *Transit*, Chi Epsilon, 1954, pp. 24-29.

Sullivan, Eleanore C. *Georgetown Visitation Since 1799*. Baltimore: French-Bray Printing Company, 1975.

Taylor, Emerson Gifford. *Gouverneur Kemble Warren: The Life and Letters of an American Soldier 1830-1882*. Boston: Houghton Mifflin Company, 1932.

Trachtenberg, Alan. *Brooklyn Bridge: Fact and Symbol*. Chicago: The University of Chicago Press, 1965.

Truman, Benjamin. *History of the World's Fair. Being a Complete and Authentic Description of the Columbian Exposition from its Inception*. Philadelphia: H.W. Kelley, 1893.

Tucker, Stephen C. *The Encyclopedia of the Spanish-American and Philippine-American Wars: A Political, Social and Military History.* Vol. 1. Santa Barbara, California: ABC-Clio, 2009.

"Up Among the Spiders or How the Great Bridge is Built." *Appleton's Journal*, January 1878.

Upton, Dell. *American Architecture: A Thematic History.* New York: Oxford University Press, 2020.

Veglahn, Nancy. *The Spider of Brooklyn Heights.* New York: Charles Scribner's Sons, 1967.

Wagner, Erica. *Chief Engineer: Washington Roebling: The Man Who Built the Brooklyn Bridge.* New York: Bloomsbury Publishing, 2017.

Walworth, Ellen Hardin. *Report on the Women's National War Relief Association Organized for the Emergency of the Spanish-American War, March 1898 to January 1899.* New York: Women's National War Relief Association, 1899.

Webster, Nancy, and Shirley, David. *A History of Brooklyn Bridge Park: How a Community Reclaimed and Transformed New York City's Waterfront.* ebook. ISBN: 97802315429440231542941. OCLC Number: 1076398356.

Weigold, Marilyn E. "Building Brooklyn's Bridge: The Newport Scenario." *Newport History: Bulletin of the Newport Historical Society*, Vol. 58, No. 3 (September 1983), 86-95.

--------- "Emily Warren Roebling." *American National Biography Online* (April 2014)

Weise, A.J. *City of Troy, New York and its Vicinity.* Troy, New York: E. Green, 1886.

Whitehead, Colson. *The Colossus of New York.* New York: Doubleday, 2003.

Wiedeman, John H. *Why We Need Our Brooklyn Bridges.* New York: Newcomen Society of the U.S., 1983.

Witty, Joanne, and Krogius, Henrik. *Brooklyn Bridge Park: A Dying Waterfront Transformed.* New York: Fordham University Press, 2022. ebook. ISBN: 9780823273584082327358X. OCLC Number: 1302164049.

Women's National War Relief Association. *Report.* New York: Board of Directors, WNWRA, 1899.

Yardley, Margaret Tufts. *The New Jersey Scrapbook of Women Writers.* Vol. II. Newark, New Jersey: Advertiser Printing House, 1893.

Zheng, Lai; Sayed, Tarek; and Guo, Yanyong. "Investigating Factors that Influence Pedestrian and Cyclist Violations on Shared Use Path: An Observational Study on the Brooklyn Bridge Promenade." *International Journal of Sustainable Transportation*, 2020, Vol. 14, Issue 7, pp 503-512.

Zink, Clifford W. *The Roebling Legacy.* Princeton, New Jersey: Landmark Publications, 2011, pp 503-512.

Newspapers

The following newspapers yielded information about Emily Warren Roebling:

Asheville Citizen
The Bernardsville News
The Brooklyn Daily Eagle
The Brooklyn Union and Argus
The Commercial Advertiser
Daily True American
Engineering News
The Evening Post
The London Times
Los Angeles Herald
The Newport Daily News
The New York Daily Graphic
The New York Herald
The New York Illustrated Times
The New York Star
The New York Times
The New York Tribune
The New York World

The Sun
The Trenton Evening Times
The Trenton Sunday Advertiser
The Trenton Sunday Times Advocate
The Trenton Times
Troy Daily Times
The Troy Record
Union
Weekly State Gazette (Trenton)

INDEX

Albany, New York   178-9,196
Albany Law Journal, The   196
Alexandra (tsarina of Russia)   159, 162
Alger, Senator R.A.   177
American Association of Engineering Societies   225
American Society of Civil Engineers   12, 93-96, 238-240
American Scenic and Historic Preservation Society   94
Anthony, Susan B.   177
Antiquarian Society (Worcester, Massachusetts)   24
Arizona   139, 159, 176, 215
Arthur, Chester A.   89, 100, 104
Asheville, North Carolina   215, 247
Aspinwall, Lloyd   72
Atlanta, Georgia   223

Barnum, P.T.   111
Barret, John   25
Barrows, Cornelia   42
Battle of Five Forks   87
Been, Vicky
Belzner, Theodore   237-239
Berlin, Germany   56
Bernardsville, New Jersey   202, 233, 248
Billy Sunday (Washington Roebling's dog)   232, 246
Blackstone's Commentaries   198
Blake, William J.   25, 88

Block Island, Rhode Island 84
Bodenstedt, F. 228
Boston, Massachusetts 24
Boulderwood (estate of John A. Roebling II, Bernardsville, New Jersey) 233
Breakneck Mountain (Cold Spring, New York) 24
Brooklyn 8, 15-7, 20, 23, 43, 48, 53-6, 60-1, 63, 66, 68, 74-7, 79, 81-4, 86, 88-90, 94, 99-100, 104, 106, 111-2, 115-7, 119, 146, 166, 182, 206, 217-8, 229, 243, 252-4, 257
Brooklyn Boys' Preparatory School 75
Brooklyn Bridge
    anniversaries 11, 15, 237, 241, 251, 140
    caissons 33-5
    delays 79, 87
    first drive across 19
    iconic symbol 243
    May 31, 1883, tragedy 108-11
    movie 251
    musical 250
    naming 118-9
    opening day 97-107
    painting 148
    plaque 240-1
    safety issues 82, 96
    September 11, 2001 16
    Smithsonian Institution exhibition 250
    Theodore Roosevelt 178
    towers 16, 71, 75, 76
    window 141, 226, 236
Brooklyn Bridge Park 242-3
Brooklyn City Hall 109
Brooklyn Daily Eagle, The 7, 18, 79, 145, 174, 223, 237-8, 240
Brooklyn Engineers Club 237-8
Brooklyn Heights 11, 81, 93, 103, 242-3,

Brooklyn Historical Society 8, 243, 250
Brooklyn Museum 250
Brooklyn Music Hall 73-4
Brown Palace Hotel (Denver, Colorado) 175
Browning, Elizabeth Barrett 42
Buck, L.L. 115-6
Burns, Ken 241

Camp Wikoff (Montauk, Long Island, New York)183, 185-7
Carolus-Duran, Charles-Émile-Auguste 250
Centennial Exposition (Philadelphia, Pennsylvania) 161
Charleston, South Carolina 230
Chicago, Illinois 159, 169, 225
Cincinnati, Ohio 20, 35-6, 43, 175
Cincinnati-Covington Bridge 20, 43, 60
Citicorp 250
Civil War 23, 29, 43, 54, 60, 67, 87, 187, 219
Clark, William A., M.D. 219, 223
Clearwater, Florida 234-6
Cleveland, Grover 100, 128
Cold Spring, New York 4, 8, 11, 17, 23-4, 26, 29, 30,
 35-8, 41-2, 83, 144, 226, 237, 263, 272,
Collegiate School, New York City 75
Collingwood, Francis Jr. 78
Colonial Dames 182, 199
Columbia Heights (Brooklyn) 68, 97, 99, 106,
 147, 243, 274
Columbian Exposition 168
Constant, Rev. Silas 221-2
Cooper, Peter 54
Cooper Union 73-4
Covington, Kentucky 20, 43
Croker, Frank 156-7
Croker, Richard 156
Cuba 184
Currie, George 237, 239

Daily True American (Trenton, New Jersey)   224
Daughters of the American Revolution   179
de Blasio, Bill   254
de Lesseps, Ferdinand   77-8,
de Maitre, Claude   24
Delamater, Claude   24
Delaware River   38, 140, 142, 252, 268
Denver, Colorado   175, 211, 241
Dixon, Rev. Dr. John   226
Dublin, Ireland   47

East Hampton, Long Island, New York   186
East River   15, 23, 43, 48, 53-5, 64, 68, 71, 81, 98, 106,
    113, 115, 166, 193, 227, 242-3,
East River Bridge   20, 54, 58, 74, 77, 99, 119, 121, 157,
Eden Museum (France)   165
Edge Moor Iron Company   76-7, 83
Edison, Thomas Alva   97
Edson, Franklin   100
Elizabeth, New Jersey   241
Emily Warren Roebling Plaza   11, 254-5
Emily Warren Roebling School (P.S. 8)   253
Emily Warren Roebling Way   11, 251, 274
Essen, Germany   44
Evelyn College (Princeton, New Jersey)   177-8

Farrington, Edwin   73
Farrow, Cornelia   230, 233
Farrow, John B.   232
Federation of Women's Clubs   172-4, 178
Fialkoff, Gabrielle   255
First Presbyterian Church (Trenton, New Jersey)   226
First Regiment, U.S. Volunteer Engineers   183
Francis, W.H.   76
Fulton ferry   56, 64

George Washington Bridge 166
George Washington Memorial Association 150, 181-2
Georgetown Visitation Convent (Washington, D.C.) 27-8
Gindhart, Mary 233
Grace, William R. 81-2, 88
Grand Union Hotel (Saratoga Springs, New York) 142
Grant, Ulysses 32
Greeley, Horace 54
Gypsum City, Kansas 175

Hanna, Mark 200
Harper's Bazaar 188
Hegel, G.W.F. 56
Herald, The (New York City) 79, 90, 113, 193, 224
Hewitt, Abram S. 9, 54, 100-2, 201, 238
Hicks Street (Brooklyn residence of Emily and Washington
   Roebling) 56-7, 62, 64, 66-7
Hildenbrand, Wilhelm 114, 117-8
Home for Consumptives (Brooklyn) 206
Hook, Eliza Warren 224, 227, 245
Howell, James 81
Hudson House River Inn (Cold Spring, New York) 23
Hudson River 23, 113, 137, 166
Hudson Valley 41
Hunt, Annie Belleville 139
Hunter, William J. 88

International Council of Women 176
Isherwood, B.F. 139

John A. Roebling's Sons Company 73, 77, 115, 118, 154,
   168, 183, 232, 234, 252-3,
John A. Roebling's Sons Construction Company, 155, 157
Journal of the Reverend Silas Constant, The 221

Kansas 175

Kansas City   175
Kavanagh, Brian   255
Kempin, Emily   189
Kingsley, William C.   55, 120, 133-4
Kremlin   163-4
Krupp Works (Essen, Germany)   44
Kunath, Mildred   233
Kunz, George Frederick   8, 93-6, 276

Lake Sunapee, New Hampshire   182
Le Havre, France   165
Lee, Robert E.   33
Levin, Stephen   251
Lickley, John   25
Lickley, William   25
Lindabury, R.V.   155
Littlejohn, A.N.   100
London, England   158-9
Long Island, New York   18, 53-4, 100, 183, 185
Los Angeles Herald   112
Low, Seth   83, 85-7, 92, 100, 106, 112
Ludington, Henry   25

MacCracken, Henry M.   189
Magna Carta   198
Manchester, Massachusetts   172
Manhattan   4, 16, 20, 48, 54, 71, 73, 93, 98, 111,
                        115, 117, 166, 170, 229, 249,
Manhattan Bridge   166, 254
Manhattan Eye and Ear Hospital   63
Mann, William d'Alton   200
Marshall, William   91
Martin, C.C.   57, 88, 110-1, 114-5, 117
Matawan, New Jersey   253
Mayflower   24
Mayflower Compact   24

McClure's Magazine	188
McCullough, David	120, 129, 132
McIlvaine, Edward Shippen	139,
McIlvaine, Joshua Hall	139, 177
McIlvaine, Margaret Shippen (Reta)	139, 148-9, 215, 233
McKim, Mead and White	193
McKinley, William	175, 187
Middleborough, Massachusetts	24
Mill, The (Roebling family business)	70, 134, 137, 139, 153, 155, 167, 215-6
Milwaukee, Wisconsin	96, 178
Mineralogical Society of America	95
Montauk Point, Long Island, New York	185
Moorestown, New Jersey	233
Moscow, Russia	110, 161-2, 165
Mühlhausen, Thüringen, Germany	45-6, 60
Murphy, Henry C.	54-5, 67, 72, 73, 80, 83, 85, 147
Music Hall (Troy, New York)	139
Narragansett Bay, Rhode Island	84
Narragansett Pier, Rhode Island	198
Nashville, Tennessee	175
National Committee of the Republican Party	200
National Museum (Le Havre, France)	165
National State Bank (Elizabeth, New Jersey)	241
National Women's Hall of Fame (Seneca Falls, New York)	250
New Haven, Connecticut	198
New Jersey Board of Lady Managers for the Columbian Exposition	168
New Jersey Society of Colonial Dames of America	199
New Jersey State Federation of Women's Clubs	172
New Jersey State Library	237
New Jersey State Museum	237
New Jersey Statehouse	236
New York Bridge Company	54, 63, 67

New York City   3, 11, 15, 87, 94, 114, 156, 170, 172,
                                                200, 250-1, 254,
New York Star, The   81
New York State Federation of Women's Clubs   178
New York State Power Authority   258
New York Times, The   65, 69, 77, 93, 96, 108, 170, 171,
                                                     187, 233
New York Tribune, The   54
New York University (NYU)   189, 192-3,197, 201
New York University School of Law   189
New York University's Woman's Law Class   189, 190,
                                              192-3, 197-9
Newport, Rhode Island   83-6, 89, 90, 92,
Newport Daily News, The (Newport, Rhode Island)   89
Niagara Bridge   138
Nicholas II (tsar of Russia)   110, 159, 162

Ohio River   35
Old Cemetery at Van Cortlandtville
        (near Peekskill, New York)   25
Oliphant, Richard   141
Oracle, Arizona   215

Pacific House (Cold Spring, New York)   23
Pagden, Alfred   167
Palm Beach, Florida   230
Palmer, Mrs. Potter   159
Panama Canal   77
Panic of 1893   154
Paris, France   44, 159, 167
Peekskill, New York   25, 95
Petersburg, Virginia   32
Philadelphia, Pennsylvania   75, 158, 161, 224,
Philipstown, New York   26
Pittsburgh, Pennsylvania   55
Plymouth, Massachusetts   24

Pocantico Hills (Westchester County, New York)   198
Ponto (the Roeblings' dog)   141-2
Price, Helen   233
Princeton, New Jersey   177
Princeton University   177

Quarry Alley (Trenton, New Jersey)   171
Queen Victoria   159, 164, 177
Once Upon a Bridge   254

Raymond, Rossiter W.   78
Raymond, Mrs. Rossiter W.   99
Red Cross   187
Reidel, Edward   39
Rensselaer Polytechnic Institute (RPI; Troy, New York)   28,
                              30, 41, 78, 119, 137, 258
Revolutionary War   25
Richfield Springs, New York   66
River Café (Brooklyn)   241
Rockefeller, John D. Sr.   198
Roebling, August   46
Roebling, Chace   252
Roebling, Charles   141, 143, 153, 155-6, 232
Roebling, Cornelia Farrow   233-2, 253
Roebling, Donald   230, 232, 234-6
Roebling, Edmund   38
Roebling, Elvira,   29, 45
Roebling, Emily Warren
    abhorrence of Seth Low   86-7
    ancestors   13, 24
    assertion concerning her role in bridge project   65,
                                       129, 225, 241
    assistant to her husband   58, 64-5, 111, 119, 169
    attitudes on race   179, 191
    author   195-6
    birth   23

birth of son 45, 47
bridge party 99
builds Trenton mansion 236
burial 227
business acumen 250, 257
childhood in Cold Spring, New York 23-4, 16
complimented on engineering skill 78, 180
courtship 28-48
death 194-5, 221
education 27, 31, 26
European trips 44, 60, 68, 158-167
first drive across the bridge 19
funeral 226
health 24, 27, 145, 179, 181, 221, 223
interviews 20, 91, 146
lecturer 74, 182, 225, 253
legal studies 189-201
lifelong involvement with the
    Brooklyn Bridge 107-120
Mill 137
opposition to husband's involvement in Williamsburg
    and Manhattan bridge projects 116
participation in the Columbian Exposition 168
plaque 237
portrait 250
praise of 9, 99, 100, 226, 238, 255
reaction to proposal to rename the
    Brooklyn Bridge 118
reception following bridge dedication 97-99
relationship with brother 25-6, 153
relationship with son 99, 140, 165, 173
role in women's and patriotic
    organizations 168-189
social and cultural life of 137, 144, 158
Spanish-American War activities 183-8
STEAM camp 253

steel and iron work for Brooklyn Bridge 70
trolley 148, 152
visit to Senator Murphy 67
walk across the bridge (December 12, 1881) 80-81
wedding 40-2, 217
Roebling, Ferdinand 38, 152, 156, 232
Roebling, Johanna 39
Roebling, John A. 16-7, 25, 28, 35-7, 39, 42-3, 47, 53-5, 57-8, 60-1, 64,
Roebling, John A. II
baptism 45-6
chemistry laboratory 202, 246
childhood 75
death of mother 221
Hudson (North) River bridge 166
marriages 139, 215, 217, 233
meteorology 247
Mill 153, 215-6
philanthropist 233
Rensselaer Polytechnic Institute student 137-8
volunteers for Spanish-American War 183
Roebling, Josephine 38
Roebling, Joy Gilmore 236
Roebling, Karl G. 232
Roebling, Kristian 241-2, 251-2, 255
Roebling, Laura 38
Roebling, Lucia Cooper 46
Roebling, Marjorie 153
Roebling, Mary 241
Roebling, Meg 252
Roebling, New Jersey 233, 236
Roebling, Paul (1893-1918) 166, 181, 215, 230, 232-3
Roebling, Paul (1934-1994) 240-1
Roebling, Siegfried 215, 225, 230, 232-3, 241
Roebling, Washington A.
absence from Brooklyn Bridge 68

appointed Chief Engineer 55
attempt to remove him from position of
    Chief Engineer 83, 88
botany 148
burial 227
Civil War service in Union Army 29, 43
concerned about bridge safety 96
contributions to design of the Brooklyn Bridge 59, 107
courtship 28-48
death 232
health 20, 60-2, 68, 70, 72, 116-7, 119, 137
interest in Hudson (North) River bridge project 166
interviews 69, 91, 146
involvement in Williamsburg and Manhattan bridge
projects 114-5, 166
marriages 18, 230-1,
mineral collection 95-6, 149, 233
opinion of wife's legal studies 156
opposition to appointment of consulting engineer 72-3
pet snake 149-151
plaque 240
portrait 250
reaction to Emily's club activities 147
resignation as Chief Engineer 111-2
role in family business 137-8, 215, 232
trolley 232
views on women's suffrage 180
Roebling Museum 9, 252-3, 273
Roosevelt, Robert 83
Roosevelt, Theodore 178, 184-5
Roosevelt Hospital (New York City) 229
Royal Polytechnic Institute (Berlin, Germany) 56
Russell, Isaac Franklin 190-2, 196-8
Russia 110, 159, 161-2, 164-5, 182

San Francisco, California 135, 191

Saratoga, New York 66, 142
Saratoga Springs, New York 142
Schuyler, Hamilton 129-130
Scituate, Massachusetts 24
Segan, Lenore 249
Semler, Ludwig 88, 90, 92
Sharon Springs, New York 222
Sheridan, General Philip 87, 127
Shropshire, England 233
Simon, Jo Anne 255
Slade, Frederick J. 77
Slocum, Henry 77
Smart Set 188
Smith, Andrew H., M.D. 63
Smithsonian Institution 96, 149, 233, 250
Society of Women Engineers 4, 250
Sorosis 169-172, 175
South Duxbury, Massachusetts 24
Spain 183-4
Spanish-American War 183, 188
Spotsylvania Court House, Virginia 33
Squibb Park Bridge 242
St. James Palace (London, England) 159, 164
St. Louis, Missouri 175
Staten Island, New York 38, 45
Steinman, David B. 238, 240
Storm King Mountain (near Cold Spring, New York) 84
Strong, William L. 200
Suez Canal 77
Swan, Charles 37, 45

Tammany Hall 55, 156, 179
Tay Bridge (Scotland) 77
Taylor Alley (Trenton, New Jersey) 171
Third Avenue Railroad (New York City) 157
Town Topics 200

Towne, Charles Hanson 188
Treaty of Paris (1898) 184
Trenton, New Jersey 28, 35, 37-8, 43, 58, 61, 65,
  68-9, 71, 113, 137, 139, 140-1, 143-5, 149, 151-3,
  158, 169, 173-5, 193, 197, 215, 217, 223-4, 227,
  229, 231-2, 236, 252,
Trenton Trust Company (Trenton, New Jersey) 143, 234
  234, 241
Tribune, The (New York City) 104
Troy, New York 41, 119, 137-9
Troy Daily Times (Troy, New York) 118
Truman, Harry 234
Twain, Mark 225
Tweed, William M. 55
Union (Brooklyn) 124
Union Army 23, 32, 35, 121
Untermarkts Kirche (Mühlhausen, Germany) 45
U.S. Illuminating Company 98
U.S. Military Academy 26, 87
U.S. Woman Engineer 250

Vanderbilt, Cornelius Jr. 89
Vassar College (Poughkeepsie, New York) 187
Victor (Washington Roebling's valet) 230
Viele, Egbert 109
Vienna, Austria 159-160

Wagner, Erica 122, 130, 132
Waldorf-Astoria Hotel (New York City) 149, 150, 152,
  170, 191, 231
Walsh, Daniel B. 249
Walterboro, South Carolina 230
Walworth, Reubena Hyde 187-8
Warren, Cornelius 26
Warren, Edgar 42
Warren, Emily 24, 29

Warren, Gouverneur Kemble — 8, 26-7, 123
Warren, John — 25
Warren, Phebe Lickley — 26
Warren, Richard — 24
Warren, Sarah Nelson — 25
Warren, Sidney — 47
Warren, Sylvanus — 25
Warsaw, Poland — 160
Washington, D.C. — 27
Washington Park (Troy, New York) — 137
Weir, Dr. A. — 221-2, 229
Wellsville, Ohio — 199
West Point Foundry (Cold Spring, New York) — 23
Westchester County, New York — 25, 198, 221-2
Wiesbaden, Germany — 68
William the Conqueror — 24
Williamsburg Bridge — 115, 118, 166
Wilson, Mrs. William G. — 99
Windsor Castle (England) — 177
Woman's Law Class — 189-93, 197-9
Woman's Legal Education Society — 189, 197, 212
Women's Hospital (New York City) — 177
Women's National War Relief Association — 185, 187, 188

Yardley, Margaret Tufts — 168
Young Women's Christian Association — 182, 206

Made in United States
Troutdale, OR
11/28/2023